The Church Struggle in South Africa

The Church Struggle
in South Africa

Twenty-fifth Anniversary Edition

John de Gruchy
and
Steve de Gruchy

Fortress Press
Minneapolis

THE CHURCH STRUGGLE IN SOUTH AFRICA
Twenty-fifth Anniversary Edition

First Fortress Press edition 2005

This volume is published in collaboration with SCM Press, London.

Cover photo: Amy de Voogd

Library of Congress Cataloging-in-Publication Data
De Gruchy, John W.
   The church struggle in South Africa / John De Gruchy and Steve De Gruchy.— Twenty-fifth anniversary ed.
   p. cm.
  Includes bibliographical references and indexes.
  ISBN 0-8006-3755-0 (alk. paper)
1. South Africa—Race relations. 2. Race relations—Religious aspects—Christianity. 3. South Africa—Church history. I. De Gruchy, Steve. II. Title.

  DT1756.D44 2005
  305.8'00968—dc22

2005011830

Contents

To Beyers Naudé
Prophet and Pastor
whose courage, integrity and hope
inspired us all

Foreword

By Archbishop Desmond Tutu

Twenty-five years ago I had the pleasure of reviewing the First Edition of John de Gruchy's *The Church Struggle in South Africa*. I commented then that I could hardly put the book down once I began reading it; I also expressed the conviction that it would one day become a classic in its field. So I am delighted that this new, updated Third Edition has been published, proving that the book has in fact become the classic I earlier predicted.

Looking back, I remember that when I first read *The Church Struggle* I was struck by the way it combined good theological and historical scholarship with commitment to the role and witness of the Church in the struggle for justice in South Africa. At the time I wrote that de Gruchy has a happy knack and God-given gift to be fair to diverse positions while retaining his right to be critical of these positions. In today's struggle for reconciliation, this combination of critical perception mixed with fairness and openness towards people of other convictions is of particular importance.

The struggle of the Church in South Africa was fundamentally how to bring about a more just society where differences of race, colour and culture were seen to be irrelevant and without theological significance. Of course, differences are not unimportant, as we have learnt over the years, but differences are meant to enrich us all not divide us from one another. Although apartheid as a system and ideology is now happily buried, we still live with its legacy, and we also face new problems that have to be addressed, not least the HIV/AIDS pandemic. We also still have to keep a watchful eye on those in power even though we celebrate and affirm all that has now been achieved by our new government. So the church struggle continues, even though in a new way and moment in history.

Given this changing situation, I am delighted that this Third Edition of *The Church Struggle* contains two new chapters. The first brings the story up to date, showing how the church helped to bring down the apartheid regime and acted as midwife in the transition to democracy. The second new chapter, the last in the book, helps us see more clearly the challenges we now face. I am delighted that Steve de Gruchy has written this final chapter, picking up, as it were, from where his father has taken us!

In September 2004 I was privileged to preach at the state funeral of Beyers Naudé, that great Dutch Reformed theologian and pastor, that giant of a man, who played such a crucial role in the church struggle. So I rejoice that this new edition of *The Church Struggle* has been dedicated to his memory. In my sermon I said that Beyers Naudé helped redeem Christianity for black people in South Africa. But already twenty-five years ago I noted: 'When Afrikaner Christians are converted and come to see the truth that apartheid, petty or grand, and separate development, applied humanely or harshly, are inconsistent with the Gospel of Jesus Christ, then there is no one to beat them for commitment to that truth.' I went on to say: 'What a wonderful day it will be when the Dutch Reformed Church is committed to that truth – all South Africa will rejoice and be glad because our land will be transfigured with justice, peace and love where now we have injustice, conflict and bitterness.'

All that has now come true, and the story of how it has happened is well told in these pages. I really do hope, as I hoped those many years ago, that this new Third Edition will have a wide readership. The de Gruchy team of father and son have put us all put us very much in their debt.

Desmond Tutu
Archbishop Emeritus of Cape Town

Preface to the
Twenty-fifth Anniversary Edition

The first edition of *The Church Struggle in South Africa* was published 25 years ago in 1979. Several other books by different authors on the same theme or related subjects have appeared since then, but for whatever reason *The Church Struggle* carved out a niche for itself as a textbook for students. It also became a standard work for all those interested in the church in South Africa. Despite the fact that the book became dated as the years passed and as South Africa went through a remarkable transition to democratic rule, *The Church Struggle* continued to be read, perhaps even living up to the comment of Desmond Tutu that it was a 'classic in its field'.

The text of the second edition, published in 1986, remained the same except for a postscript in which I responded to some of the criticisms levelled at the first edition, and also included an expanded bibliography. However, in the preface to that edition I indicated that I was busy working on a sequel that would bring the text up to date. That promise was not kept at the time though I did write many essays on the issues over the ensuing years which have been published in a variety of places. In the meantime South Africa went through almost two decades of repression and resistance before the apartheid edifice crumbled and the new South Africa was born. The ongoing story of the church struggle during these 25 years had to be told if *The Church Struggle* was to continue to serve its purpose. So this new 25th anniversary expanded edition was conceived. The fact that its publication coincides with the celebration of ten years of the democratic South Africa makes it more pertinent.

A few comments are necessary on what has been kept, what has been omitted, and what has been added. The first four chapters of the original text have been retained, and while they are substantially the same as before some changes, as indicated below, have been made. The decision to retain these chapters much as they were, was not taken lightly, especially in view of the fact that reading them in retrospect made me aware of their inadequacies and gaps. Nomenclature has changed, fresh information has come to light, and perceptions have been sharpened. Different typologies from my own have been employed to try to give some order and coherence to the diversity and ever-expanding multiplicity of churches. Many of these churches, such as those formed by Francophone-speaking African refugees, or new independent charismatic churches of one kind or another, simply did not exist previously. So if I had to start from scratch today I would undoubtedly write some of it differently. Yet I would not fundamentally change the story line or the content. Sometimes I am a little embarrassed by my style and some of my comments, but that is how it was and I am prepared to stand by it now 25 years later. The alternative, of course, was to rewrite all the material, taking into account the vast amount of research others and I myself have subsequently done. But that would have meant a quite different and much larger book, and would have been a much greater undertaking. For guidance on the subject, I can only point readers to the new and expanded bibliography and especially to the work on the social history of Christianity in South Africa that was undertaken over the past two decades by a number of people, including my colleagues and me, at RICSA, the Research Institute at the University of Cape Town.

One important change to the text should, however, be noted. The text was published in the 'present tense' in 1979, and this no longer made sense for a book that is published in 2004, given the dramatic change within those 25 years. Readers who are familiar with the earlier editions will note that the first four chapters (the original text) are now generally written in the past tense. Hopefully that will help new post-apartheid readers, and especially those from beyond South Africa, to make better sense of the story of the struggle as it was then. Times have, indeed, changed. For similar reasons, a few sentences and paragraphs have been deleted as they no longer serve any purpose in the text. This is especially true of Chapter 4 where the final section in the original on 'white evangelical liberation' has been reworked and conflated with the preceding section on 'black liberation'. The present-day reader may well regard some of the theological debates of the past as now somewhat arcane, but the story of the church struggle makes little sense if these intense discussions, which at the time were heated, risky and highly relevant, are forgotten. After all, the church struggle was as much an ideological one as it was one of practical engagement, and the original telling of the story was not simply for the sake of the record, but also a contribution to the struggle through both its telling and theological reflection on the narrative.

Alongside the textual changes to the original chapters, several sections, including the whole of Chapter 5, have been taken out. Although I remain greatly indebted to Alan Paton for his foreword to the first edition, it has now served its purpose, and I am delighted that Desmond Tutu so readily agreed to provide one for this anniversary edition. The statistical appendices on 'Population in South Africa' and 'Church Membership' in the 1985 edition have been updated on the basis of the 1996 census to reflect the situation in the country at the time the struggle against apartheid had come to an end. But what about the exclusion of the original Chapter 5 entitled 'The Kingdom of God in South Africa'? Unlike the other four chapters it was not so much historical narrative as it was theological commentary and reflection. Much of my writing in the years that followed the publishing of *The Church Struggle* was, in fact, an expanded commentary on these themes. So while the chapter no longer fits appropriately into the telling of the story, the themes remain pertinent even if their formulation today might be different. A brief summary may be helpful.

The providential reign of God within human history remains a key conviction of Christian faith, even though God's redemptive purposes often seem hidden. Such a notion is, of course, contested and is by no means self-evident amid the ambiguities and ironies of history. Christians sensitive to the problems are well aware of the dangers of a triumphalist 'grand narrative' that is used to dominate and control others, not least by the colonial churches. So it is important to affirm that God's reign in human history should not be confused with any ideology or political programme, including those of the church. God's reign in Jesus Christ is always on behalf of those who suffer and are oppressed, and therefore critically transcends our efforts to shape the world in which we live. At the same time, there is a connection between our penultimate struggles for justice and God's justice, and there are some political programmes that more clearly anticipate God's ultimate purpose than others. To opt out of political decision and action, to try to be neutral in the face of injustice and violence, is irresponsible and unchristian. There is a 'politics of the kingdom' that requires engagement not withdrawal; one that requires identification with the victims of oppression and with their struggle for justice.

Christian engagement in politics seeks, however, to embody a particular character and concern. The character is shaped by what Christians believe about Jesus Christ, and especially his assuming the redemptive role of the 'suffering servant' rather than trying to dominate and control. The concern is the 'common good' rather than political or material advantage, and a commitment to peace-making rather than violence and war. But there is one other dimension to the 'politics of the kingdom' that remains of paramount importance, namely what St Paul referred to as 'hope against hope'. The 'hope of the kingdom', as the final section of Chapter 5 was entitled, was particularly important in the late 1970s when apartheid repression was becoming more intense and government power ever more draconian in its intent, range and execution. What kept the struggle against apartheid alive was not any romantic optimism that all would eventually work out for the good, but a 'hope against hope' that engendered action. Such hope is unprepared to accept things as they are because it is founded on the conviction that this is not how the world is meant to be, and that good will triumph over evil. Keeping such hope alive is at the heart of Christian political witness, a hope that celebrates every achievement of justice, no matter how small, en route to the coming of God's kingdom.

In place of the previous Chapter 5, two new chapters have been included. The new Chapter 5 tells the story of the church struggle from 1979 through the process to declare apartheid a 'heresy', and the publication of the *Kairos Document*, to the birth of the new South Africa in 1994. Then an additional Chapter 6 discusses the work of the Truth and Reconciliation Commission, and reflects on the new agenda that now faces both the church and the nation. Throughout the book we have changed the text to reflect a more inclusive use of language, although we have retained sexist language where this is used in original sources. Finally, a new and expanded bibliography has been included.

I am particularly delighted that my elder son, Steve de Gruchy of the School of Religion and Theology at the University of KwaZulu-Natal (Pietermaritzburg) has participated with me in producing this new expanded edition of *The Church Struggle*. Aware of a new generation of students that struggles to keep the 'dangerous memory' of the church struggle alive, Steve was largely responsible for convincing me that the book needed to be expanded and republished. Without his encouragement and support I probably would not have gone ahead. He also took special responsibility for writing Chapter 6, and for updating the index, producing the updated bibliography, and writing the postscript to this third edition which reflects on the historiographical contribution of the book. I am not sure whether it is appropriate to dedicate a book to someone who has shared in its production, but if I could I would dedicate this new edition to him with gratitude for all that we have shared together over the years in pursuing a common vocation.

John W. de Gruchy
Easter 2004

Preface to the Second Edition
(1986)

For some time now I have been working on a sequel to *The Church Struggle in South Africa*, which will update the story and reflect upon its significance. In the meantime the publishers have expressed their desire to keep *The Church Struggle* in print, a decision which is, for me, both gratifying and problematic. I am gratified to know that the book has met a need and continues to do so both in South Africa and elsewhere. It is, evidently, a helpful introduction to the church situation in South Africa for the general reader as well as a useful textbook for students. My problem derives from the fact that not only have ten years of tumultuous events passed since it was first conceived, profoundly affecting both church and society, but also during this decade a large and growing amount of research has been done on the church in South Africa which needs to be taken into account. Moreover, while my own theological convictions have not altered a great deal, some of my social perceptions and theological insights have changed and developed.

In the light of this problem I have considered two alternatives. The first was a complete rewriting of *The Church Struggle*, which would not only bring the story up to date but would also reflect throughout the text the changes in my own analysis. After consultation with colleagues, however, I have decided against this. *The Church Struggle* belongs to the period in which it was first written and remains, I believe, a substantially accurate account of the story as far as it goes. This is confirmed, for me at any rate, by a rereading of the reviews the book received, and by references to it in more recent literature. At the same time the book is by no means beyond criticism, and it would be both unhelpful and foolish to reprint it without taking such criticism into account. Indeed, I believe the value of the book can only be enhanced by indicating what these criticisms are and by responding to them.

The second alternative, then, and the one I have decided to follow, is to leave the substance of the text unaltered but to provide a postscript in which I examine the major criticisms. This will enable the reader to approach the text with some awareness of its weaknesses and their remedies. It will also indicate some of the ways in which my own thinking has developed. An extended and updated bibliography (which is totally new to the American edition), together with a subject index, will also make it a more useful textbook.[1] As already intimated, there is a considerable and growing literature on the church in South Africa, and no one who is really interested need remain uninformed. In any event, the bibliography will enable the reader to explore the subject beyond the parameters and limitations of *The Church Struggle*, and so, in some measure, bring the story up to date.

Much has indeed happened in southern and South Africa during the past decade, not least with regard to the struggle of the church for justice and genuine reconciliation. It is now widely believed that South Africa has reached a critical moment in the struggle between those who cling to white power and dominance and the vast majority of South Africans who look towards a future without apartheid, however disguised. Unless present perceptions are totally misguided, I do not believe that the birth of a new South Africa is too far away, though it would be falsely optimistic to expect that it will be born without continuing conflict, pain, and suffering. I also do not believe that the birth of a new South Africa will usher in the kingdom of God or some Utopia in which the prophetic responsibility of the church will somehow cease. In the meantime, the church struggle in South Africa has entered a new phase as the struggle for a just society has intensified. If the continued publication of this volume makes some contribution to that struggle I shall be gratified, but in any event I dedicate it to that end and to all who are committed to the birth of a just and truly free society in South Africa.

Cape Town
January 1986
John W. de Gruchy

---

[1] The postscript, together with an updated bibliography and subject index are retained in this edition.

xvii

Preface to the Original Edition
(1979)

When I received an invitation in 1975 from Bethel College in North Newton, Kansas, to present the Menno Simons Lectures in 1977 on The Church Struggle in South Africa, neither those responsible for the invitation nor I had any premonition that by the time they would be given, South Africa would be so much in the news headlines of the world. In fact, the lectures were scheduled for and given within a few days of the banning of the Christian Institute, and amid the widespread publicity which surrounded the death in police detention of black student leader Steve Biko.

Prior to presenting the lectures at Bethel College, I was privileged to give them a trial run in seminars at Wesley Theological Seminary in Washington, DC, and at the Iliff School of Theology in Denver, Colorado, as part of their summer school programmes. The lectures were also given at the Canadian Mennonite Bible College in Winnipeg, and in January of this year they formed the basis for a winter inter-term seminar at the Associated Mennonite Biblical Seminaries in Elkhart, Indiana.

I am most grateful, therefore, to Bethel College, its president, Dr Harold Schultz, and the Menno Simons lectureship committee, Drs Alvin Beachy, Robert Kreider, and James Juhnke, for the original invitation to give the lectures. I count this a great honour and privilege. But thanks are also due to the college community as a whole, both faculty and students, for the warm welcome and friendship we experienced as a family throughout our stay during the fall semester. I am also grateful to the other institutions already mentioned, to their presidents, and to those members of their faculties responsible for the invitations and our well-being, and particularly to those students whose stimulating participation helped me to clarify many of my own thoughts.

Since returning home, I have expanded the lectures and attempted to produce a readable book. In doing so, I have benefited from the critical comments and encouragement of colleagues and friends, especially Alex Boraine, Jim Cochrane, Jo Dunstan, Jaap Durand, James Leatt, James Moulder, and Francis Wilson. In expressing my gratitude to them, I naturally absolve them from responsibility for errors of fact or judgment which may be found in the text.

In thanking Alan Paton for so willingly and graciously writing the foreword, I wish to pay tribute to him as a man, a Christian, and a South African. His prophetic concern for justice, his dogged struggle against racism in all its forms, and his capacity for genuine hope are an encouragement to many people, both here and in other parts of the world.[1]

At many times during the writing of this book, I have been conscious of my identity as a white, English-speaking South African, and the limitations that this inevitably means in terms of insight and perspective. I cannot speak for either Afrikaners or blacks, nor, indeed, for the English-speaking community. If I have misrepresented any, I ask for pardon. But I have written as one involved in the situation, and out of the conviction that the Christian gospel contains the word of hope for present and future South Africans, irrespective of race or culture.

Among the many people who have helped me complete my task, I would like to thank those in the Secretarial School at Bethel College, and Suzanne Lind at the Mennonite Seminary in Elkhart, who typed the first drafts of the manuscript, and especially our departmental secretary, Shaan Ellinghouse, who prepared the final draft with amazing patience and considerable skill. Professor John Cumpsty, head of the Department of Religious Studies at the University of Cape Town, has supported and encouraged me throughout my labours, and I am most grateful to him for this. It has also been a privilege to have the help and guidance of the editorial staff at Wm. B. Eerdmans, and in particular, the confidence and support of Mr Marlin Van Elderen, the Editor-in-Chief.

Finally, I wish to thank my wife, Isobel, and my children. As they

---

[1] Alan Paton wrote the foreword for the first edition (1979), which was also reprinted in the second edition (1986). Owing to its datedness it has been omitted from this edition.

enjoyed my sabbatical in the United States as much as I, I do not feel unduly guilty about the time devoted to these pages rather than to them. But without my wife's constant encouragement, and the badgering of Stephen, Jeanelle, and Anton, who also enthusiastically prepared the index, I would still be writing.

University of Cape Town
Pentecost 1978
John W. de Gruchy

Postscript to the Second Edition (1986)

A Response to Major Criticisms

As far as I am aware, four major criticisms have been made of *The Church Struggle*, each of which relates to critical issues facing the church in South Africa today. The first criticism concerns my social analysis and, related to this, my failure to take the Marxist critique of the church sufficiently seriously.

James Cochrane has rightly argued that my analysis of the role of the church in South African society failed to take the relationship of the church to the historical development of the economy into account. In particular, Cochrane maintained, I failed to show the extent to which the so-called English-speaking churches have been captive to capitalism.[1] Thus *The Church Struggle* not only does not deal with a serious weakness within the English-speaking churches themselves but it also reveals the extent to which my analysis has been affected by my church and cultural heritage as well as my class position as a white English-speaking South African. During the past few years I have become increasingly aware of this analytical weakness, and have begun to correct it.[2]

For several years now a debate has raged about whether race or class is the primary category for analyzing South African society. Broadly speaking, the debate has been between liberals and Marxists.[3] *The Church*

---

[1] James R. Cochrane, *Servants of Power: The Role of English-speaking Churches in South Africa 1903–1930* (Johannesburg: Ravan, 1986).

[2] John W. de Gruchy, 'Theologies in Conflict: The South African Debate', in Charles Villa-Vicencio and John W. de Gruchy (eds.), *Resistance and Hope: South African Essays in Honour of Beyers Naudé* (Cape Town: David Philip; Grand Rapids: Eerdmans, 1985).

[3] See esp. the discussion in *Social Dynamics*, a journal of the Centre for African Studies at the University of Cape Town, vol. 9, no. 1 (1983).

Struggle assumes that race is the fundamental problem, and pays very little attention to questions of class and therefore to the economic gulf that separates rich and poor, the oppressor and the oppressed. It now seems clear to me that neither race nor class is primary, but that both categories are fundamental and interrelated. A rewriting of *The Church Struggle* would therefore require a much more thorough-going social analysis, and I would need to respond more adequately than I did to the practical as well as the theoretical challenge which Marxism presents to the church in southern Africa today. Central to such a discussion would be the relationship of the church to labour and the trade unions, a subject which is quite crucial both for the future of the church and the country as a whole.[4]

The second major criticism of *The Church Struggle*, made by Bob Clarke, centred on Chapter 2 of the book. In an otherwise very positive review, Clarke wrote:

> I cannot understand how any book which purports to discuss *The Church Struggle* in South Africa, makes no reference whatsoever to Bishop Clayton's Church and Nation Report of 1944, Michael Scott, and the Church's response to the compulsory takeover of Mission Schools under the terms of the Bantu Education Act of 1953. Incredibly Bishop Reeves is not mentioned at all, nor is his deportation nor that of four other Anglican Bishops nor is Dr Arthur Blaxall. The briefest of reference is made to Father Trevor Huddleston . . . No mention is made of the Freedom Charter, the Treason Trial, nor the Treason Trial Defence Fund, nor of Canon John Collins. No attempt is made to assess the role and effectiveness of overseas pressure groups. He scarcely does justice to the significance of the churches' resistance to the Church Clause Legislation of 1957 . . .[5]

As I intimated at the time in a response to Clarke's criticism, I was and remain grateful for the detailed and helpful comments which he made, but in mitigation I would say that *The Church Struggle* was not intended

---

[4] See Buti Tlhagale, 'Towards a Black Theology of Labour', and James R. Cochrane, 'The Churches and the Trade Unions', in Villa-Vicencio and de Gruchy (eds.), *Resistance and Hope*.

[5] Bob Clarke, 'A Review of "The Church Struggle in South Africa"', *Reality* (November 1979), p. 17.

to be an exhaustive account of the church's struggle against apartheid, let alone a history of the church in South Africa. Indeed, I am not primarily a church historian engaged in detailed research and analysis, but a theologian seeking to reflect on the social history of the church in South Africa. There are many omissions in *The Church Struggle* which, if it were to be rewritten as a comprehensive history textbook, would have to be remedied. Much more, for example, would have to be said about both the Roman Catholic and the Lutheran Churches. But the original intention of the book was to paint some broad strokes on the canvas – a more Breughel-like detailed portrayal might have increased its usefulness in some respects but it might also have clouded the issues. Certainly the canvas would have had to be enlarged beyond its present size.

The third major criticism of *The Church Struggle* came from Allan Boesak in a review in *Social Dynamics*.[6] Dr Boesak's review was generally positive but he argued that while my 'treatment of the relationships between Black theology, Black consciousness and the church is in fact better than most', I did not take the challenge of black theology as seriously as I should have in my final chapter on 'The Kingdom of God in South Africa'.[7] Moreover, Boesak pointed out that I failed to deal adequately with the black Dutch Reformed churches and the role of the 'coloured' community.

Once again I must not only admit the validity of these criticisms, especially of the first, but also express my gratitude for having them pointed out. In response I would say that since writing *The Church Struggle* I have been engaged in reworking my approach to theology, and the challenge of black theology has continued to be one of the major reasons and sources for doing so. During the past decade black theology in South Africa has grown in stature and significance, and there is no doubt in my own mind that it has begun to reshape the church in spite of strong resistance to it.[8]

On the question of the black Dutch Reformed churches, and particularly Dr Boesak's own D. R. Mission Church (NG Sendingkerk), I would argue that their involvement in *The Church Struggle* against

---

[6] *Social Dynamics*, vol. 5, no. 1 (1979).

[7] Note that this fifth chapter of the 1979 and 1986 editions has been left out of this edition. Chapter 5 in this edition is of an entirely different nature.

[8] See my essay 'Theologies in Conflict', in Villa-Vicencio and de Gruchy (eds.), *Resistance and Hope*.

apartheid only really got underway in the second half of the 1970s. Nevertheless, it is true that its beginning was marked by the synod of the black NG Kerk in Africa in 1975 at which, inter alia, the church decided to become an observer member of the South African Council of Churches, and this historic event should have been discussed in *The Church Struggle*. Subsequently, it should be noted, the NG Sendingkerk at its synod in 1978, and the Indian Reformed Church in 1980, took similar decisions which also expressed their rejection of the white DRC's support of government policy. That part of the story, and Dr Boesak's own role within it, belongs to more recent times rather than to the period dealt with in *The Church Struggle*.[9] Without doubt, however, the involvement of the black Dutch Reformed churches in the South African Council of Churches, the emergence of 'the Belydende Kring' and the Alliance of Black Reformed Christians in South Africa, together with the declaration 'Apartheid is a Heresy' and the exclusion of the white DRC from the World Alliance of Reformed Churches, have been crucial developments during these past few years.[10]

A variation on Dr Boesak's criticism was that of Nicholas Wolterstorff who felt that I had downplayed the significance of the black church for the future.[11] If that is the message *The Church Struggle* conveyed, then it is clearly wrong and in need of correction. From a purely statistical point of view, the church in South Africa is a black church with some white members, rather than the other way around, as commonly perceived. According to the 1980 government census, 77 per cent of all South Africans belong to some church denomination, and of these, 88 per cent are black and only 12 per cent white. Not only do the multi-racial or so-called English-speaking churches have a large majority of black members, but the black Dutch Reformed churches' membership is, taken together, comparable in size to the white DRC. Moreover, the largest and fastest-growing church group is the African Independent, or, more accurately, Indigenous church movement. Approximately six

---

[9] This is now included as the new Chapter 5.

[10] See John W. de Gruchy and Charles Villa-Vicencio (eds.), *Apartheid Is a Heresy* (Cape Town: David Philip; Grand Rapids: Eerdmans; London: SPCK, 1983); see also my article 'The Revitalization of Calvinism', *Journal for Religious Ethics* (Spring 1986).

[11] Review of *The Church Struggle* in *The Reformed Journal* (February 1981), p. 28.

million blacks belong to churches within this group, almost 30 per cent of the black population as a whole.[12]

But quite apart from statistics, it is clearly the case that the black membership within the churches, whether they be mainline denominations or independent, is increasingly providing the leadership in the struggle against apartheid and for a just and liberated society. When *The Church Struggle* was written, by way of illustration, Bishop Desmond Tutu had yet to become General Secretary of the South African Council of Churches, and the national leadership of the mainstream churches was almost totally in the hands of its white membership. This situation has dramatically changed during the past ten years. At the same time it must be noted that the most radical theological critique of apartheid yet to appear, the *Kairos Document*, published late in 1985, which was largely the work of black theologians, is also the most critical of the failure of the established, traditionally white-dominated churches to fulfil their task.[13]

A fourth major criticism of *The Church Struggle* was that I failed to deal adequately with the problem of violence, an issue which is also raised very sharply in the *Kairos Document*. This criticism was made by several reviewers, who rightly noted that my own orientation was towards a Christian pacifism, particularly as articulated by the North American theologian John Howard Yoder.[14] During the past decade violence has spiralled in South Africa and it has undoubtedly become the most serious issue facing the church as well as the nation. There is no doubt in my mind that it is no longer meaningful to ask whether social change can come about without violence – the fact is, violence has become a reality, and many would argue with some justification that it is the only language that speaks to those in power. What is required, then, is an accurate analysis of the causes and nature of the violence, and an ability to distinguish between the violence of apartheid and the repression that goes with it, and the struggle of those who have been driven to

---

[12] See my article 'Christians in Conflict: The Social Reality of the South African Church', *Journal of Theology for Southern Africa*, no. 51 (June 1985), pp. 16ff.

[13] *The Kairos Document: Challenge to the Church: A Theological Comment on the Political Crisis in South Africa* (Johannesburg: The Kairus Theologians, 1985); repr. in *Journal of Theology for Southern Africa*, no. 53 (September 1985); 2nd rev. edn. (Johannesburg: Institute for Contextual Theology; Grand Rapids: Eerdmans, 1986).

[14] This criticism relates to the original Chapter 5 in the 1979 and 1986 editions.

use violence in their quest for liberation.[15] This does not necessarily justify the latter, but it avoids the facile response of so many white Christians to what is happening. It remains my conviction, nonetheless, that the church has a special responsibility to pursue non-violent strategies for change. This is the context within which, for example, the disinvestment debate and the End Conscription Campaign have to be considered. Non-violence is not passivity, and it may well require acts of civil disobedience in faithfulness to the apostolic injunction that we should 'obey God rather than man' in bearing witness to the gospel and our confession that 'Jesus Christ is Lord'.

The confession that 'Jesus Christ is Lord' remains at the centre of my theological understanding. It is a confession shared by all Christians, though many fail to discern its social and political implications. I remain convinced that the task of the church in South Africa today is to be a church that is faithful to this confession – therein lies its identity and its relevance. In this sense theology is a radical project; it is always seeking to relate the church of today and the issues and conflicts facing it to its biblical and apostolic roots. An example of this is the theological basis upon which the call was made on 16 June 1985 to pray for the end to unjust rule in South Africa.[16] As already indicated, my theological understanding has developed during the past ten years largely in response to the challenge presented by black theology, but I do not believe that this has led me away from the central affirmations of the Christian faith, nor from what I regard as the essence of the tradition, both ecumenical and Reformed, in which I stand. If anything, it has sharpened these affirmations and shown how important they are for the future of the church in South Africa, indeed, for the future of the country itself.

---

[15] The best discussion of this issue in the South African context is David Russell, 'A Theological Critique of the Christian Pacifist Perspective with Special Reference to the Position of John Howard Yoder', PhD Thesis (University of Cape Town, 1985).

[16] See Allan A. Boesak and Charles Villa-Vicencio (eds.), *When Prayer Makes News: Churches and Apartheid, a Call to Prayer* (Philadelphia: Westminster Press, 1986).

Postscript to the Third Edition

Locating *The Church Struggle in South Africa* in the Wider Historiography of the Church in South Africa

STEVE DE GRUCHY

In the postscript to the second edition of *The Church Struggle* (reprinted in this edition) there is a reference to four major criticisms of the book, two of which raise important issues to do with historiography and the telling of the story of the church's struggle in South Africa. One criticism of the book had to do with gaps in the telling of the story. The reviewer noted – correctly – that some important parts of the history of the church's struggle are missing, including the impact of the Bantu Education Act of 1953, the Freedom Charter and the Treason Trial. John de Gruchy accepted the criticism, but pointed out that he had never understood the book to be a history of the church in South Africa. He went on to write: 'there are many omissions in *The Church Struggle* which, if it were to be rewritten as a comprehensive history textbook, would have to be remedied.' This comment provides us with an important clue in understanding the book and placing it within the wider body of work on the history of the church in South Africa. It is a matter to which we shall presently return.

A second and perhaps more significant criticism was that, because the book used 'race' rather than 'class' as its primary analytical tool, the history focused upon the church and its response to racism and apartheid rather than to colonialism and capitalism. This meant that while the relationship between blacks and whites received attention, the relationship between rich and poor, owners of capital and wage-earners, the state and trade unions, was avoided. In effect this meant that serious weaknesses in the social witness of the English-speaking churches were overlooked, and possibly even legitimated.

At the time of the second edition in 1986, John de Gruchy accepted the validity of this criticism and noted that 'a rewriting of *The Church Struggle* would therefore require a much more thorough-going social analysis', in words that drew on the work of the Latin American liberation theologians, and echoed the *Kairos Document* which was then being written. Yet this third edition has not been able to provide this 'thorough-going social analysis', because the decision was taken not to rewrite the early material, but rather to bring the story up to date in the same style. The criticism, however, still stands even though the final chapter does draw attention to wider issues that continue to face the church in South Africa following the demise of apartheid, and specifically the economic issues underlying people's livelihoods.

It is important to draw attention to these criticisms to do with omissions and analytical frameworks in the writing of the history of the church in South Africa. These are crucial matters of which the student of the church struggle ought to be aware. Precisely because the way we understand our history is shaped by that very history, and because we choose to tell certain things in certain ways and not other things in other ways, the *writing* of history is as shot through with politics, passion and prejudice as the subject matter itself. If this is true in general it is even more so when it comes to a Christian minister and theologian writing the story of the church in a struggle against what was declared a heresy, just four years after the book was published.

Something of this perspective emerged when John de Gruchy responded to these criticisms with this revealing comment: 'I am not primarily a church historian engaged in detailed research and analysis, but a theologian seeking to reflect on the social history of the church in South Africa.' *The Church Struggle*, published in 1979, was his first book, and in many ways his subsequent published work as an academic theologian has borne out this comment. The work on Bonhoeffer, Reformed theology, democracy, reconciliation and aesthetics has pointed to a wider theological interest, while countless conference papers, chapters of books, edited volumes and journal articles have provided a sustained theological reflection on the social and political issues confronting the church in South Africa. Indeed it is just possible that part of the value of *The Church Struggle* as a theological work was that it not only reflected upon history, but also was itself a significant *theological* contribution to the subsequent witness of the church against apartheid.

From a historiographic perspective, however, it is important to note that *The Church Struggle* triggered off two important impulses concerning the wider social history of the church in South Africa. In the first instance, for all his disavowal of himself as one involved in detailed historical research, the book did signal a commitment to the historical task. John de Gruchy has continued to research and publish in the area of the history of the English-speaking churches in South Africa, and in his work as an academic he has supervised a large amount of student research in this area. Much of this has culminated in his leadership of and participation in the hugely significant undertaking of the Research Institute for Christianity in South Africa (RICSA) into the social history of Christianity in South Africa.

Second, in many ways the book opened the floodgates for others to write and reflect upon that history. For all its shortcomings, it was the first book to provide a comprehensive historical and theological framework in which to understand the relationship between the church and the apartheid state, and therefore to provide a much needed historical dignity to those who were concerned about the situation. Ironically, this makes it vulnerable to another significant criticism that is important for the student of the church in South Africa to note, namely, that *The Church Struggle* is so concerned with the 'meta-narrative' of the grand and glorious struggle against apartheid that it cannot possibly do justice to the thousands of micro-narratives that make up the story: to the ambiguities of those caught in the middle, the voices of the silent and silenced (such as women and the rural poor), the contribution of the laity – those who really are the 'church' – the failures of witness, the incredible sacrifices of ordinary people, the personality clashes, the financial and sexual scandals, the acts of compassion and integrity, the textures and sights and sounds that are uppermost in the minds of those who happened 'to be there'.

Such a criticism, coupled with those noted earlier, helps us understand what *The Church Struggle* is not, and therefore to understand what it is, and to place it within the wider historiographic picture. *The Church Struggle* is not a comprehensive history of the church in South Africa, nor even a full history of the church witness against apartheid. It does not use a class analysis to understand history, choosing 'race' as its major analytical category; and it seldom touches on the everyday stories of ordinary people. In this sense it takes its place as but one book in a library of *histories* of the church in South Africa. But having said this, the book's significance lies precisely in the fact that it does unashamedly seek to provide a meta-narrative, a broad theoretical and theological framework to understand the meaning of the present time in terms of the past. It helps the reader to understand how and why black theology emerged; how and why conscientious objection became a key focus of white Christian witness; how and why apartheid was declared a heresy; how and why the *Kairos Document* was written; how and why the church celebrated the coming of democracy; and how and why other struggles have emerged.

But – and here my own prejudices emerge – I have a suspicion that the book never intended to stop there. It is not just history. But neither is it just theology. It does not end with explaining 'how and why', it wants to invite the reader to make a choice and to take a stand. Let us not forget that the first edition was written in a context in which Steve Biko and many others were murdered, Beyers Naudé and many others were banned, young white Christian South African conscripts were learning to kill young black Christian South African freedom fighters, and many good people were questioning the relevance of the gospel. The book was written as part of that context, not as an unconcerned analysis, but as a contribution to the struggle and an invitation to others to participate. In that sense John de Gruchy was not just being a historian, and not even just being a theologian – he was also being a preacher. Thus I would argue that *The Church Struggle* takes its place in the wider bibliography on the church in South Africa somewhere in the interface between history, theology, and sermon.

1

Historical Origins

Settler Church – Mission Church

It has been a failure of European colonialist historians to write about South African history as though it began with the arrival of Portuguese explorers in the sixteenth century and the Dutch settlers in the next. Some recent historiography has attempted to correct this false assumption.[1] But it is true that the history of the church begins with the coming *Church* of the Dutch (1652), the French Huguenots (1668), and the early German *history* settlers a little later. With few exceptions these settlers were Protestants, and the Dutch and French were Calvinist. Portuguese Catholics had predated the Dutch in landing at the Cape – a small Catholic chapel was built at Mossel Bay in 1501, but by 1652 this very temporary presence had long since gone. Indeed, even though there were Catholics residing at the Cape, the Dutch East India Company forbade the practice of Roman Catholicism.[2] The Dutch Reformed Church (DRC), known in Dutch and Afrikaans as the Nederduitse Gereformeerde Kerk (NGK),[3] controlled by the classis in Amsterdam, was the established church, into which the Huguenots were soon assimilated. The German Lutherans were more successful in their struggle to retain their own identity, but it was only in 1779 that they finally obtained permission to erect their own church building.[4]

---

[1] Cf. Monica Wilson and Leonard Thompson (eds.), *The Oxford History of South Africa*, vols. 1 and 2 (Oxford: Oxford University Press, 1969 & 1971).

[2] Cf. W. E. Brown, *The Catholic Church in South Africa, from its Origin to the Present Day* (London: Burns & Oates, 1960).

[3] The official title of the DRC is the Nederduitse Gereformeerde Kerk (NGK). In previous editions of this book the English title and its acronym are used. In this new edition NGK is used throughout.

[4] A short, basic introduction to the history of the church in South Africa is Peter Hinchliff's *The Church in South Africa* (London: SPCK, 1968). See also Jane M. Sales, *The Planting of the Churches in South Africa* (Grand Rapids: Eerdmans, 1971).

MISSIONS

As the Cape colony expanded during the eighteenth century, so the NGK grew, but its growth was almost totally confined to white settler congregations. Early attempts to evangelize the indigenous San and Khoi populations were sporadic and eventually declined, until the birth of the nineteenth-century international missionary movement provided new impetus and concern for the evangelization of the 'heathen'. Indeed, the first European missionary specifically sent to minister to the indigenous population at the Cape was not Dutch Reformed but a Moravian, George Schmidt, who in 1738 commenced his work at Genadendal, about a hundred miles east of Cape Town.[5] Within ten years he had to stop. One reason for this was that the evangelistic piety and gospel of universal grace proclaimed to the indigenous peoples collided with the Calvinist orthodoxy of the Dutch church. There was, at this time, considerable opposition to the Moravian Brethren in Holland itself, and this had begun to influence opinion at the Cape. But the teaching and practice of George Schmidt was not only regarded as a threat to the theology and authority of the church, it was also seen as a threat to the social life of the settler community to which the church ministered.

This conflict between 'settler' church and 'mission' church became a dominant issue for church and society at the Cape during the nineteenth century. When Britain finally gained occupation of the Cape in 1806, and the NGK and the small Lutheran congregations were no longer the only churches in the colony, Protestant missionaries of other persuasions arrived by the score from Europe and America 'to Christianize the heathen'. But they soon discovered that the white settlers were largely unconvinced about the need for and desirability of such missionary enthusiasm and endeavour. Again and again, missionaries had to answer objections to Christian missions, objections that were by no means strictly theological. Charles Brownlee, a mid-nineteenth-century missionary of the London Missionary Society, tells how he had to convince his audience that it was not true 'that Christian Natives are not such good servants as the wild heathen'.[6] As we proceed, we shall show how this tension between church and mission played a crucial role in the social history of South Africa. It provides one of the clues for

---

[5] Bernard Kruger, *The Pear Tree Blossoms: The History of the Moravian Church in South Africa, 1737–1869* (Genadendal: Moravian Church Board, 1967).

[6] Charles Brownlee, *Reminiscences of Kafir Life and History*, 2nd edn (Lovedale: Lovedale Press, 1896), p. 349.

understanding the struggle of the church for faithfulness and relevance during the apartheid era.

By 1824 the NGK at the Cape had gained its autonomy from the church in Holland, symbolized by the constitution of its own synod.[7] Though it remained dependent upon its distant mother church in many ways, this was a momentous step for the NGK. Indeed, it was the establishment of the first independent church in southern Africa. The church had finally taken root, even though the soil was largely white. What precipitated this development, however, was not simply the inevitable desire of and need for congregations to organize and control their own affairs in a new land, but the fact that the Cape colony was now British. It was undesirable and impractical for the established church to be controlled from an enemy country. And the NGK was the official church even after the British took control of the Cape. Included in the terms of Dutch surrender was the stipulation that the position and privileges of the NGK would be maintained by the new colonial administration. A somewhat strange and anomalous situation ensued. The NGK was now free from the Calvinist control of Amsterdam, but its synodical decisions required the sanction of the Anglican governor at the Cape. Meanwhile, the Church of England, to which the governor belonged, not only had little influence, it had no parishes. It existed to serve the spiritual needs of the colonial officials and militia. Its first sanctuary was the Dutch Groote Kerk in Cape Town; its growth was sporadic, and its life remained disjointed and haphazard until the arrival of the first Anglican bishop of Cape Town, Robert Gray, in 1848.

The cutting of the umbilical cord linking the NGK with its mother church in Holland came at a time when the church in the Netherlands was shedding some of its strict Calvinist theology under the impact of the Enlightenment. By 1817 the ultra-Calvinistic decrees of Dort were no longer binding, and rationalism had made considerable gains in the church. Unlike the church in the Netherlands, the NGK did not jettison Dort, but neither did it escape these European developments. It was only after a protracted struggle that it managed to curtail the influence of its more liberal theologians and pastors.[8] Even so, in spite of official

---

[7] The early history of the Dutch Reformed Church is told in A. Moorrees, *Die Nederduitse Gereformeerde Kerk in Suid-Africa, 1652–1873* (Cape Town: Bible Society, 1937).

[8] Moorrees, *Die Nederduitse Gereformeerde Kerk*, pp. 881ff.

adherence to Dort, the theology of the NGK during the nineteenth century was not pure Calvinism.

After the Cape Synod was constituted, long debates were held about the desirability of establishing a theological seminary. This became increasingly necessary because of the difficulties facing the church in calling Dutch pastors, and in sending students for training in Holland. There were those who opposed the formation of the seminary on the grounds that it would shut the door on participation in the important theological developments taking place in Europe at the time. But the majority supported the move for precisely that reason.[9] With the establishment of the theological seminary at Stellenbosch in 1859, the NGK was able to control its own theological teaching, and in spite of sporadic attempts to introduce more liberal emphases, it was able to plough a conservative furrow for its ministers and members to follow.

Another decisive development in the NGK was the arrival of a number of Scottish Presbyterian ministers from about 1820 onwards. The need for them arose because the British disliked the calling of Dutch ministers to the colony, and there were delays in establishing the Stellenbosch Seminary. Thus, in the interim, the church was encouraged by the British authorities to obtain the help of Scottish dominees whose churchmanship was acceptable to the NGK and whose citizenship was acceptable to the government. Notable among these divines, some of whom had received part of their training in Holland, was Andrew Murray, who arrived at the Cape in 1822. More famous was his son Andrew Murray, Jr, who with his brother John went to Scotland and Holland to train for the ministry in the mid-nineteenth century. The younger Andrew became moderator of the NGK Synod on six occasions. Together with John, Andrew Murray, Jr injected a new evangelical enthusiasm into the church, profoundly shaping Dutch Reformed theology and piety at a critical moment in its development. The Murrays had personal experience of the church–state controversies which had split the Church of Scotland in 1843; they had also encountered firsthand the rationalism of the church in the Netherlands. Thus, they were ideally equipped to steer the church through this crucial period when liberalism and state relations were the dominant issues. That their evangelical piety did not logically fit pure Calvinism did not really matter because the

---

[9] Moorrees, *Die Nederduitse Gereformeerde Kerk*, pp. 863f.

NGK, though conservative, was not strictly Calvinist anyway. The astonishing revivals under the ministry of Andrew Murray, Jr, to which modern Pentecostalism owes a great deal,[10] produced a crop of new theological students ready to fill the desks at Stellenbosch. The spiritual life of the church was immeasurably enriched, and considerable impetus was given to education, especially the training of devout Christian teachers. This evangelical theology and revivalist piety also corresponded well with the international missionary movement of the time, now well into its stride at the Cape. Around 1857, the NGK began to embark more seriously than before upon missionary work among the Coloured peoples on its doorstep,[11] and the Murray influence gave this mission motivation, direction, and personnel.

At the same time, Murray's influence created tension. Although evangelicals now dominated the church, orthodox Calvinists coexisted in an uneasy relationship. Both found a common enemy in rationalism and liberal theology, but there were those who were critical of the pietist and foreign input, an influence made more suspicious by the fact that the Murrays were of British descent. Moreover, Calvinism was being revived in Holland. Rationalism, having split the church there, led to various schisms, beginning in 1834 with the founding of the Separated Christian Reformed Church, inspired by Groen van Prinsterer. Van Prinsterer was highly critical of the liberalism of both the state and the established church. He was convinced that this would eventually lead to atheism and revolution. Europe was going through revolutionary years as it was. Thus, under the banner of Christian Nationalism, and with the motto, 'In isolation is our strength', van Prinsterer waged an intense political and ecclesiastical war on behalf of his brand of Calvinism. Liberalism was the enemy.[12] Try as he did to prevent its spread, van Prinsterer failed in his lifetime. However, he profoundly influenced Abraham Kuyper,

---

[10] Cf. Walter J. Hollenweger, *The Pentecostals* (London: SCM Press, 1972), pp. 111f.

[11] Cf. J. du Plessis, *A History of Christian Missions in South Africa* (London: Longmans, Green & Co., 1911; repr. Cape Town C. Struik, 1965), ch. 28. On the history of the Coloured people, see J. S. Marais, *The Cape Coloured People, 1652–1937* (Johannesburg: University of Witwatersrand Press, 1968); Sheila Patterson, *Colour and Culture in South Africa: A Study of the Cape Coloured People within the Social Structure of the Union of South Africa* (London: Routledge & Kegan Paul, 1953).

[12] Cf. Guillaume Groen van Prinsterer, *Unbelief and Revolution*, trans. and ed. Harry van Dyke with Donald Morton (Amsterdam: Kampert & Helm, 1975), first published in 1847.

the person who did succeed to a remarkable degree in achieving his neo-Calvinist goals.

Schism in Holland stabilized with the formation of the Christelijke Gereformeerde Kerken in 1869. Kuyper was the most important influence within these new Gereformeerde Kerken. A statesman and theologian of considerable stature, Kuyper not only gave fresh expression to the strict Calvinism of Dort, but also developed van Prinsterer's idea of Calvinism as an all-embracing philosophy and lifestyle.[13] A valiant fighter for the separation of church and state, Kuyper insisted that all spheres of life exist by virtue of God's common grace, and that therefore each has a sovereignty over its own affairs under God. Education, art, economics, family life, are all spheres through which God operates directly. This common grace, as distinct from saving grace, is built into the structures of creation and provides the basis for Christian Nationalism in its various dimensions.

Kuyper eventually founded the Free University of Amsterdam, at which many Dutch Reformed theologians were trained in the course of the following century. But already by the middle of the nineteenth century, these neo-Calvinist developments were being propagated and assimilated at the Cape. An important leader in this was the Revd S. J. du Toit, a father of Afrikaner Nationalism. Not only did this movement offer an articulate alternative to evangelical pietism, but it also laid the foundation for Christian National education, a cornerstone of later Afrikaner Nationalist policy. The pietism of Murray and the neo-Calvinism of Kuyper, the one so intensely personal, the other so much more directly socio-political in significance, never came together in a creative synthesis. On the contrary, it led to schism when S. J. du Toit left the NGK to form his own church. Later, when the Gereformeerde Kerk (the 'Dopper Kerk') was established in Potchefstroom, Transvaal, in 1859 after the Great Trek, it embodied this neo-Calvinism and attracted many from the NGK who had been influenced by du Toit and others like him. It was this church, rather than the NGK, that was strictly Calvinist, at least in the Kuyperian sense, during the nineteenth century. It is important to keep this distinction in mind, for 'the existence of this truly Calvinist Church alongside the Dutch Reformed Church has led many commentators to attribute Calvinist attitudes to the Dutch Reformed

---

[13] Cf. Abraham Kuyper, *Calvinism* (Grand Rapids: Eerdmans, 1939).

Church which in fact come from the Reformed Church (i.e., the Gereformeerde Kerk).'[14]

This was not the only tension heightened by evangelicalism within the NGK. Expanding missionary work produced as much, perhaps even more. In the very early days at the Cape colony, discrimination practised between white and black, slave and free person, was ostensibly based more on religion than race. Though racism and a European sense of cultural superiority were rife, the first Dutch commandant at the Cape issued a proclamation in which it was decreed that 'everyone is . . . earnestly admonished and ordered to show all friendliness and amiability to the natives . . .' A decisive criterion for interracial relationships was Christian baptism. A Khoi convert, Eva, who was baptized in 1661, married an influential European official, and such mixed marriages between Christians of different races, though rare, were initially tolerated. But race proved more powerful than religion. When, in the nineteenth century, missionary work met with the success it did, the NGK was confronted with a crisis similar to that which beset the early Jewish-Christian community when, to their amazement, the gospel was so readily accepted by gentiles. While baptism theoretically rendered all distinctions void, whether in church or society, a fact demonstrated at the Lord's Table, not all white settlers warmed to this theology in practice. Racial prejudice and the interests of labour and land clashed with theology.

The Synod of 1829 stood firm and undeterred. Holy Communion, it maintained, was to be administered 'simultaneously to all members without distinction of colour or origin' because this was 'an unshakable principle based on the infallible Word of God'. This refusal to allow race to determine church practice was re-affirmed at several subsequent synods. But taking into account the great social rift that did exist between the settler community and the indigenous people, many of whom were slaves, it is not surprising that social pressures eventually proved stronger than synodical resolutions.

By 1857, the synod had to change its stance and depart from the plain sense of the Word of God. It decided that, though not desirable or

---

[14] Irving Hexham, 'Dutch Calvinism and the Development of Afrikaner Calvinism', in Christopher R. Hill and Peter Warwick (eds.), *Southern African Research in Progress, Collected Papers*, vol. 1, Centre for Southern African Studies (York: University of York Press, 1974), p. 14.

scriptural, due to the weakness of some (i.e., whites), it was permissible to hold separate services for whites and blacks.[15] Its resolution read:

> The Synod considers it desirable and scriptural that our members from the Heathen be received and absorbed into our existing congregations wherever possible; but where this measure, as a result of the weakness of some, impedes the furtherance of the cause of Christ among the Heathen, the congregation from the Heathen, already founded or still to be founded, shall enjoy its Christian privileges in a separate building or institution.

This permitted separation was not allowed simply for racial reasons. Social pressures found an ally among missionary strategists such as Andrew Murray, Jr. In line with much nineteenth-century European Protestant missionary strategy, this separation was regarded as a way of facilitating mission work. Influential German missiologists such as Gustav Warneck taught that the gospel should not be proclaimed to humankind in general, but to each nation and group in ways appropriate to their culture.[16] There was, and still is, sufficient sense and biblical sanction ('a missionary to the gentiles') in the proposal to give it plausibility. But the cost was high – it was a policy that divided the church along ethnic and cultural lines. Although mixed congregations continued to exist, what was meant in 1857 to be an exception became the rule. Separate parallel congregations were formed, leading eventually to separate mission or 'daughter' churches. The first of these was the *Sendingkerk* (Mission Church), established in 1881 for Coloured people. This was followed later by the N. G. Kerk in Africa, for blacks (Africans), and the Indian Reformed Church. Churches were also established in other African countries as a result of extensive mission work.

This separate development within the NGK, reluctantly accepted by some, had enormous ramifications for the church. While it facilitated the growth of indigenous congregations, it divided the church along racial lines in a way that was recognized even then as theologically

---

[15] Cf. Moorrees, *Die Nederduitse Gereformeerde Kerk*, p. 595; the text of the Resolution is taken from 'The Dutch Reformed Churches and the Non-Whites', Fact Paper 14, July 1956, where the issues are also discussed.

[16] Cf. J. C. Hoekendijk, *Kerk en Volk in de Duitse Zendingswetenschap* (Amsterdam: Kampert & Helm, 1948), pp. 83f.

(margin annotation: Segregation, continuing to Spirit or flesh?)

unsound. It is debatable that what was gained by this development was of greater value for the church than what was lost. It is also debatable that it was necessary on cultural grounds, for the separation did not begin initially among black African converts, with their very different Nguni or Sotho cultures and languages, but in the western Cape, where settler and Coloured communities shared much in common. Would the church not have been more faithful and thus eventually more relevant if it had attempted to provide a bridge between people rather than serve as an instrument whereby social and racial differences were legitimized? However understandable from a cultural and evangelistic perspective, it was an example of social pressure and pragmatism, custom and culture, rather than theology and scripture, determining the life of the church. The Dutch Reformed theologian, Professor B. B. Keet, critically commenting on this, wrote: 'Why could the Coloured Christian not have come into his own inside the Church of the Europeans? The answer is obvious: It is because the white man was not prepared to give him the opportunity of doing so.'[17] In any event, the missionary programme of the NGK as it developed during the next hundred years followed custom and culture consistently, thus providing an ecclesiological blueprint for the Nationalist policy of separate development. This separation of settler and mission churches had implications far beyond the ecclesiastical realm.

It is evident, then, that the theology and practice of the NGK has been influenced by a great deal more than the authentic teaching of John Calvin. The original Dutch Calvinism at the Cape was affected by liberalism, then transformed by the Murrays' evangelicalism. It was also profoundly influenced by the neo-Calvinism of Abraham Kuyper.[18] Even though Kuyper's theology was much more dominant in the Gereformeerde Kerk in the Transvaal, neo-Calvinism penetrated and influenced the NGK to an ever increasing extent. Kuyper's idea of separate spheres of sovereignty embedded in creation corresponded well

---

[17] B. B. Keet, *Whither South Africa?* (Stellenbosch: Stellenbosch University Publishers, 1956), p. 38. For a detailed study of the issues from a sympathetic viewpoint see N. J. Smith, 'Die Planting van Afsonderlike Kerke vir Nie-Blanke Berolkingsgroepe deur die Nederduitse Gereformeerde Kerk in Suid-Afrika', *Annale, Universiteit van Stellenbosch*, vol. 34, Serie B, no. 2, 1973.

[18] Cf. H. G. Stoker and F. J. M. Potgieter (eds.), *Koers in die Krisis*, vol. 1 (Stellenbosch: Pro Ecclesia, 1935).

with the Lutheran doctrine of the 'orders of creation' as expounded by German missionary science and embodied in NGK policy. Together they have had considerable influence on South African social history. Indeed, it helps explain why at a later date the NGK could give its support to the Nationalist policy of separate development as being in accord with the will of God. It was this theological position that provided the religious ground for the policy. But it was a position somewhat removed from the theology propounded by the reformer of Geneva.

Throughout the nineteenth century, British administrative influence at the Cape was strengthened by the growing numbers of British immigrants. Many of these immigrants were casualties of the Napoleonic wars, escaping from severe hardships at home to start a new life in the colony. By this time, many of the Dutch settlers, most of whom were farmers (Boers) often living in remote country areas, had begun to lose touch with their own European culture and were beginning to mould a new one with its own language and traditions (Afrikaans and Afrikaner). The British colonial agents and the British settlers who came in increasing numbers after about 1820, to settle largely along the eastern Cape frontier, were a different European breed.

In particular, the British settlers were townspeople rather than farmers, though they soon had to learn to use the plough in order to survive. They were the products of working-class England. Independent-minded grocers and labourers hit by the economic recessions of the day, they were more often than not Nonconformists and Wesleyans by religious conviction and of a social class that disliked the British aristocratic establishment and its Anglican faith. But they were British. As the century passed and their numbers grew, they were proud to belong to an expanding empire, even though they still had to fight for their rights, especially the liberty to express their opinions in the press. They were part of the Victorian Age, an outpost of a culture which they regarded as inferior to none, and superior to most, including those they encountered at the Cape. 'The Victorians', Owen Chadwick reminds us, 'changed the face of the world because they were assured. Untroubled by doubt whether Europe's civilization and politics were suited to Africa or Asia, they saw vast opportunities open to energy and enterprise, and identified progress with the spread of English intelligence and English industry.'[19]

---

[19] Owen Chadwick, *The Victorian Church*, vol. 1 (London: A. & C. Black, 1971), p. 1.

The Boers were probably a little overawed, even though they had arrived to possess the land 150 years before; they were certainly apprehensive, if not of the English-speaking settlers themselves, then of the British authorities and the policies they would adopt. They had every reason to be. Rumours of English liberalism were sufficient cause for concern. Moreover, they were increasingly unhappy about the missionaries who emanated from London, and who seemed to embody such liberalism in religious guise. Their struggle against imperialism, an alien culture, liberalism, and interfering missionaries was about to begin, and it would not end until it had produced an Afrikaner Nationalism equal to the task of subduing the land and reshaping society. All of this had significant ramifications for the NGK, for if it was to be relevant to Afrikaner fears and aspirations, it could not stand aloof from the Afrikaner struggle. If it became involved, it could not but be affected by political developments. To this dilemma we must return later. For the moment let us consider the British settlers and their churches.

Whereas the NGK missionary enterprise began only after the Dutch church had taken root in the country, the British churches came to the Cape in two forms from the outset. They came to serve the needs of the colonial administrators and the 1820 settlers. But even before that, they came as part of the great nineteenth-century missionary thrust. In 1799 the first and much maligned London Missionary Society (LMS) missionary, Dr Johannes van der Kemp, arrived in Cape Town. It is ironical that a Dutchman should have been the first English missionary to become the bane of the Afrikaner farmers. But he was. And so were many other LMS missionaries, including Robert Moffat in Kuruman, and especially Dr John Philip, who served as the Cape superintendent of the society from 1819 until 1851, and who in that period became the best known and most hated of all.[20] Some LMS missionaries, including van der Kemp, who married a Coloured woman, were accused of immorality, and others of treason. The trouble was that they were not serving the apparent needs of the white settlers and farmers, but striving to be relevant to the conditions and struggles of the Coloureds and Africans. Not only were these 'non-Europeans' regarded as inferior, the majority

---

[20] Cf. Moorrees, *Die Nederduitse Gereformeerde Kerk*, pp. 410f.; du Plessis, *History of Christian Missions*, pp. 99ff. For a sympathetic account of John Philip, see W. M. Macmillan, *Bantu, Boer, and Briton: The Making of the South African Native Problem* (Oxford: Oxford University Press, 1963).

of settlers considered them born to be their servants. Moreover, they were often considered cattle-thieves, and the frontier wars made the Xhosa enemies of the settlers. To be sympathetic to their needs, to champion their cause, and to do so by enlisting both the authority of the British administration and overseas opinion was, to say the very least, regarded as reprehensible. Such was the opinion not only of Afrikaner Boers, but also of British settlers, and even of some English clergy. A Scottish Presbyterian, the Revd John M'Carter of Ladysmith in Natal, wrote an apologia for the NGK in 1869 in which he exclaimed to his British readers accustomed only to the reports of missionaries: 'We cannot avoid giving utterance to our impression that missionaries and their friends have sometimes overstated their case . . . we have been astonished at the one-sidedness of some . . .'[21] Even Robert Gray, the Anglican bishop in Cape Town, charged that some LMS missionaries had been the cause, albeit unintentionally, of the Kat River Rebellion.

The problem which has continuously dogged relationships between the white community and the missionaries who have come to serve black South Africans is simply, how do you relate to the needs of both at the same time? Jane Sales sums it up well:

> There was some validity to the charge of 'traitor' which the Dutch farmers had levelled at Vanderkemp when he negotiated with Klaas Stuurman in 1802, and again at James Read at the time of the Black Circuit. The attacks which the Grahamstown merchants made on John Philip in 1838 and on Nicholas Smit, Dutch-background pastor of the Coloured LMS Church in Grahamstown in 1851, also indicated this charge of treason. To deny the charge was, in a sense, to forsake the Coloured people, the 'objects' of their missionary concern. If social welfare is conceived only on a racialistic basis, then Vanderkemp, Philip, the Reads, and others, even Stockenstroom, were 'traitors' to white society in South Africa.[22]

This is an interesting comment, not only for its perception of the problem we are considering, but also because it shows how the English-

---

[21] John M'Carter, *The Dutch Reformed Church in South Africa* (Edinburgh, 1869), p. 141.

[22] Jane M. Sales, *Mission Stations and the Coloured Communities of the Eastern Cape, 1800–1852* (Cape Town: A. A. Balkema, 1975). Klaas Stuurman was a Khoi leader allied with the Xhosas; the Black Circuit, initiated at the request of John Philip, was a travelling court which tried white farmers for the ill-treatment of their labourers.

speaking settlers and their churches had also begun to follow the pattern established by their Afrikaner or Dutch counterparts. The 'Grahamstown merchants' to whom Sales refers were British, not Boers. The London Missionary Society Church was Coloured, not multiracial – there was a separate Congregational Church in the town which served the English Independents and Presbyterians. The same was true for the Wesleyan Methodists, who were numerically the strongest among the eastern Cape settlers centred in Grahamstown.

The basic reason that Dutch and English settlers alike resented the presence of some missionaries was thus precisely because the missionaries not only evangelized the indigenous peoples, but took their side in the struggle for justice, rights, and land. Such missionaries, being white, regarded themselves as the conscience of the settlers and the protectors of the 'natives'. A great deal of the bitterness had to do with the way the missionaries went about their task, for some, as the Revd John M'Carter complained, were quite unwilling to listen to settler grievances and automatically presumed that their mission flock was in the right. But whatever the faults of the missionaries, from a black as well as a white perspective, it is true to say that the church's struggle against racism and injustice in South Africa only really begins in earnest with their witness in the nineteenth century.

Although Anglican chaplains served the spiritual needs of the British civil servants and soldiers, and occasional services were permitted for Congregationalists and Presbyterians alike, Methodists were less fortunate. The first Methodist minister left Cape Town for Ceylon after waiting 18 months for permission to preach. His successor, Barnabas Shaw, who arrived in 1816, preached without permission, like John Wesley, but within ten years he left the white Methodists at Cape Town in order to pioneer missionary work in the north. Methodism really began to flourish when the 1820 settlers arrived, among whom was William Shaw, no relative of Barnabas but also a Wesleyan minister. His prime responsibility was to minister to the settlers, but he soon became restless: 'There is not a single missionary between my residence and the northern extremity of the Red Sea,' he wrote in a report to the Mission House in London.[23] By 1823 he had pioneered the first step in that

---

[23] Horton Davies, *Great South African Christians* (Cape Town: Oxford University Press, 1951), p. 35; cf. L. A. Hewson, *An Introduction to South African Methodists* (Cape Town: Methodist Publishing House, 1951).

direction by establishing a chain of mission stations from the eastern frontier towards Natal, and ensured that the Methodist Church would eventually have the most black African members of any mainline denomination. At the same time, the Methodist Church grew to be the largest English-speaking church in the country. Continual streams of Englishmen swelled the settler community. Cornish miners and Yorkshire entrepreneurs, Wesleyans to the core, were attracted by work opportunities resulting from the discovery of diamonds in Kimberly and gold in the Transvaal as the nineteenth century drew to a close. But though white and black Methodists belonged to the same church, they worshipped in different buildings and belonged to separate circuits. The settler/mission-church pattern was adopted by them as well.

Segregation

It is perhaps strange to note that the most articulate exponents of the need for separating settler and mission churches were not always the settlers but often the missionaries, van der Kemp and John Philip leading the way. They regarded this as necessary for the sake of the indigenous peoples. One of the founders of the London Missionary Society, Thomas Love, became secretary of the Glasgow Missionary Society in 1800. From knowledge gained while with the LMS, he soon encouraged the Scots to send missionaries to the Cape. By 1824 the famous Lovedale Mission, forerunner of the University of Fort Hare, was established, and had begun what was to be a long and very distinguished ministry to black South Africans, especially the Xhosa people. Eventually, as a result of Scottish missionary work, the Bantu Presbyterian Church was born. It is interesting to read the rationale for the foundation of this church:

> The Bantu Presbyterian Church claims to be a true Church of Christ, with no barriers of colour or race, though from the circumstances of its place and service its membership will be preponderatingly of people of the Bantu races ... The Bantu Presbyterian Church however is in no sense a secessionist Church. It is the natural development of the hundred years of South African missionary work of the two Scottish Churches . . . It is the declared missionary policy of that Church to work through its missions towards the formation of self-governing and self-supporting Churches. So the 'mission' from overseas fosters a Native 'Church', and as the latter increases in strength,

the work of the 'mission' reaches completion, and a time comes when the Native Church is able to take upon itself its full responsibilities.[24]

This only happened in the 1920s, but it was the goal of many Protestant missionaries of all traditions from the outset.[25]

This question – 'Should the native churches of this country develop on independent lines, or should they be brought into organic connection with the European churches of the same denominations?'[26] – was widely debated by the various European missionary societies at the turn of the nineteenth century as missionary work came to fruition in South Africa. Successive missionary conferences stressed, as the NGK had earlier, the need to keep them apart for their own sake. 'Christianity', pleaded the French missionary Edouard Jacottet in 1907,

> is here far more foreign and exotic than it ever was among the Saxons and the Slavs. If ever it should exert on the bulk of the Native races the same attraction it did once in Europe, so as to draw them into its bosom, it must needs become thoroughly African and present itself to the Africans in such a form that they will be able to understand it and to accept it as something of their own.[27]

To insist otherwise, it was argued, was to keep Christianity alien in Africa. Thus, the Scottish missionaries helped to create the Bantu Presbyterian Church; the Swiss, the Tsonga Presbyterian Church; the French, the Evangelical Church of Lesotho; the American Board missionaries, the Bantu Congregational Church among the Zulu; and the LMS, a mission church in Botswana. Each was dependent on foreign mission boards and missionary leadership, but they were independent of the settler churches. Seperate but 'equal'

But at the same time, there was development in the opposite direction. The Coloured congregations of the LMS joined with the white Congregationalists in the Evangelical Voluntary Union in 1864, which

---

[24] Francis Wilson and Dominique Perrot (eds.), *Outlook on a Century: South Africa, 1870–1970* (Lovedale: Lovedale Press & Spro-cas, 1973), p. 390.

[25] The Bantu Presbyterian Church, later named the Reformed Presbyterian Church, united with the largely white Presbyterian Church of Southern Africa in 1999 to form the Uniting Presbyterian Church of South Africa.

[26] Wilson and Perrot (eds.), *Outlook*, p. 378.

[27] Wilson and Perrot (eds.), *Outlook*, p. 379.

became the Congregational Union in 1883 and included a fair number of Africans.[28] The white Presbyterians gradually developed their own mission work and so became multiracial in principle, though, like the Congregationalists, seldom in practice, except in the higher courts of the church. The Baptists took a similar approach, with a multiracial union, but separate congregations and work. To begin with, this was not an issue for the Roman Catholics, who, though permitted to worship and have their own chaplains, were at first discouraged by both the NGK and the Anglican authorities from undertaking missionary work. When they did, it grew with amazing rapidity; there was no separate autonomous church for black Catholics. This did not mean that there was no discrimination, or that the problem of race was resolved. In fact, the problem was far from resolved, but in principle the issue of separate churches for different ethnic groups of Catholics did not arise in the same way. Both the Roman Catholic and Anglican doctrines of the church prevented this. Separation would have meant schism.

What, then, of the Anglicans, the communion to which the governor himself belonged? We must return to 1829. There was no bishop, and the nine colonial chaplains, according to Anglican historian Peter Hinchliff, 'were not, on the whole, an inspiring body of men'.[29] The bishop of Calcutta performed the necessary episcopal functions as he journeyed between India and Britain! Robert Gray transformed the situation, and his coming in 1848 as bishop of Cape Town really marks the beginning of growth for the Anglican Church in the country. Gradually the church, with its vast diocese of about 20,000 square miles, took shape, ministering to black and white alike. By 1853 there were bishops in Grahamstown and Natal, and in 1857 Gray convened the first synod of the church, confiding in a letter to England that now he had 'transplanted the system and organization of the Church of England to this land . . .'[30]

---

[28] The story of Congregationalism in Southern Africa, including the LMS and the American Board Mission, is told in D. R. Briggs and J. Wing, *The Harvest and the Hope* (Johannesburg: UCCSA, 1970), and S. de Gruchy (ed.), *Changing Frontiers: The Mission Story of the UCCSA* (Gaborone: Pula Press, 1999).

[29] Cf. Peter Hinchliff, *The Anglican Church in South Africa* (London: Darton, Longman & Todd, 1963).

[30] Letter to Edward Gray, 10 February 1857, published in Charles Gray, *Life of Robert Gray: Bishop of Cape Town and Metropolitan of Africa*, vol. 1 (London: Rivingtons, 1876), p. 420.

There was, as might be expected, a certain amount of tension between the church in England and this fledgling Church of the Province of South Africa. A major issue concerned the appointment and therefore the dismissal of bishops. The tension reached its climax when Gray charged his erstwhile friend, Bishop Colenso of Natal, with heresy. The heresy trials against liberals in the NGK were being repeated by Anglicans. In the process Gray fought for the independence of the church in South Africa to decide its own affairs, and eventually won. This led, after many legal battles, to the formation of two separate autonomous churches – the Church of the Province (Gray's church), and the Church of England in South Africa. The latter was much smaller than the Church of the Province, but claimed continuity with the church in England. When Gray died in 1872, he left behind him a well-organized church, rapidly growing among all the races of the land, and recognized by Canterbury as the Anglican Church in South Africa.[31]

The deposed Bishop of Natal also left an important legacy. Not only had he introduced critical biblical scholarship to the country, and thus been found wanting by the Anglo-Catholic and conservative Gray, but he had also forced the issue, in spite of himself, which made the Anglican Church become an autonomous province within the Anglican communion. He also, as Peter Hinchliff reminds us, 'advocated revolutionary and unpopular missionary policies' and 'asserted very firmly that the Christian gospel possessed definite social implications'.[32] With regard to his missionary policies, Colenso was convinced that the way forward was not to reject African religious traditions and customs out of hand, as other missionaries tended to do, but to leaven African culture and its social system with the gospel. What was required was the transformation of African society, not the detribalization of individuals by turning them into black Europeans. On this, as on biblical criticism, Colenso and Gray disagreed. Zonnebloem College in Cape Town, founded by Gray for the education of the sons of African chiefs, was designed to take them out of their traditional culture and turn them into good Anglicans fitted for English society.[33]

---

[31] Hinchliff, *Anglican Church*, pp. 91f.; see also his *John William Colenso, Bishop of Natal* (London: Nelson, 1964); cf. C. Lewis and G. E. Edwards (eds.), *The Historical Records of the Church of the Province of South Africa* (London: SPCK, 1934).

[32] Hinchliff, *Church in South Africa*, p. 71.

[33] Cf. Janet Hodgson, 'Zonnebloem College, 1858–1870', unpublished MA thesis (University of Cape Town, 1975).

The struggle to make the Anglican Church and other churches of British origin relevant to South Africa was not easy, nor were its leading architects agreed on how it should be done. But they agreed that it must be attempted if the church was to survive and grow. One thing is tragically clear, however. Few if any black Christians were consulted on the subject. Paternalism was rife. Eventually, the English-speaking churches adopted a different way of relating settler church and mission church from that followed by the NGK. But during the nineteenth century, the pattern was similar if not always the same. The English-speaking churches were in fact divided along ethnic lines, even if this did not usually mean separate synods or denominations.

Afrikaner Church – English Church

The distinction between settler and mission churches is only one of the cleavages that has shaped the church in South Africa. Equally significant is the division between the NGK and the so-called English-speaking churches, that is, churches of British origin. This division is integrally related to the first, for the two groups of churches eventually took different positions on the racial composition of the church. But it is also an issue of great importance in itself. Thus, we return to the history of the NGK, especially in relation to the struggles of the Afrikaner against British imperialism.

By the late 1820s, many Afrikaners along the eastern Cape frontier had grown disenchanted with the British administration. This was largely because of the promulgation of Ordinance Fifty in 1828, at the instigation of Dr John Philip, which established the principle of equality in the sight of the law for all free persons irrespective of colour or race. Disenchantment turned to disgust when, five years later in 1833, slavery was abolished. Thus, from about 1834, numbers of Boers decided to trek beyond British rule. Anna Steenkamp gave as one of her reasons for joining the Great Trek 'the shameful and unjust proceedings with reference to the freedom of the slaves'. 'Yet', she continued, 'it is not their freedom that drove us to such lengths, as their being placed on an equal footing with Christians, contrary to the laws of God and the natural distinction of race and religion, so that it was intolerable for any decent Christian to bow beneath such a yoke; wherefore we withdrew in order to preserve our doctrines in purity.'[34]

Language was also an issue, for English was now the official language of the colony. But there was another reason for the trek: the economic. It is just as false to gloss over the economic factor in interpreting South African social history as it is to make this the key to everything else.[35] Analytically, it may be possible to separate the ethnic, cultural, religious, and economic aspects from each other, and claim the priority of one over the others. But this is not possible when the complexities of historical development are taken seriously and not simply interpreted in the light of later theories. From the earliest days at the Cape, the 'natives' were regarded as inferior, their culture was despised, and they were mistreated. Moments of enlightenment on the part of the authorities and settlers proves the rule. And in all this, economic factors played an important part. After all, the Cape was colonized in order to facilitate trade with the East. Settlement necessitated the acquisition of land and labour. A critical development in this respect was the decision very early in the life of the colony to employ slaves. Thus, when we come to analyze the reasons for the trek, as well as the rationale for much else in the growth of racial discrimination in South Africa, the question of land and labour looms large. Was Anna Steenkamp only worried about the freedom of the slaves because this placed them on an equal footing with white Christians? Was she, and was the embryonic Trekker community, not equally concerned about the economic ramifications of such liberation? Methodist church historian Leslie Hewson, in sketching the historical background to the racial problem in South Africa at a church conference in 1949, commented:

Land and Labour! No one understands the complexities of the racial situation in South Africa until he has given due consideration to the significance of land and land hunger, until he has sought to under-

---

[34] Quoted by I. D. MacCrone, *Race Attitudes in South Africa* (Oxford: Oxford University Press, 1937), p. 126.

[35] Cf. Harrison M. Wright, *The Burden of the Present: Liberal–Radical Controversy over South African History* (Cape Town & London: David Philip, 1977). See also the debate in *Social Dynamics, A Journal of the Social Sciences*, University of Cape Town, vol. 3, no. 1 (June 1977).

stand the necessity for labour, and attempted to assess the exorbitant cost of what is called 'cheap' labour.[36]

The Trekkers went north from the Cape, in search of a new land where they could build a republic of their own. They were devout men and women; avid readers of the family Bible, and able marksmen as well. But they went without the blessing of their church. In 1837 the Synod of the NGK denounced the trek, and refused permission for any of its ministers to leave the colony with the Trekkers. It is worth noting, then, that the Great Trek went ahead led by devout laymen, and sometimes ministered to by preachers of other traditions, but without the NGK clergy.[37] The theological interpreters of the events that were to shape Afrikaner tradition indelibly were not trained by Dutch or Scottish faculties of Calvinist theology, but by their own experience and their reading of the sacred book. As they journeyed, the pages came alive with meaning and relevance. The exodus of the people of Israel and their testing in the wilderness were happening again.[38] Any obstacle along the way to the promised land had to be overcome, by sheer grit and by the gun. Any doubt of divine providence was not only unthinkable, but blasphemy, a harbinger of disaster. The church at the Cape was no longer relevant, but the saga of Israel in the holy book was.

Once across the borders of the Cape, the Trekkers passed beyond the jurisdiction of both the British and the NGK. This was what the NGK had feared. But there was dissension among the Trekkers. In spite of what had happened, some wished to remain faithful to the Cape church, but schism became inevitable. In 1853 the Nederduitsch Hervormde Kerk (NHK) was born. This *Voortrekker* Church became the *volkskerk* of the South African Republic, founded by the Trekkers in the Transvaal. Six years later, also in the Republic, a further split took place, to which we referred earlier, and the Gereformeerde Kerk was born. This division was not directly the result of the trek, but a consequence of theo-

(margin note, vertical: Weaponizing the Bible)

---

[36] L. A. Hewson, 'The Historical Background', in *The Christian Citizen in a Multi-racial Society*, a report of the Rosettenville Conference, 1949 (Christian Council of South Africa), p. 44.

[37] Cf. A. Dreyer, *Die Kaapse Kerk en die Groot Trek* (Cape Town: van de Sandt de Villiers, 1929).

[38] Cf. T. Dunbar Moodie, *The Rise of Afrikanerdom: Power, Apartheid and Afrikaner Civil Religion* (Berkeley, CA: University of California Press, 1975).

logical controversy and schism in Holland. Eventually centred in Potchefstroom, the Gereformeerde Kerk adopted the neo-Calvinism of Kuyper. The Cape NGK, or, to use its proper title, the 'Nederduitse Gereformeerde Kerk' (NGK), eventually established its own synod in the Transvaal. The story is a complex one, but the result was three separate white Afrikaner Reformed churches: the NGK, with its autonomous synods; the NHK, which sought to be the true *volkskerk* of the Transvaal Republic; and the Gereformeerdes, with their ultra-Calvinist theology.

It is worth noting that the NHK regarded the NGK as tainted by Scottish Calvinism, and saw itself as theologically more flexible in the tradition of Dutch Calvinism. However, on the question of race and mission work it was the NGK, both in the Cape and Transvaal, that took the more liberal position. NGK ministers in the Transvaal expressed concern for blacks and sometimes denounced Boer race attitudes, considering them a threat to the Republic.

One reason why the NGK had been unhappy about the Great Trek was the fact that this church, after all, was the established church, and had a special relationship with the British authorities. The Anglicans were only too ready to take over in this capacity. However, by the 1860s both churches were increasingly unhappy about too close a relationship with the state. Their reasons were similar. Both churches were involved in heresy trials, the Anglicans against Bishop Colenso and the NGK against three of its theologians who were indicted on the charge of being theological liberals. In both cases, when the accused appealed to the state against the verdict of their respective churches, the state upheld their appeal. This was an intolerable situation for the leaders of the two churches, and disestablishment was the only plausible option open to them. Thus, contrary to their traditional position on church–state connections, they both supported a Congregationalist Member of Parliament, Saul Solomon, who had been trying for some time to get Parliament to withdraw state aid from the churches.

Eventually, in 1875, following the example of the colony of Natal, the Cape Parliament conceded under pressure from the NGK and the Anglicans, and Solomon's 'Voluntary Bill' was passed. Since then, there has been no established church in South Africa. Of course, this did not affect the position of the NHK, which remained the state church of the South African Republic until 1910. But all the churches in the Cape became 'free churches', free to pursue their affairs in their own way. At the same time, because of the widespread strength and unique position of the NGK, it continued to fulfil many of the social roles of an established church. And, because of the peculiar relationship of the Anglican Church to the government, and despite the 'Voluntary Bill', there was continued tension between the NGK and the Anglican Church concerning their respective positions in the country. A great deal depended on who was in political power.

It is, therefore, somewhat surprising to discover that in 1870 a short-lived attempt was made by the Anglicans, under the leadership of Bishop Gray, to unite with the Cape Dutch Reformed Church. Indeed, this was the first attempt at church union in the country. The NGK leaders were interested, if rather sceptical. Negotiations began, but they were soon shipwrecked on the issue of episcopacy. Of course, there was more to it than such theological issues. Michael Nuttall puts it tersely: 'The Dutch found no place for themselves in the English Church any more than the English found themselves a place in the Dutch.'[39] For one thing, there were very few white South-African-born priests in the Church of the Province, and even fewer who could communicate in Dutch; in this respect, the Anglicans had not taken root in the larger white Cape society. On the other hand, however, by the end of the century it was not uncommon for black priests to be members of synod, though the Anglicans were behind the Methodists, Presbyterians, and Congregationalists in this respect. As the years passed, it became increasingly significant that these English-speaking churches were becoming more multiracial in character, which meant that they had less in common on this crucial issue with the NGK and the other Afrikaner churches. This multiracialism did not mean a great deal at the time, either in terms of black leadership or in the life of local congregations. Discrimination abounded. Nevertheless, the principle of multiracialism was established, and this was potentially of great significance.

One reason for the parting of the ways between the English-speaking churches and the NGK at the end of the nineteenth century was the fact that tension between the Afrikaners and the British had spread from the Cape to the republics in the Orange Free State and the Transvaal. This fact was related to the discovery of gold and diamonds, and the attempt

---

[39] M. Nuttall, *The Making of a Tradition, 1870–1970* (Johannesburg: CPSA, 1970), pp. llf.

by the British authorities to annex Afrikaner republican territory. War broke out in the late 1880s. More significantly, a Second War of Independence, or the Anglo-Boer War, erupted in 1899, producing a legacy of bitterness that would bedevil relationships for decades to come. Relations between the Afrikaans churches (NGK, NHK, and Gereformeerdes) and the English-speaking, particularly the Anglican, were virtually non-existent, as each church generally sided with its own group. The NGK congregations nearer the western Cape were in a particularly difficult situation, as many of their members were of British descent.

The racial issue, as far as whites were concerned, was tangential to this conflict between the Afrikaner republics and Britain. While the Afrikaners wanted to retain their independence, and while the British posed as benefactors of the 'natives', control of the newly found mineral wealth was a much more powerful motive than either acknowledged. In this regard, the Africans were not seen as contestants. The general feeling was that they should be kept out of the fray altogether. It is clear, nonetheless, that most blacks identified with the imperialist cause. They hoped that a British victory would mean the extension of the franchise to include them, and the establishment of equitable land and labour rights.[40] Nevertheless, blacks became virtual spectators as the emerging Afrikaner nation took on the British imperial giant, or, perhaps more significantly for the blacks, as Christian killed Christian. Christianity could not win. Dutch Reformed ministers, like their English-speaking counterparts, found it difficult to remain neutral, and both British and Boer soldiers found appropriate moral support from within their respective ecclesiastical institutions. Perhaps this was more true of the Afrikaans churches, for their nation had its back to the wall. From their perspective they had justice on their side, a view widely held in Europe at the time. This was their country. The Boer soldiers were not alien conscripts but the fathers and sons of families who worshipped and prayed week by week in homestead and congregation throughout the land that was now a battlefield.

---

[40] Cf. the 'Statement of the Executive of the South African Native Congress, 1903' to the Rt Hon. Joseph Chamberlain, in Thomas Karis and Gwendolen M. Carter (eds.), *From Protest to Challenge: A Documentary History of African Politics in South Africa, 1882–1964*, vol. 1 (Stanford: Hoover Institution Press, 1972), pp. 18f.

As we have mentioned, this civil war created much bitterness. Indeed, some Afrikaners regarded England as a horn of the apocalyptic beast. Given the 'methods of barbarism', as British Liberal leader in the House of Commons, Campbell-Bannerman, himself described British military methods, this is not surprising. Twenty-seven thousand Afrikaner women and children, and many black servants, died in concentration camps, as superior British armoury gradually crushed the highly mobile but ill-equipped Boer commandos. As is well known, the courageous Boers had the support not only of their own people, but also of many in Europe. An illuminating example of this is found in a sermon preached by F. C. Fleischer, a Mennonite minister in Holland. The sermon was preached in Glasgow at the end of a Conference of Christian Churches on Peace, in September 1901, and later published and sold on behalf of the International Boer Women and Children's Distress Fund of Alcmaria.[41]

Fleischer's sermon was entitled 'September 15th, A Day of Tears, Not Only in South Africa'. September 15 was the day in 1901 which General Kitchener had set for the surrender of all Boer soldiers. Failing their surrender, Kitchener had decreed that they would be banished and the cost of maintaining their families charged against their property. While this had the opposite effect on the Boer soldiers than was intended, it certainly moved the Mennonite preacher of peace to understandably righteous anger:

> I think it is well, that the day begins at midnight. For the red of daybreak might seem to be the red of blushing. The beauty of sunshine is too good to welcome such a day of abomination.
>
> Who can imagine how the morning sun, symbol of Truth and Happiness, was greeted today in the Refugee-Camps of South Africa? O Sunshine, they have longed for you in the calm of a sleepless night, and yet they feared for you, the 100,000 old men, women and children, crowded into cold, shivering, damp and dark tents where the helpless young can not be properly cared for and cried in vain for food.

---

[41] A copy of the sermon is in the Bethel College Historical Library, North Newton, Kansas.

It would be a hideous irony if they should call this Sunday there a holiday of rest.

Is it a mere chance or is it a cruel purpose, that for this tyrant's date the dear Lord's Day has been chosen?

Our hearts bleed for them in their distress.

Blood is thicker than water. Kinship in itself is something. But more than our kinship speaks our sorrow, our anger because holy justice has been violated, because might is above right, because of the violence done to children who are not yet boys, to feeling women, mothers, wives, brides, daughters, to old men worn out with age . . .

Fleischer continued by lambasting the British government and war effort, and decrying war in general and this war in particular:

We address the proud Government on the banks of the silvern Thames and our eyes are filled with sorrow and reproach and we say: Even entering this war for the maintenance of your Empire, even if it be undeniable that you have not been impelled by the arrogance of pride, the passion of revenge nor the lust of gold . . . for God's sake! What right have you to carry on this war as you do?

And we sum up our grievances, many and grave grievances. Have you not armed your soldiers with dum-dum bullets, an inhuman crime, condemned by civilization and martial laws? Did not your generals in the beginning of the war like Antiochus Epiphanes selecting the Lord's Day to attack the Boers and deliberately fall upon their camps when engaged in worship? Have you not like Tiglath Pilezer Nebuchadnezzar carried off your prisoners of war into foreign regions?

The sermon continues, page after page, in similar vein. The warfare is hideous. It is doubly so because it is Protestant Britain at war with Protestant Boers. In fact, Fleischer concludes, it is all beyond understanding; 'at present we wander in darkness and grief'.

British imperialism has a great deal to answer for; it helped spawn a nationalism whose racial policies have become as hideous to the world at large as the war Britain waged against the Afrikaner. As far as black Africans were concerned, however, the British victory in 1902 held out promise of better things. Indeed, the executive of the South African

Native Congress in 1903 not only expressed loyalty to the British government, but also indebtedness for bringing the gospel to the native peoples. The executive declared:

> The question of loyalty raises the larger question of the indebtedness of the Native races to the Government and people of Great Britain. How much is implied in the thought that out of the self-sacrificing faith of the Christian nations, foremost among whom are the people of the British Isles, the Gospel of Salvation has been brought to the people that sit in darkness and the shadow of death, cannot be adequately expressed . . .[42]

But black confidence in the British government gradually dwindled away during the years following the war, as the government began to create a Union of South Africa out of the British provinces and the Afrikaner republics. Time and again, black leaders, especially church leaders and Christian spokesmen such as the Revd John L. Dube and J. Tengo Jabavu, represented black grievances and hopes before the British authorities and local commissions.[43] Every effort was made to persuade Westminster to make sure that black political and land rights were firmly established in any new constitution for a united country. But all of this was to little avail. The black voice was left crying in the wilderness, as Westminster tried to meet the conditions of the republican leaders. Moreover, it was not only the republicans who demanded segregation and white control. In fact, the roots of segregation as a political policy to ensure white supremacy and survival were part of British policy as developed by Sir Theophilus Shepstone in Natal.[44] The British settlers in that colony were strongly opposed to any kind of power-sharing and integration. The missionaries there, including Bishop Colenso, found themselves as much at odds with the colonial administration on 'native policy', as did missionaries in the other regions of southern Africa.

By 1909, after years of negotiation, Afrikaner and Englishman agreed to differ within a united country. But union under one constitution,

---

[42] Karis and Carter (eds.), *Protest*, p. 18.

[43] Karis and Carter (eds.), *Protest*, pp. 18–61.

[44] Cf. David Welsh, *The Roots of Segregation: Native Policy in Natal, 1845–1910* (Oxford: Oxford University Press, 1971).

approved by both the British Parliament in Westminster and representatives of the republics and the Cape and Natal colonies, tragically meant that the enfranchisement of the Coloureds and blacks in the Cape remained limited and was not extended beyond that colony. This was part of the bargain demanded by the republican leaders in return for approving the union. The constitution was racially discriminatory, in order to ensure the participation of the Transvaal and the Orange Free State. The verdict of *The Oxford History of South Africa* is sharp and sobering: 'In withdrawing from South Africa, Great Britain left behind a caste-like society, dominated by its white minority. The price of unity and conciliation was the institutionalization of white supremacy.'[45] In 1910, the first Parliament of the Union of South Africa was convened in Cape Town, with Pretoria as the executive capital.

Interestingly, the modern ecumenical movement was also born in 1910, in Edinburgh, with the first great international missionary conference held under the inspiration of John Mott. William Carey, the father of modern Protestant missions, had suggested such a conference as long before as 1810 and, strangely enough, had recommended Cape Town as its venue. His plan came to nothing. But the events of 1910 in Edinburgh and Cape Town have both been of great significance for South Africa. As J. du Plessis, a noted Dutch Reformed historian, wrote: 'Contemporary mission history and contemporary Cape history find a point of meeting in the year of grace 1910.'[46]

A number of South African church leaders were inspired by the Edinburgh Conference, and as a result the South African General Missionary Conference formed in 1904 took a new lease on life. It brought together missionaries and ministers of both the English- and Afrikaans-speaking churches in a series of important conferences until 1932. Two years later, John Mott himself visited the country. With him he brought the vision which was later to take form as the World Council of Churches. But before that dream was realized in Amsterdam in 1948, it became real in South Africa in 1936, when the Christian Council of South Africa was constituted in Bloemfontein. Members of the NGK Cape and Transvaal Synods played leading roles in this development. But this fledgling attempt on the part of English and Afrikaans

---

[45] Wilson and Thompson (eds.), *Oxford History of South Africa*, vol. 2, p. 364.
[46] Du Plessis, *History of Christian Missions*, p. vii.

Christians to discover each other in fellowship and service was to be short-lived. It fell victim to the nationalist aspirations of the Afrikaner and the insensitivities of the English.

The years after 1910 were years of intense struggle for the Afrikaner people, a struggle for identity in a land which they had lost through war but which they regarded as their own, a land dominated by a foreign government, economy, and culture. In 1914 the National party was launched in Bloemfontein, with the conviction that the way to regain what had been lost by conquest was through the development of a sepa-rate nation (*volk*) within the Union, stressing its own distinct language, traditions, religion, and institutions. While the motto of the Union was 'Unity is Strength', the Nationalists echoed the slogan of nineteenth-century Dutch Nationalism, 'Isolation is Strength'. The story of this struggle is a relatively complex one, and does not need to be repeated here, but it is nonetheless an important factor in the history of the churches in the land. It is also important because it gave birth to what has more recently been described as Afrikaner civil religion, a phenom-enon to which we will return.

Afrikaners were by no means united in the struggle for identity and power. The other major political party, the South African Party (SAP), which later became the United Party (UP), was led by ex-Boer generals Louis Botha and Jan Smuts, and included many Afrikaans-speaking people. Smuts believed that the future depended on white unity between the Afrikaner and English-speaking South Africans; but others such as General Barry Hertzog, and later Dr D. F. Malan, were convinced that the way into a secure future was through an Afrikaner Nationalism that carefully strove to maintain its own distinct identity, separate from the English community as well as the 'non-Europeans'. This division among Afrikaners had its impact upon the Afrikaans churches, especially the NGK in the Cape. Many ministers and members of this church favoured co-operation with the English-speaking community and their churches. But on the whole, the Afrikaans churches could not remain aloof from the Nationalist aspirations of their people, for they were very much churches of the people. This was especially so in the area of social welfare. Many Afrikaners, especially in the cities, were very poor, and the church was their main source of solidarity and comfort, Some Dutch Reformed ministers left the pulpit and entered politics, while many others supported the struggle through social and cultural organizations.

Political ministers were as much in evidence then as political priests became once the National party came to power in 1948.

But quite apart from any direct involvement in political activity, the NGK held the key to the birth of Afrikanerdom. In every town and village, the NGK and its sister Afrikaner churches provided continuity with the traditions of the Afrikaner. They provided educated and articulate leadership, and offered a moral and spiritual basis for personal and social life. They were the spiritual home for the potentially great but slowly emerging Afrikaner Nationalism that was to dominate so much of twentieth-century South African history.

The struggle against British imperialism was more than a military one. The war with weapons had been fought and lost – for the moment. The spiritual and cultural struggle had to continue, or begin again and be sustained on other flanks: education and language, welfare and economics. Cultural and particularly language (Afrikaans) rights had to be achieved; children had to be educated in ways consonant with their Afrikaner heritage; the Afrikaner had to gain access to the growing economy of the country and find ways of adapting to the alien environment of burgeoning cities and towns. And, above all, the Afrikaner needed to develop a sense of history, a vision for the future, and a strategy which could inspire action, create an identity and solidarity, and so lay the foundations for eventual victory.

A defeated people need an interpretation of their history, a *mythos*, which can enable them to discover significance in what has happened to them. The continuity of the Afrikaner demanded such a world-view which would provide coherence to their shattered hopes. Such a *mythos* was not difficult to construct, especially for a people with such a strong belief in providence and an existential awareness of the plight of ancient Israel as it sought liberation from the Egyptian yoke. So it is not surprising that Afrikaner history, like that of other nations, took on a sacred character. This was especially true of history since the Great Trek. While such 'holy history', with its vivid use of Old Testament motifs, was not official Dutch Reformed theology, it was certainly fundamental to Afrikaner self-understanding.[47]

---

[47] Cf. F. A. van Jaarsveld, *The Afrikaners' Interpretation of South African History* (Cape Town: Simondium, 1964); Moodie, *Rise*; W. A. de Klerk, *The Puritans in Africa: A History of Afrikanerdom* (Harmondsworth: Penguin Books, 1975).

Dr D. F. Malan, a former minister and the Nationalist leader who became Prime Minister in 1948, described this history as follows:

> Our history is the greatest masterpiece of the centuries. We hold this nationhood as our due for it was given to us by the Architect of the universe. [His] aim was the formation of a new nation among the nations of the world. . . . The last hundred years have witnessed a miracle behind which must lie a divine plan. Indeed, the history of the Afrikaner reveals a will and a determination which makes one feel that Afrikanerdom is not the work of men but the creation of God.[48]

In their struggle against British imperialism, especially in the aftermath of the Anglo-Boer War, or the Second War of Independence, the Afrikaners drew immense strength from this interpretation of history. They detected a sacred thread running through all the events of their past, beginning with the Great Trek into the unknown (the exodus) and including the encounter with and victory over the black nations (Philistines), especially at the Battle of Blood River, where they entered into a sacred covenant with God, the entry into the promised land of the Transvaal and Orange Free State, and the encounter with the pursuing British. Though they believed defeat on the battlefield in 1902 was the judgment of God calling his people back to their covenant as his people, they knew it was not the cancellation of the call to be his people and bring light to the dark continent. Their struggle was not over. They still had that eschatological vision which anticipated once again the rebirth of a republic in which the Afrikaner would be the free and undisputed ruler under the providence of the Almighty.

The Afrikaner churches fulfilled a central role not just in this struggle for identity, but also in providing a theological base upon which nationalism could flourish.[49] G. D. Scholtz, a prominent Afrikaner author, wrote: 'Without hesitation it can be said that it is principally due to the Church that the Afrikaner nation has not gone under . . . With the dilution of this philosophy [i.e., the unity of nation, church and party] it [the Afrikaner nation] must inevitably disappear . . . that is the great difference between the Afrikaner nation and other nations'.[50] Here we

---

[48] Quoted by Moodie, *Rise*, p. 1.

[49] Moodie, *Rise*, pp. 52ff.

[50] Quoted in Wilson and Thompson (eds.), *Oxford History of South Africa*, vol. 2, p. 373. Quoted in Moodie, *Rise*, p. 67.

see the powerful impact of Dutch nationalistic thought adapted to the Afrikaner situation. Mediated through philosophers such as Herman Dooyeweerd in Holland, and interpreted by men such as H. G. Stoker at the University for Christian Higher Education at Potchefstroom, it provided the framework for and the necessary legitimation of both Afrikaner Nationalism and its racial policies:

> God willed the diversity of Peoples. Thus far He has preserved the identity of our People. Such preservation was not for naught, for God allows nothing to happen for naught. He might have allowed our People to be bastardized with the native tribes as happened with other Europeans. He did not allow it . . . He has a future task for us, a calling laid away. On this I base my fullest conviction that our People will again win back their freedom as a People. This lesson of our history must always be kept before our eyes.[51]

As Dunbar Moodie says,

> For Stoker, the People (volk) was a separate social sphere with its own structure and purpose, grounded in the ordinances of God's creation. Here Stoker's Calvinism was able to accommodate the Afrikaner civil religion, indeed to undergird it, for the Afrikaner People, too, was sovereign in its own circle, acknowledging no other master than God, whose purpose was to be seen in its structures and calling, its historical destiny.[52]

This was, in sum, a civil religion based on a doctrine of creation, history, culture, and calling, designed to uphold the Afrikaner people in their struggle for identity, survival, and power, against all odds.

But it was also a theology that included the corollary that every other ethnic group should also retain its identity as part of the will of God. A main drafter of the National party constitution and policy was J. D. du Toit, the son of a founding father of the Gereformeerde Kerk. Like his father, du Toit was deeply committed to Kuyper's theology and Christian National principles. Indeed, it has been cogently argued that it was the Gereformeerde Kerk rather than the NGK, Potchefstroom rather than Pretoria or Stellenbosch, that really provided the theological

---

[51] Quoted in Moodie, *Rise*, p. 67.

[52] Moodie, *Rise*, p. 66; cf. Charles Villa-Vicencio, 'South African Civil Religion: An Introduction', *Journal of Theology for Southern Africa*, no. 19 (June 1977), pp. 8ff.

basis for Afrikaner Nationalism.[53] But such nationalist convictions also had a significant following within the NGK itself. It was a Dutch Reformed missionary conference in 1950 that was to recommend 'territorial apartheid', and so prepare the ground not only for one of the most controversial and heartbreaking pieces of apartheid legislation, the Group Areas Act, which has caused such tremendous bitterness within the black community, but for separate development itself. It is indicative of the vast difference in perspective between Afrikaner Nationalists and those opposed to separate development that a man such as J. C. G. Kotze, who was opposed to racial discrimination, could regard the resolution of this conference in such a positive light. Total segregation was not wrong or bad; it was right and good. Separate development was the will of God. Commenting on the recommendation, Kotze said:

> It must be remembered that no people in the world who is worth its salt, will always be content with no, or even an indirect, voice in the political and social economic organizations of the country whose decisions are taken with regard to its interests or future. To expect such a thing from the Bantu, is not only unfair to the Bantu, but it will eventually lead to the greatest disillusionment and strife.[54]

It was to certain Afrikaner theologians that the National party ideologists turned for scriptural and theological justification for their racial policies and too readily obtained them, to the dismay of other Christians, including other Dutch Reformed theologians and ministers. Thus, the seeds of apartheid, or separate development, as it was officially called in NGK and National Party documents, were sown in the fertile soil of Afrikaner religious belief and fed with the conviction that a Christian National policy and way of life was fundamental to the survival and proper growth of Afrikanerdom, and therefore necessary for South Africa as a whole.[55]

However, if some Afrikaner theologians provided the framework

---

[53] Hexham, 'Dutch Calvinism'.

[54] J. C. G. Kotze, *Principle and Practice in Race Relations* (Stellenbosch: CSA Publishers, 1962), p. 15.

[55] My use of the term 'separate development', which was a euphemism for apartheid, was, at that time, part of my attempt to address NGK theologians and church members in a way that sought to critically engage them rather than alienate them from the outset. Many used to say 'we do not support apartheid; we promote separate development'.

and justification for what eventually became apartheid, it was not they who filled the framework with its full ideological content. Those responsible for this were a group of well-educated, highly articulate Afrikaners who were gradually replacing the old Boer generals in the Afrikaner hierarchy and struggle for power. Bound together in a secret society known as the *Broederbond*, they believed that the Afrikaner nation was specifically put in this land by God to fulfil a particular calling as a nation, and that the maintenance of Afrikaner identity was essential to this task, and therefore part of the will of God. Profoundly influenced by German idealism and what Moodie calls 'neoFichteanism', this new generation of thinkers and political visionaries was able to stir the hopes and direct the steps of their people – first, in overthrowing the British yoke, and second, in developing an ideology that enabled them to meet the growing threat of the black races. These men, especially Dr D. F. Malan, Dr H. Verwoerd, Dr N. Diederichs, Dr P. J. Meyer, and Dr Geoff Cronje, were the ideological pioneers of the National party. It was largely in connection with this ideological development that W. A. de Klerk wrote: 'Afrikaner politics was slowly but fatally being theologized. There was a grow-ing urge to set the South African world aright, once and for all, to reconstruct it and redeem it in terms of a newly-defined Afrikaner "lewens-en-wereldbeskouing" – a world view.' The National party, he comments, 'was itself becoming, if not a church, then a party imbued with religion – a secular religion – at its very roots.'[56]

What can we now say about English-speaking South Africa? Unlike Afrikaner Nationalism, the English in South Africa had few leaders with a sense of national calling and destiny. But there were some who regarded South Africa as crucial to the designs of British imperialism. Notable among these was Cecil John Rhodes. It was the ambition of Rhodes to paint Africa red from Cape to Cairo – a somewhat ironical vision once red no longer referred to British territory, but Soviet Communism, on maps of the world. Rhodes' imperial dream of political and economic power, no less than Afrikaner Nationalism, claimed religious sanction. 'Only one race', he declared, 'approached God's ideal type, his own Anglo-Saxon race; God's purpose then was to make the Anglo-Saxon race predominant.'[57] The will-to-power was justified in the name

[56] De Klerk, *Puritans in Africa*, p. 199.
[57] Quoted by David Bosch, 'The Church and the Liberation of Peoples?', *Missionalia*, vol. 5, no. 2 (August 1977), p. 33.

of God, on behalf of the Queen and the empire. Military flags and memorials in Anglican cathedrals throughout the country testify to this English civil religion that pervaded South Africa at the turn of the century. An inseparable relationship existed between God and the empire. Anglicans apparently found nothing incongruous about the Union Jack coexisting with cross and altar, even when blood-stained from encounters with Boers and 'natives'. Somehow, British success in battle was ordained and blessed by God.[58]

In his rather idealized account of English-speaking South Africans, John Bond described them as a community with 'restless energy, the freshness of ideas' and the inventiveness needed to break into South Africa's history and transform it.[59] They had something of that vision, commitment, and drive characteristic of Victorian England, which inspired missionaries, public servants, and settlers all over the world, and which made the empire what it was. But the South African English were rather different in ethos from their Puritan fellow-countrymen who had settled in New England, and from their newly found Afrikaner countrymen, the 'Puritans in Africa'. The British settlers in South Africa were the products of a Europe in transition. It was a very different Europe from the one which the Puritans of North America and those of South Africa had left two centuries before. No European could remain untouched by the social, political, and industrial revolutions of the eighteenth and nineteenth centuries. Moreover, the social vision that inspired the British settlers was not theocratic Calvinism, but the imperial dream – a sense of belonging to a mighty empire whose will was supreme and whose ways were always just.

⌐A concomitant of this civil religion was the tendency for the Christian faith to become highly individualistic.⌐And when the full impact of the Enlightenment and revolutionary Europe finally destroyed the Christian convictions of many, at about the same time as the imperial dream began to fade away, all that really remained to characterize the English as a group was secular individualism. This has often degenerated into

---

[58] Cf. Peter Hinchliff, 'The "English-speaking Churches" and South Africa in the Nineteenth Century', *Journal of Theology for Southern Africa*, no. 9 (December 1974), pp. 32f.; John W. de Gruchy, 'English-speaking South Africans and Civil Religion', *Journal of Theology for Southern Africa*, no. 19 (June 1977), pp. 45ff.

[59] John Bond, *They Were South Africans* (Oxford: Oxford University Press, 1956), p. 5.

apathy, cynicism, and indifference towards social and political issues, and it was precisely this laissez-faire approach to life that the Afrikaner Calvinist and Nationalist regarded as symptomatic of their age-long arch-enemy, 'liberalism'. For the Afrikaner, liberalism was generally regarded as the essence of unbelief.[60] It is important to keep this distinction in mind, for it is a significant example of the cultural and thus communication gap that existed between the two major white communities in South Africa. This gap has affected the life of the English-speaking churches, giving them an image in the eyes of the Afrikaner that they have not always relished. It has dogged attempts to break out of imported theological traditions and provide afresh theology for a new situation.

Shortly after 1910, two-thirds of the white population was English-speaking; from then on, this proportion gradually decreased.[61] English-speaking South Africa was at its zenith. It dominated the civil service, controlled finance and industry, had a firm grip on education, commanded the major cities, and was part of a larger empire that ruled the world. Yet, it should be remembered that the English could never govern South Africa alone. Their political power depended on unity with those Afrikaners who, like Jan Smuts, sought to bridge the gap between the white sections of the population. Thus, while the English could dominate much of Parliament, they were always in need of Afrikaner support.

Similarly, after the Anglo-Boer War and the founding of the union, the NGK still dominated the church scene in South Africa. At the same time, the English-speaking churches benefited from the advantages that were accruing to the English-speaking community as a whole. This was particularly true for the Anglican Church, whose synods were now attended by high-ranking state officials. On more than one occasion the church was able to address the fledgling nation in the presence of the Governor General.[62] The shades of English establishment were not too

---

[60] Cf. James Leatt, 'Liberalism, Ideology, and the Christian in the South African Context', *Journal of Theology for Southern Africa*, no. 22 (March 1978), pp. 31ff.

[61] H. L. Watts, 'A Social and Demographic Portrait of English-Speaking White South Africans', in Andre de Villiers (ed.), *English-Speaking South Africa Today* (Cape Town: Oxford University Press, 1976), pp. 46f.

[62] Cf. Hinchliff, *Anglican Church*, pp. 183ff.; Louis Bank, 'An Analytical Outline of the Socio-Political Role of the Church of the Province of South Africa, as Reflected in the Resolutions of Provincial Synods from 1910–1948' (Research paper, University of Cape Town, 1976).

far away. Indeed, throughout the period 1910–48, the majority of the upper crust of English South Africans who held positions of power and responsibility in the country belonged to the Church of the Province. It is important, then, to inquire about the role of the Anglican Church with regard to the unfolding socio-political situation. This is particularly important in view of the criticism by both Marxist and Nationalist commentators that the English-speaking churches only became critical of racism in South Africa after 1948.

Although synodical resolutions cannot be regarded as synonymous with church action or practice, it is nevertheless striking that virtually all the resolutions of the Synod of the Church of the Province on social issues during the post-union pre-apartheid period were related to the race problem.[63] The church was outspoken on the question of justice for the African population, especially in terms of land distribution; African education; the need for effective and proper consultation with Africans on matters affecting them; and the need for better housing and living conditions. The synod in 1915 reacted to the Native Land Act of 1913 by asking that it be 'immediately repealed until such a time as more generous and comprehensive legislation is forthcoming'.

At the same time, the Church of the Province was ambivalent on some issues, and was not critical of all racially discriminatory legislation. By and large, the church was conservative. On occasion it intimated that it did not wish to disturb social custom, whether in the life of the church itself or the state. Yet, the Synod of 1924 stated that 'the relations prevailing between Christians of different races belonging to our own Church are not what they should be' and so desired 'an adjustment of the relations between groups of Christians living in the same places, without aiming at any interference with social customs'. This adjustment was meant to express in an unmistakable way 'the Brotherhood of all in Christ, the equality of all before God, and the unity of the Body' and to 'witness to our desire for the inclusion of all races in the one Church of Christ'. Similarly, in 1930, the Anglican bishops stated plainly: 'We believe that rights to full citizenship in any country are not dependent on race or colour, but on men's fitness to discharge the responsibilities which such citizenship involves.'[64]

---

[63] Cf. Bank, 'Analytical Outline'.

[64] Cf. 'What my Church Has Said', a pamphlet published by the Church of the Province, n.d., p. 1.

It is difficult to determine the impact of these resolutions upon society at the time. That some of them were never followed up by the church itself is obvious from the fact that committees appointed for this purpose sometimes never reported back. The gap between synodical resolve and congregational involvement was as real then as it is today. But the fact that the church did try to influence the state in its pleas on behalf of African rights is also obvious. At first the state was not regarded as the enemy, but as the years passed and discrimination became more intransigent, the state appeared more and more as an opponent in the struggle for justice. The church persistently called upon the state to consult with Africans 'for the well-being of the Native People and the security of the country'. But like the church's other pleas, this one remained unheeded and unheard by those to whom it was addressed. On reflection, it is tragic that neither the church nor the state was finally able to work successfully for the kinds of changes that Christian insight proclaimed then as essential for the future. Yet, nothing can alter the fact that the church attempted to speak the prophetic word, and on occasion to implement it.

It is helpful in understanding the life of the Church of the Province, to remember that many of its bishops, priests, and missionaries were influenced by Anglican Christian socialism in England. The theology of F. D. Maurice, and later of William Temple, had considerable impact. As Peter Hinchliff puts it:

> The heroic crusades of Anglo-Catholic priests in the English slums had a profound effect upon the Anglican Church in this country. The ideal of the priest became that of the Christian socialist, struggling to bring the Faith to the poor and underprivileged, fighting their battles in matters of housing, of political and civic rights, striving for social justice, for fair wages, and no sweated labour. And just as the Union of South Africa came into existence the Province received its first Archbishop who possessed an Anglo-Catholic and Christian socialist background . . . the proclamation of Union and the emergence of the Catholic-socialist ideal coincided.[65]

This social witness of the Anglican Church during the period 1910–48 was more or less the same as that of the English-speaking churches as a

---

[65] Hinchliff, *Anglican Church*, p. 231.

whole. The basic difference was the special place the Church of the Province had as a result of its connection with the British establishment. From a contemporary perspective, much of what it said and did was undoubtedly paternalistic. The concept of white guardianship was prevalent. There were no black Anglican bishops, and the leadership of the churches was firmly in the hands of missionaries and other whites. Yet, throughout the period, the number of black delegates to the synods of the churches increased. It was during this era that men such as Z. K. Matthews and Albert Luthuli came to prominence as dedicated Christians and articulate leaders of their people within the churches as well as the nation. Indeed, the churches and the country were blessed with increasing numbers of black leaders of Christian commitment, stature, and ability.

In spite of the tension between Afrikaner and English-speaking South Africa during the decades following Union and the First World War, relations between the NGK and the English-speaking churches were cordial, and attempts were made to foster co-operation between them. These were the years of ecumenical stirring which led in 1936 to the formation of the Christian Council of South Africa. The Cape and Transvaal Synods of the NGK were foundation members, and very active as such.[66] But such co-operation was gradually undermined by the twin factors of nationalism and race, which eventually led to the departure of the NGK from participation in the Christian Council.

In 1941, in the midst of the Second World War, the Transvaal Synod of the NGK withdrew from the Christian Council. This was one of many signs that the Afrikaner wanted to go it alone. Dr William Nicol, who was both a moderator of the NGK and the president of the Christian Council, gave three reasons for this withdrawal, all of them significant for understanding inter-church relations between the Afrikaner and the English South African. First, the council was not really bilingual, but English in its orientation; second, there were fundamental differences of opinion between the churches on the 'native question'; third, the other synods of the NGK (Natal and Orange Free State) were not prepared to join the council.[67] None of these issues was ostensibly theological,

---

[66] Cf. E. Strassberger, *Ecumenism in South Africa: 1936–1960* (Johannesburg: SACC, 1974), pp. 134ff.

[67] Strassberger, *Ecumenism*, pp. 157f.

though each had considerable theological implication. But they were of great consequence to the NGK Synods of the Transvaal and Cape, and caused their withdrawal. It is painfully true that the council was not very relevant to the needs of the NGK and its Afrikaans constituency. Few of those attending council meetings were able to speak or understand Afrikaans. There was also a sense of English superiority. Many of those involved were foreign missionaries, not South Africans. It is also painfully true that the members of the council could not agree on the 'native question'. Throughout the 1930s the NGK was more and more influenced by the concept of apartheid, for which it was partly responsible, while the other members of the council tended to be more liberal on racial issues. The NGK was primarily concerned about the plight of the Afrikaner. And, as the third point indicates, the NGK was by no means united. The Synods of Natal and the Free State were more conservative than those of the Transvaal and Cape, and wanted nothing to do with the ecumenical movement, which they believed would liberalize the church and even lead to flirtation with Rome.

[margin note: NGK – pro Afrikaaner]

It is interesting to note that when the Transvaal Synod announced its withdrawal, the Anglican Church of the Province chose to do the same because it saw no purpose in remaining in a body from which the NGK was absent. However, it was persuaded to rejoin a short while later. This nevertheless indicates how much the English-speaking churches felt the need for co-operation with their Afrikaner counterparts. It also suggests that there was very little by way of an 'English-speaking church front'. Most Anglican bishops from the time of Gray were more concerned about relationships with the NGK than with the English-speaking Nonconformists. The ecclesiastical and social divisions imported from Britain were far too real to permit much ecumenical co-operation between them. Indeed, the English-speaking Nonconformists and Scottish Presbyterians sometimes felt more affinity with the NGK than with the Anglicans. They had little in common with the latter, except language and perhaps racial attitudes. And yet, in the long term, it was their consensus on the racial issue that was of the greater significance.

Shortly after the end of the Second World War, the 1945 Anglican Synod addressed the nation on 'social righteousness'. It declared: 'It is the duty of all Christian people to apply, consistently and unsparingly, the highest tests of Christian conduct to the social and industrial organization of any State which claims to be, in any sense, a Christian country.'

[margin note: Xstians are to be Socially responsible]

39

Society, not just individuals, had to be transformed in terms of Christian ethics. This, too, was the conviction of the NGK and the Gereformeerde Kerk. But what the Anglicans and the other English-speaking churches envisaged was not the same, as was already evident by then and as would become more obvious within the next decade.

Black Church – White Church

There were three ecclesiastical alternatives for black Christians in South Africa by the turn of the twentieth century. They could be members of mission churches, whose membership was wholly black, but which were under the control of white missionaries and their mission boards in Europe, North America, or, in the case of the NGK, South Africa, and which would only much later achieve their autonomy. A second possibility was that they could be members of multiracial denominations, those churches largely of British origin where the line between settler and mission church had not been clearly drawn. But here, likewise, the black members were dominated by white leadership, European customs, discrimination, and a great deal of paternalism. In some respects, this was worse than belonging to the wholly black mission churches. There was a third option. They could leave the mission and the multiracial churches and initiate their own.

In the *Christian Express*, a Church of Scotland missionary journal published at Lovedale, the editorial of June 1906 discussed the problem of the rise of what it termed independent 'Native Churches' in the country:

> During the past dozen years, the South African Mission Field has unhappily witnessed a number of secessions of Native Church members. Some of these have been from Churches with both European and Native members. Others have been from Churches where the membership was entirely Native; so that these secessions have not been entirely due to racial feeling. Various reasons have been given by the seceders for the course they have followed. Most frequently the alleged cause has been difficulty of working together, a feeling of being curbed, or overshadowed, or otherwise restricted in the exercise of their activities, or a lack of mutual trust and confidence. In some cases

these reasons have no doubt been sincerely believed and acted upon. In others they have been a mere pretext, cloaking less worthy motives. The number and extent of these secessions call for earnest consideration, if for no other reason than the danger they constitute to the Native Church.[68]

The editor spelled out the dangers. The schisms, he claimed, were 'the occasion of much bitterness' in the native areas; they 'lowered the vitality of the Native Church' and 'led to great laxity of Church discipline'. Moreover, the editor warned, the Christian creed itself would be affected. 'Already', he declared, 'there have been two Native Messiahs!' But he also recognized that the fault was not entirely on the side of the native schismatics:

> It may be that the Missionary Churches have been slow to recognise that the Native Church is quickly leaving its childhood behind, and is able to take upon itself an increased measure of self-control. It is conscious of new powers and is impatient of dictation. Because the parent has been slow to observe the development which was bound to come, and has not been quick enough to recognise the need of directing these new energies to work on useful and absorbing enterprises, the Native Church has in these separatist movements wrested from the parent's hand what it regards as its rights, and has asserted its ability to manage its own affairs.[69]

However, not all these so-called independent churches were the same, and their motives were, as the editor indicates, varied.

Something of the thinking of the founders of the independent church movement can be gathered from the following extract taken from the 'Testimony of the Rev. Samuel Jacobus Brander, the Rev. Joshua Mphothleng, and Stephen Nquato of the Ethiopian Catholic Church in Zion, before the South African Native Affairs Commission' in October 1904. The answers were given by Samuel Brander:

Q. Who do you represent?
A. I represent the Ethiopian Catholic Church in Zion.

---

[68] Wilson and Perrot (eds.), *Outlook*, p. 375.
[69] Wilson and Perrot (eds.), *Outlook*, p. 377.

Q. What is that?

A. It is an organisation which we have commenced lately since we resigned from the A.M.E. Church.

Q. Are you the head of it?

A. Yes.

Q. What were you belonging to before?

A. To the A.M.E. Church.

Q. And before that?

A. We belonged to the Church of England before we joined the A.M.E. Church.

Q. Why did you leave that Church and start your own?

A. When we found that we could not get ahead, Makone and myself came together to raise the Church of Ethiopia, and later on we joined the A.M.E. Church of America, because we found at that time that it would go better if we joined the American Church, as they had education and other things better than we had. We considered that it would be better for us to join them, so that they could help us, being coloured people themselves.

Q. What was your object in leaving the A.M.E. Church and starting a Church of your own?

A. We left on account of the promises they gave us when we joined them not being kept . . .

Q. During the six years you were a minister of the American Church, did you receive any grants from America at all?

A. Not one.

Q. Was there any political teaching in the Church during the six years you were a member of it?

A. Not to my knowledge.

Q. Have you in the Church that you have just lately started no white supervision whatever?

A. No.

Q. What is your object in starting a Church independent of the white man and of white control; seeing that your first attempt at that was a failure, what is the reason that you made a second attempt?

A. We have not seen that we have become a failure as yet.

Q. Did you not say you made a mistake by joining the A.M.E. Church?

A. In joining the American Church we thought that, as they were our own colour, they would help us up, but we found they helped us down, and they took all the best positions without telling us a word, sending men from America . . .

The inquiry turned to political questions. The black church leaders acknowledged that the 'natives' were not yet ready for political control. For one thing, they lacked adequate education. But in time this would be overcome:

> Q. And you would also like in time by constitutional methods, that is by lawful measures, to get yourselves into the control and management of public affairs in the Government as you have done in the Church?
> A. Yes, I should think so.
> Q. And where would you end; would you like the races to amalgamate?
> A. Yes.

After further questioning, the Revd Samuel Brander explained that he did not mean that the 'natives' would ever have control over the whites:

> Q. You recognise that the white man must always govern in this country?
> A. I recognise it that way.
> Q. What is it then you desire: religious freedom?
> A. Yes, religious freedom.
> Q. Do you in your church preach loyalty to the Government and obedience to the white man?
> A. Yes.[70]

The authorities clearly perceived something of a political threat in the rise of the independent churches.[71] And when the representations which some of the leaders made to the authorities on questions of voting rights, wages, land, and labour are carefully read, there remains little doubt that

---

[70] Karis and Carter (eds.), *Protest*, pp. 39f. The A.M.E. Church is the African Methodist Episcopalian Church.

[71] Cf. Leo Kuper, 'African Nationalism in South Africa, 1910–1964', in Wilson and Thompson (eds.), *Oxford History of South Africa*, vol. 2, pp. 434f.

the independent churches were concerned about more than just religious freedom. They wanted the liberation of their people from all unjust bondages, including control by black Americans in the African Methodist Episcopalian Church. But, at least for the time being, they had to be content with religious freedom.\

The first major study of the African independent churches, later referred to as African indigenous or initiated, was done by a Lutheran missionary in Zululand, Bengt Sundkler.[72] Sundkler distinguished between three types of independent churches. There were those that retained the outward forms, structure, and much of the theology of their parent body, and usually continued to use the name of that church as part of their new title. These churches Sundkler labelled 'Ethiopian', a name that clearly stressed the fact that Christianity came to Africa long before any European missionary. The main reason for their breakaway was racial, the desire to control their own affairs, and sometimes the desire for prestige as well as power. Then there were those Sundkler described as 'Zionist', church groups within which Christian faith and African tradition blended together in a dynamic synthesis, and sometimes syncretism. Considerable emphasis was given to ecstatic utterances, prophecy, dreams, healing, purification rites, and taboos. A third type, 'Messianic', referred to those churches that apparently followed the leadership of 'Native Messiahs', as the editorial in the Christian Express called them. Many years later Sundkler was to reject the use of this third category as pejorative, unwarranted, and misleading.[73]

There were various reasons for this separatist movement.[74] First it was a rejection of white control both in the mission and the multiracial churches, especially with regard to questions concerning church discipline. Second, it was a rejection in many instances, and especially in the case of the 'Zionists', of European culture and of the suppression of African culture in the life of the church. African culture was customarily rejected by missionaries, including men of the stature of Robert Moffat, as heathen or at least inferior. Third, particularly in the multiracial churches, the cause was plainly racial discrimination and paternalism.

---

[72] Bengt Sundkler, *Bantu Prophets in South Africa* (London: Lutterworth, 1948).

[73] Bengt Sundkler, *Zulu Zion and Some Swazi Zionists* (Oxford: Oxford University Press, 1976), pp. 308f.

[74] Cf. Trevor Verryn, *A History of the Order of Ethiopia* (Johannesburg: Central Mission Press, 1972), pp. 17ff.

Fourth, the desire for power and prestige partially explains the myriad of subsequent splinter groups within the independent church movement itself. By 1970, it included perhaps as many as 3,000 different groups with a combined total of more than three and a half million members.

Opinions varied about the significance of this rapidly growing movement. Sundkler first regarded it negatively as a bridge across which black Africans would return from Christianity to heathenism. He discerned the danger of syncretism, the confusion of culture and Christ. This was the view of most missionaries and the mainline churches until the 1960s. Later, opinions slowly changed. Sundkler's view became more and more positive. For one thing, it was recognized that every form of Christianity is in danger of syncretism, European Christianity as much as any other. One of the very reasons why the independent churches arose in the first place was because the white-dominated churches were so captive to European culture. The church cannot escape from the culture in which it is set. It has to relate to it if it is to exist and witness at all. So the African initiated churches were increasingly recognized as legitimate expressions, by and large, of Christian faith in Africa, and as legitimate protests against many of the spiritually deadening influences in the more traditional churches.

The independent churches served another significant purpose. The rapid growth of black urbanization, stimulated by migratory labour and post-war industrialization, had radically altered the socio-cultural existence of the black community since early in the twentieth century. As a result, much of the former tribal cohesion was fragmented and many personal and social problems arose without traditional resources available to handle them. The independent churches enabled many urban blacks to cope with this alien world of the townships.[75]

The groups vary a great deal, and some have been more successful than others in developing an indigenous Christian lifestyle. Generalizations are difficult. Whatever their faults, however, these churches stand as a legitimate protest against white racism and ecclesiastical imperialism, and in their own right as remarkable attempts to bring together Christian faith and the traditions of Africa. It was to take the mission and

---

[75] Cf. Monica Wilson and Archie Mafeje, *Langa: A Study of Social Groups in an African Township* (Oxford: Oxford University Press, 1963), pp. 91ff., 175f.; Martin West, *Bishops and Prophets in a Black City: African Independent Churches in Soweto, Johannesburg* (Cape Town: David Philip, 1975).

multiracial churches years to fully understand the theological and social significance of the movement, though the authorities were aware of its political potential very early. It is our contention that whatever the reasons given for the birth and growth of this African independent church movement, and whatever its problems and failures, it is properly understood as part of the story of the struggle of the Christian church in South Africa.

These independent churches symbolize the black revolt against European spiritual and cultural domination. However, while some soon appeared to become largely apolitical, their rise was coterminous with and paralleled by the awakening of black nationalism. And since Christians led the way, this development becomes part of our story. The African National Congress was born in 1912, in the same place, Bloemfontein, as the Afrikaner National party two years later. The history of African and black nationalism is as complex as that of Afrikaner Nationalism.[76] All the while the Afrikaner was struggling for power among white South Africans, black Africans saw their own rights being curtailed and denied. It was an even more burdensome task for the African to pick himself up after centuries of defeat and servitude than it was for the Afrikaner, for the African did not even have the vote. And, in one sense, this task could not truly be undertaken until after the Afrikaner had completed his own struggle for power. White politicians had continually turned black people into pawns in their own efforts to control Parliament.

It is very sobering, in the light of the history of apartheid, to read the story of the birth and struggles of the African National Congress. As during the period 1903–9, the pleas and petitions of black leaders for the political rights of their people fell on deaf ears for most of the time. Document after document tells the story of one disappointment after another, whether in dealing with Britain or with the South African government. And all the time, political rights dwindled, beginning with the Native Land Act of 1913, which, in the name of territorial separation, not only failed to distribute land on anything like an equitable basis, but also deprived the 'natives' of basic rights regarding the acquisition of land and the freedom to sell their labour through bargaining in the open

---

[76] Cf. A. P. Walshe, *The Rise of African Nationalism in South Africa* (London: University of California Press, 1970); Kuper, 'African Nationalism'.

market, and thus severely limited 'all opportunities for their economic improvement and independence'.[77] It is interesting to note that during many of the early years of the black political struggle, the principle of separation was accepted by some black nationalist leaders, provided that, as the Revd John Dube, president of the South African Native National Congress in 1914, put it, 'it can be fairly and practically carried out'. But, with reference to the Native Land Act of 1913, Dube made it clear:

> We do not see how it is possible for this law to effect any greater separation between the races than obtains now. It is evident that the aim of this law is to compel service by taking away the means of independence and self-improvement. This compulsory service at reduced wages and high rents will not be separation, but an intermingling of the most injurious character of both races.[78]

Without going further into the details of the early post-union struggles of black leaders, it is important to comment on the role of the church. First, it is obvious that much of the leadership of the black nationalist movement was Christian, and that many of the leaders were ministers within the mission and English-speaking churches. Virtually all the leaders were trained and educated at missionary institutions, and their petitions and protests stress the fact that their motivation stemmed from Christian principles and convictions. African nationalism depended heavily on educated Christian leadership. Second, while the churches to which they belonged usually supported the principles for which they fought, such as those related to the land act already mentioned, the black leaders realized that the struggle was their own. They did not depend on the white-dominated churches, whether mission or 'multiracial'. At the same time, as Leo Kuper stated, 'The Christian missions brought Africans and whites together in new structures of relationship, and under dedication to a universal ethic, conditions which might be expected to counteract tendencies toward the expression of an exclusive nationalism.'[79]

Third, there was no dualism between their religious convictions and

---

[77] Karis and Carter (eds.), *Protest*, pp. 86f.

[78] Karis and Carter (eds.), *Protest*, p. 85.

[79] Kuper, 'African Nationalism', p. 434.

their political aspirations. For them, Christianity could not be divorced from life as a whole; certainly, it could not be divorced from the plight of their fellow black people in the land. In this respect, these black Christian leaders were no different in their understanding of Christian political responsibility from the Afrikaner theologians and ministers who shared the burden of the day in the Afrikaner struggle against the British. Fourth, and arising out of the last observation, the crux of the struggle had to do with land and political rights. It is important to see that racism was never regarded as a phenomenon on its own; it was almost always related to educational, economic, and political issues. It would be untrue to the facts to maintain that the Christian gospel, or the education provided by the missionary institutions, prevented blacks from a critical analysis of their situation. Their understanding was penetrating and sharp – it invariably went to the heart of the matter. This is shown in an address by Dr A. B. Xuma delivered at a Conference of European and Bantu Christian student associations at Fort Hare in 1930.[80] Entitled 'Bridging the Gap between White and Black in South Africa', Dr Xuma's speech powerfully describes how racism works itself out in practice, or, more accurately, how racism is used to justify injustice in every walk of life. The only way to build bridges between white and black, Xuma maintained, was by getting rid of the 'Union Native Policy' through the establishment of justice.

Finally, it has been cogently argued that Christianity encouraged patience rather than angry revolt, dialogue rather than violent reaction, and that this delayed the black political advance over the years. Yet, the proponents of this hypothesis, even though partly correct, cannot deny the freedom with which blacks have espoused Christ and their willingness to be true to the gospel. Their hypothesis denies the leading and active role of black Christians in the political realm. Black Christians continued to lead the way in the black struggle for political and other rights well into the apartheid era. To mention only a few: Albert Luthuli was a Congregationalist; Robert Sobukwe, the founder of the Pan African Congress, was a devout Methodist; and Professor Z. K. Matthews, an Anglican and the first student to graduate from Fort Hare (1924), was at one time leader of the Cape branch of the African National Congress, and through his distinguished career as an academic, political leader,

---

[80] Karis and Carter (eds.), *Protest*, pp. 218ff.

and ecumenical spokesman, influenced more than a generation of black leaders in Africa. He was also, towards the end of his life, Botswana's Ambassador to the United States of America. Whatever the failures of the missions, they did stress a genuinely liberal education, which in turn helped nurture articulate leaders dedicated to the service of their people. Apart from Fort Hare, there were many other fine institutions of all denominations; Heraldtown (Methodist), Tigerkloof (Congregational), St Peters (Anglican), and Mariannhill (Catholic) are but a few examples.

During these years there emerged what was increasingly referred to as 'the black church' in South Africa. This does not refer to a denomination, nor does it simply refer to the independent churches. Rather, it suggests a black Christian solidarity that straddled the theological confessions and the ecclesiastical divisions imported into the country with the arrival of the missionaries in the nineteenth century. Something of this was expressed in IDAMASA, the black Interdenominational African Ministers' Association of South Africa, which began as a Transvaal organization in 1915, and in 1946 became a nation-wide movement. Many black Christians regarded denominationalism as another aspect of the political policy of 'divide and rule'. Indeed, as long ago as 1883, we find a black Christian spokesman decrying this divisiveness in the name of Christ, and for the sake of political rights:

> Anyone looking at things as they are, could even go so far as to say it was a great mistake to bring so many church denominations to the Black people. For the Black man makes the fatal mistake of thinking that if he is an Anglican, he has nothing to do with anything suggested by a Wesleyan, and the Wesleyan also thinks so, and so does the Presbyterian. *Imbumba* must make sure that all these three are represented at the conference, for we must be united on political matters. In fighting for national rights, we must fight together. Although they look as if they belong to various churches, the White people are solidly united when it comes to matters of this nature. We Blacks think that these churches are hostile to one another, and in that way we lose our political rights.[81]

Certainly, denominationalism was, as Kuper says, 'highly fragmenting

---

[81] Statement by S. N. Mvambo on the Purpose of Imbumba, December 1883, in Karis and Carter (eds.), *Protest*, p. 12. Imbumba Yama Afrika, founded in 1882, was a forerunner of the African National Congress.

and exclusive, analogous to tribalism', but the potentially unifying power of Christianity was also a basis for African nationalism.[82] At the centre of the church struggle throughout South African history is the struggle of the black church to prove to its fellow blacks that Christianity is not the 'opiate of the people' but the hope for the future and therefore the word of salvation for today. It is no easy task, for the white church has too often failed to be faithful to the gospel, and in the name of Christ given its support to policies and systems that oppress others.

This brief sketch has attempted to show the origin of the church struggle in South Africa. The origins were complex; the struggle had many facets. But we have described some of the fundamental issues that bind the story together, not in a neat bundle, but hopefully in one that makes sense of this data. The basic thesis is that the church in South Africa has been, and remains, divided not only along theological and confessional lines, but also by race and culture. In this, the church in South Africa is not unique. But the problem is exacerbated in South Africa because of the social and political situation. The church cannot avoid relating to the cultural milieu in which it is set if it is to fulfil its task; neither can it simply stand aloof from the social and political aspirations of groups within society. But in some way divisions created by race and culture have to be transcended in the church so that its identity as the reconciled and reconciling community can be demonstrated. This does not deny the place of cultural diversity in the life of the church, but it rejects any captivity to culture whereby unjust social structures are reinforced and legitimated.

The next four chapters are not exhaustive treatments of church history in South Africa. They pick up some of the threads we regard as important in our discussion thus far, as these were in evidence between the advent of apartheid in 1948 and its end in 1994. The divisions we have noted provide the underlying theme; the questions we have raised about Christianity and politics, about culture and the ideological captivity of the church, become more and more urgent. The struggle against racism brings the church face to face with the human will to power, with all its demonic potential; it also confronts the church with the cry of the oppressed, the powerless, and the dehumanized.[83]

---

[82] Kuper, 'African Nationalism', p. 435.

[83] This paragraph has been reworked to reflect the structure of this revised edition.

2

Apartheid and the Churches

The Advent of Apartheid

In 1942 the Christian Council of South Africa convened a conference at the University of Fort Hare. The purpose of the conference was to discuss the task of the churches in 'Christian Reconstruction' after the war. That was an important year for those involved in the struggle against Hitler. The tide had turned, and now it seemed only a matter of time before the world would be at peace. South Africans were becoming optimistic, and that was the prevailing mood of those who gathered at Fort Hare to reflect together on the future role of the churches. Seven years later the Christian Council convened another conference, this time at Rosettenville near Johannesburg. The theme on this occasion was 'The Christian Citizen in a Multi-Racial Society'. By this time, however, the optimism of Fort Hare had gone. The mood was one of apprehension. Apartheid had arrived.[1]

We have seen enough already to know that racism in South Africa did not arrive when the National party came to power in 1948 with its clarion call to apartheid. But 1948 is symbolic of a dramatic change in the meaning of racism for South Africans. Although racial discrimination was entrenched in the Union Constitution and determined much of the legislation between 1910 and 1948, it did not have the rigid, ideological character that it began to assume under the apartheid slogan. A distinction can be made between the segregation policies before 1948 and the apartheid policy after that year. R. H. Davenport puts it succinctly: 'They differed in degree and direction, rather than in kind, from the policies

---

[1] Cf. Stanley G. Pitts' (ed.) 'Introduction' to *The Christian Citizen in a Multi-Racial Society* (Christian Council of South Africa, 1949), p. 5.

which had gone before.'[2] We cannot go into all the details about the apartheid policy and the way it evolved over the years into separate development. Some of this will emerge as we proceed; it is fully documented elsewhere.[3] There is no doubt, however, that the English-speaking churches and other denominations belonging to the Christian Council realized that a new political phenomenon had entered the scene, and that it contradicted the hopes they had for the future of the churches and the country.

In September 1948, the General Assembly of the Presbyterian Church of South Africa criticized proposed legislation aimed at depriving Africans of their limited Parliamentary representation as a retrograde step contrary to the claims of Christian responsibility. 'Our earnest prayer', the General Assembly said, 'is that white South Africa may be saved from the contempt in the eyes of the world which such action is bound to produce.'[4] The Methodist Conference that same month stated that

> no person of any race should be deprived of constitutional rights or privileges merely on the grounds of race, and morally binding contracts protecting such rights or privileges should be regarded on the high level of a pledged word. Political and social rights especially of the underprivileged groups should not be reduced but rather developed and expanded into greater usefulness.[5]

Similar sentiments were expressed by the Congregational Assembly, which stated: 'It is our sincere conviction that the Government's policy of "apartheid" has no sanction in the New Testament Scriptures ...'[6] The Assembly of the Baptist Union condemned 'any tampering with the accepted constitutional understanding that the franchise rights of non-Europeans will continue to be entrenched as provided in the South Africa Act'. Furthermore, it was

> gravely concerned at the rising tide of bitterness and resentment,

---

[2] T. R. H. Davenport, *South Africa: A Modern History* (Johannesburg: Macmillan, 1977), p. 254. On the development of the concept of apartheid, see ch. 18.

[3] See E. H. Brookes, *Apartheid: A Documentary Study of Modern South Africa* (London: Routledge & Kegan Paul, 1968).

[4] *The Churches' Judgment on Apartheid* (Cape Town: The Civil Rights League, 1948), p. 13.

[5] *Churches' Judgment*, p. 11.

[6] *Churches' Judgment*, p. 7.

noncooperation and hatred, which is evident among those people concerned by any suggestion of the limitation of their existing rights and legitimate aspirations, and the Assembly resolutely dissociates itself from any policy which would restrict or reduce the present rights of representation in Parliament or Senate of any section of the community.[7]

Finally, in November 1948, the Episcopal Synod of the Church of the Province issued a lengthy statement on the race issue. The bishops identified themselves fully with the resolutions of the Lambeth Conference earlier that year which declared 'that discrimination between men on the grounds of race alone is inconsistent with the principles of the Christian religion'. The South African bishops then stated that human rights are not extraneous to Christianity but rooted in Christian anthropology. They condemned the newly proposed apartheid legislation and stated:

> The only hope in our judgment for the future of the men, the women and the children of Southern Africa lies in the creation of harmonious relationships between our various racial groups. And harmony can only be achieved if the Europeans, who at present wield power, engender a spirit of confidence amongst the non-Europeans. But if, on the other hand, Europeans seek to preserve to themselves the exclusive benefits of Western Civilization, and to allow the non-Europeans merely its burdens, South Africans will inexorably draw apart into mutually antagonistic racial groups.[8]

The Rosettenville Conference in 1949, mentioned at the beginning of this chapter, was significant for a number of reasons. This was the first ecumenical conference since the National party came to power, and its affirmations characterize the position of the English-speaking churches of that period. With the exception of one fraternal delegate, the NGK did not participate in the conference. The participating churches never retracted the position they took at Rosettenville:

> We affirm that the fundamental truths we shall neglect at our peril include:
> 1. God has created all men in His image. Consequently, beyond all differences remains the essential unity.

[7] *Churches' Judgment*, p. 6.
[8] *Churches' Judgment*, pp. 4f.

2. Individuals who have progressed from a primitive social structure to one more advanced should share in the responsibilities and rights of their new status.

3. The real need of South Africa is not 'Apartheid' but 'Eendrag' (i.e. unity through teamwork).

4. Citizenship involves participation in responsible government. The franchise should be accorded to all capable of exercising it.

5. Every child should have the opportunity of receiving the best education that the community can give, and for which the child has the capacity.

6. Every man has the right to work in that sphere in which he can make the best use of his abilities for the common good.[9]

In retrospect, these Rosettenville affirmations do not appear very radical; they smack a little of paternalism, but they were a direct attack on the unfolding policy of apartheid. One of the major papers at the conference was given by Chief Albert Luthuli, at that time a member of the Native Representative Council. Luthuli remarked:

> The spirit of selfish exclusiveness shows itself [again] in a tendency to regard civilization as the sole possession and production of White people. Hence the plea that Africans must develop along their own lines. This claim ignores the fact that in its historical development western civilization has been indebted to many sources, ancient and modern. The tragedy of the attitude behind this claim is that white South Africa tends to forget its God-given mission to spread civilization and not to hoard it, and thus to ensure its survival and growth.[10]

Rosettenville proved to be the first of a series of ecumenical conferences assembled by the churches after 1948 to deal with the racial problem. The next major conference following Rosettenville was convened by the Federal Missionary Council of the NGK. It was held in Pretoria in November 1953. Prior to this, the Federal Council had held five conferences on the racial situation in the country, attended by both black and white delegates from the various NGK synods. We have already referred

---

[9] Pitts (ed.), *Christian Citizen*, pp. 7f.

[10] A. Luthuli, 'The Christian and Political Issues', in Pitts (ed.), *Christian Citizen*, p. 72.

to the important 1950 NGK Missionary Conference with its recommendation of 'territorial apartheid'. But the Pretoria Conference was particularly significant because the NGK invited church leaders from other denominations to attend, especially churches belonging to the Christian Council, of which the NGK was no longer a member. What is more, the addresses given were evenly distributed among speakers representing the various denominations present. These were hopeful signs.

After two days of frank but respectful interchange, during which agreement was reached on a number of matters pertaining to missionary work and to mutual understanding between the churches, the conference adopted a statement in which the following was expressed:

3. . . . No effort was made to conceal or minimise differences.

4. In the words of one of the representatives, these differences divided the conference into three groups, [firstly,] those who sincerely believed in a righteous racial separation in the Church based on the Scriptures; secondly, those who made no such confession but nevertheless practised some form of separation because circumstances demanded it although such separation did not correspond with the ideals of the Christian Church; thirdly, those who were convinced that separation in the Church was wrong and stood condemned according to Scripture.

5. A strong desire was felt by all present to reach solutions and some understanding; there was also a sense of urgency arising from a realisation of the seriousness of racial tensions in our country and of the unhappy effect on Non-Europeans when European Christians were at variance.[11]

A number of noteworthy points emerged from this Pretoria Conference. First, while nothing like the consensus at Rosettenville was achieved, it was significant that the NGK was willing to enter into such frank discussion of racial affairs at that moment in South African history with members of churches who were so strongly critical of the NGK for not condemning apartheid. Second, the list of 107 delegates does not appear to include any black representatives, a situation that would later

---

[11] 'Christian Principles in a Multi-Racial South Africa', a report of the NGK Conference of Church Leaders, Pretoria, November 1953, pp. 176f.

become unthinkable and intolerable to the English-speaking churches. Third, the differences dividing the delegates, so well expressed in point 4 of the statement, is an accurate description of the dividing lines that separated white Christians virtually until the demise of apartheid. While the statement refers specifically to the church, it had implications for society as a whole. Some regarded racial separation as scriptural, some as blatantly unscriptural, and others as pragmatically necessary but not the ideal.

It must not be supposed that all the delegates of the NGK stood firmly opposed to the position of the delegates from the other churches. The opening address given by Professor B. B. Keet of the Dutch Reformed seminary in Stellenbosch certainly suggests otherwise:

> Personally, I believe that our brethren who want to maintain apartheid on biblical grounds are labouring under this misunderstanding. They confuse apartheid, which is an attitude of life, with a diversity which includes unity. Christian unity, I know, will include diversity but it must never be seen as separation; and apartheid is separation.

For Keet, 'our brethren' meant fellow members of the NGK. He went on to say:

> My Bible teaches me that God is no respecter of persons and that His compassion is for the miserable, the underprivileged, the neglected children of the human race. Surely, the Gospel, though far more than mere humanism, as founded on the compassion of Him who gave His life for all peoples and nations, cannot be inhuman. To love God above all, and your neighbour as yourself – on these two commandments hang all the Law and Prophets. Of a truth there is no way to God that bypasses my neighbour . . .

After rejecting the slur of 'liberalism' which so many attach to words such as these, he declared: 'The relationship at present existing between white and coloured Christians can well be termed as a cynic has described it, "Brothers in Christ, Limited"!'[12]

---

[12] 'Christian Principles', pp. 17ff.

The Pretoria Conference Statement avoided any directly political utterance, except for the short eighth paragraph, where we find: 'It was generally felt that Non-Europeans have a claim to right and justice in all matters, great and small, but that there should be no talk of rights if there were not also admittance of fundamental duties.' This coupling of rights and duties appears in a number of NGK pronouncements over the years, but very seldom, if ever, do we find any elaboration on the subject. For example, what duties need to be performed or accepted before rights are conferred? What duties have whites fulfilled in order to receive the rights they have? Have blacks been given the opportunity to fulfil such duties as required for receiving rights? What duties have blacks failed to perform, seeing that rights have been taken away from them?

The reticence of the Pretoria gathering to pronounce on political issues and the meaning of rights and duties was not reflected in Parliament. By the mid-1950s, apartheid legislation was being introduced and implemented at full speed as act after act was introduced, and bill after bill adopted. At the same time, the government began to develop an increasing array of security laws by means of which it could suppress any radical opposition, black or white. The cornerstone of this legislation was the Suppression of Communism Act of 1950, amended in 1954, with its very wide definition of Communism.[13]

In spite of failures in their own fellowship, the English-speaking churches spoke out strongly against what was happening at virtually every step along the apartheid route during the first decade of National party rule. They were not alone. Quite apart from the critique of opposition politicians, academics, newspaper editors, professional and other community leaders, black and white, apartheid came in for rigorous attack by leading theologians in the NGK. Professor Ben Marais scrutinized racism with rigor and perception in his *Colour: The Unsolved Problem of the West*,[14] and Professor Keet demolished the false myths used by many in his own church to support apartheid in his brief but powerful statement *Suid-Afrika-Waarheen? (Whither, South Africa?)*. Keet's profound grasp of Scripture and his incisive theological insight cut through all the racial shibboleths of the past and present. 'The more one examines the case for complete, permanent apartheid', he wrote,

---

[13] Cf. Davenport, *South Africa*, ch. 14.
[14] Ben Marais, *Colour: The Unsolved Problem of the West* (Cape Town: Timmins, 1952).

'the less can one avoid the conclusion that its supporters are labouring under a delusion that belongs to a world of make-believe.'[15]

The most provocative attack on apartheid came, however, from another quarter, and this evoked a response from the government that provided a foretaste of things to come. As of old, many missionaries continued their role of speaking out on behalf of the voiceless. No one fulfilled this role more ably than an Anglican missionary priest working in Sophiatown, outside Johannesburg. His name, Father Trevor Huddleston, was soon to reverberate around the British Commonwealth. In 1956 Huddleston published his book *Naught for Your Comfort*. In it he told the story of his parish, especially the agonies and heartbreaks caused by apartheid in the lives of his black parishioners. He concluded:

In opposing the policies of the present Government, therefore, I am not prepared to concede that any momentary good which might conceivably emerge from them is good. Nor am I prepared to concede that the motives which inspire such policies have any quality of goodness about them. For both the acts and the motives are inspired by a desire which is itself fundamentally evil and basically un-Christian; the desire to dominate in order to preserve a position of racial superiority, and in that process of domination to destroy personal relationships, the foundation of love itself. That is anti-Christ.[16]

Huddleston was recalled to England shortly after by his order, the Community of the Resurrection. While the order supported him, they wanted him to serve elsewhere. But even though he left, his book remained behind to sear the consciences of the government and white South Africa. It was even too strongly worded for his own bishop, Geoffrey Clayton, in Johannesburg. Nonetheless, it was a sign that church–state relations were going to grow more tense, as Clayton himself soon discovered. During the years that followed, more and more foreign missionaries, especially Anglicans, were deported by the government. They were regarded not only as a source of irritation by the authorities, but also as perpetrators of unrest among the black popula-

---

[15] B. B. Keet, *Whither South Africa?* (Stellenbosch: Stellenbosch University Publishers, 1956), p. 85.

[16] Trevor Huddleston, *Naught for Your Comfort* (London: Fontana, 1956), p. 182.

tion. The churches could do little about this except protest and accept the situation.⌡

The first major crunch in church–state relations came in 1957 with the promulgation of Clause 29(c) of the Native Laws Amendment Bill. This was a very different matter from the deportation of some missionaries. In effect, the bill made it very difficult for black people to attend worship in churches in so-called white areas. In other words, apartheid was beginning to affect the life and worship of the churches in a direct way. The bill caused an immediate outcry, even from those who felt that missionaries such as Huddleston had gone too far. Geoffrey Clayton, who was now Anglican Archbishop of Cape Town, saw the issues of the bill very clearly. In a strong letter to Dr Verwoerd, the Minister responsible for the bill, Clayton accused the state of trespassing on the freedom of the church. He wrote: '. . . we feel bound to state that if the Bill were to become law in its present form we should ourselves be unable to obey it or counsel our clergy and people to do so.'[17] Similar sentiments were expressed by other churches and by the Christian Council. The Baptist Union, generally more cautious on political matters, declared that 'the proposed bill will compel law-abiding Baptists, together with members of many other Churches, to violate the law. This we do not desire to do, but where conscience and legislation conflict we must take our stand with our conscience, whatever the consequences may be.'[18]

The NGK was also perturbed by the bill. The Federal Council of the Church produced an eight-point statement on the subject, of which only the first four points were initially made public. The NGK stressed the duty of the state to allow the church the freedom to fulfil its calling: 'The right to determine how, when, and to whom the Gospel shall be proclaimed is exclusively in the competence of the Church.'[19] The unpublished points specifically criticized the bill as going beyond the bounds of what the state, from a Christian perspective, was entitled to do. Rather than publish these specific criticisms, the NGK leaders preferred to discuss the whole matter with Dr Verwoerd. After doing so, they felt reassured that the government would not in fact trespass on the

---

[17] 'Open Letter to the Prime Minister', 6 March 1957; cf. Alan Paton, *Apartheid and the Archbishop: The Life and Times of Geoffrey Clayton* (Cape Town: David Philip, 1973), p. 279.

[18] Statement of the Executive of the Baptist Union of South Africa, March 1957.

[19] A Statement of Principles issued by the Council of the NGK, March 1957.

freedom of the church, and thus the need to publish their critique fell away. But the fact remained that the state now had the power to act against multiracial worship if the cabinet minister felt that this was necessary.

Services of worship were never affected by this legislation. The state acted on a few occasions against black services held in 'white areas' where residents complained about them creating a public disturbance. But multiracial services, particularly in the large cathedral churches of the cities, Catholic and Anglican, remained a common feature of church life throughout the years.[20]

Perhaps as a sign of protest against the bill, a black Dutch Reformed minister was invited to preach to a white Dutch Reformed congregation in Pinelands, a fairly conservative middle-class suburb of Cape Town, during the period of its debate. For although the NGK and the English-speaking churches differed in their interpretation of its significance, they all found the bill undesirable. 'It would have been better', declared Dr A. J. van der Merwe, moderator of the NGK in the Cape,

> if it had not been introduced, because any practical advantage which it may have does not weigh up against its propaganda value against the minister. In arriving at our conclusions we have tried to be completely honest and sincere. We credit our brother Churches with the same sincerity in arriving at an opposite conclusion, and where we do not see eye to eye in this matter we must agree to differ in brotherly love.[21]

Brotherly love between the churches was soon to be severely tested.

Cottesloe Consultation

If the 'church clause' shocked the churches into action, the whole country was rudely awakened by Sharpeville. This name of a small town in the Transvaal rang around the world in March 1960, signalling a

---

[20] Early in 1978, the government relaxed the law at the request of the NGK. Those churches that had refused to acknowledge it in the first place did not regard this as of great significance, for they had never obeyed it.

[21] Quoted in the *Cape Times*, 30 April 1957.

dramatic turn in world-opinion against South Africa and ushering in a new era of racial discord and protest. At Sharpeville on 21 March, 69 black people, mainly women, were shot and killed by the police, and 186 were wounded, according to official figures. It was a shocking and terrible event, precipitated by the discriminatory pass laws against which the people were protesting when fired upon. Opinions vary greatly as to what actually happened. The police claimed that the protesters were storming the police station, which was manned by a few policemen whose lives were thus endangered. The protesters maintained that the demonstration, sponsored by the recently formed Pan African Congress, was peaceful and, as the records show, the only violence done was by the police. Many of the dead were shot in the back.[22]

In the post-Sharpeville 'state of emergency', thousands of black people were arrested and many banned. The leadership of the African National Congress and the Pan African Congress, including Albert Luthuli, Nelson Mandela, and Robert Sobukwe, was arrested, and the organizations were declared illegal.[23] Many blacks fled the country to participate in anti-apartheid exile movements in Europe and North America. Others went underground. Whites, too, left the country out of fear for the future, and foreign investments in South Africa suffered severely. White morale reached an all-time low. Perhaps never before, and not again until the Soweto protests in 1976, were those struggling for justice and reconciliation in South Africa in such despair. What could the churches do amid all this bitterness and frustration, especially when, humanly speaking, all power resided in the hands of authorities who were unbending in their responses to the situation?

One powerful, emotive reaction came from Archbishop Joost de Blank, the successor to Geoffrey Clayton, who let off a furious broadside against the NGK for what he regarded as its connivance at apartheid. He went so far as to demand that the World Council of Churches expel the Cape and Transvaal Synods who, along with the Nederduitsch Hervormde Kerk, were then members. In a letter to the General Secretary of the WCC, Dr W. A. Visser 't Hooft, de Blank stated: 'The future of Christianity in this country demands our complete dissociation from

---

[22] Cf. Davenport, *South Africa*, pp. 286f.

[23] Cf. A. P. Walshe, *The Rise of African Nationalism in South Africa* (London: University of California Press, 1970).

the Dutch Reformed attitude . . . Either they must be expelled or we shall be compelled to withdraw.'[24]

The leaders of the WCC did not accede to de Blank's harsh and hasty request. Indeed, members of the WCC executive committee were very unhappy about de Blank's ultimatum, and expressed considerable sympathy for the NGK. The Anglican Bishop of Ceylon, Ladkasa de Mel, reasoned 'that the expulsion of the NGK would be in effect a kind of ecclesiastical apartheid adding one more scandal to an already scandalous situation'.[25] Thus, instead of such action, and after much discussion with other member churches in South Africa, the WCC agreed to help arrange a 'consultation on Christian race relations and social problems in South Africa'. This in itself was a remarkable achievement. For not only did de Blank's hostile attitude towards the NGK create resentment within that church, but his aggressive and strident assault on the government and the manner in which he exercised his episcopal authority were alienating all around and were often counterproductive. Even those who agreed with him in principle found him to be an uncomfortable ally.

Before continuing the story of Cottesloe, we must comment a little on the episcopate of Joost de Blank. Without doubt, he was a major figure in the history of the confrontation between the church and apartheid. Formerly the Bishop of Stepney in London, de Blank burst on the South African scene like a latter-day van der Kemp and Thomas a Becket rolled into one. Like van der Kemp, he too was born in Holland, a fact which had some influence on those responsible for his election to the see of Cape Town. And like the missionary of the London Missionary Society, the Archbishop soon became one of the most controversial clerics in South Africa's history. He was applauded by blacks, but intensely disliked by most whites, especially those in authority. Though he started his adult life as a conservative evangelical, by the time of his enthronement as Archbishop in 1957, de Blank's views on episcopacy were more Roman than Protestant. Like a medieval lord bishop, he demanded the allegiance of his church to his person and his views as he confronted the government on apartheid. In the process, he polarized opinion in his

---

[24] Cf. A. H. Liickhoff, 'Die Cottesloe-Kerkeberaad', unpublished PhD thesis (University of the Witwatersrand, Johannesburg, 1975), pp. 19f.

[25] Liickhoff, 'Die Cottesloe-Kerkeberaad', pp. 38f.

own church, and created bitter feelings throughout the country – not always because of his ideas, but often because of the way he expressed them.

Opinions vary a great deal on de Blank's ministry. None can doubt that he had a razor-sharp, theologically incisive mind. His views commanded attention, even from his worst enemies. Further, there can be little doubt that he was an important catalyst in the Christian struggle against racism in South Africa. His trenchant criticism of apartheid went to the heart of the matter, and it was always based on Christian doctrine, especially the incarnation. His diaries reveal a man who could be highly self-critical, and along with his books and addresses, they also tell the story of a man who was totally committed to his Lord. It was this commitment that led him to attack racism with passion and zeal, sparing no person, high or low, least of all himself. But he failed during his episcopate to stem the tide of government policy and public attitudes. As his years in Cape Town drew to an end, he grew increasingly disappointed with the fruit of his ministry, and disillusioned with his own church, to say nothing of the NGK. De Blank returned to London in 1963, a disheartened and broken man. But before he left, he commented on his ministry in a final sermon: 'Some people have hinted that I have tried to go too fast too quickly. But how far and how fast are you supposed to go when you are running away from sin and seeking to do God's will?'[26]

The official history of the ecumenical movement has only one passing reference to the Cottesloe Consultation, held in a Johannesburg suburb 7–14 December 1960.[27] But it was a gathering of great importance for the churches in South Africa. Presided over by Dr Franklin Clark Fry of the United States, chairman of the central committee of the WCC, the consultation was attended by ten delegates from each of the eight South African member churches, and five representatives of the WCC, including its General Secretary, Dr Visser 't Hooft. There were 18 black participants, including Bishop Alphaeus Zulu and Professor Z. K. Matthews; there were eight laypeople, including author Alan Paton and the anthropologist Monica Wilson, the only woman delegate; and the ministers

---

[26] Quoted by Victor Charles Paine, 'The Confrontation between the Archbishop of Cape Town, Joost de Blank, and the South African Government on Racial Policies, 1957–1963', unpublished MA thesis (University of Cape Town, 1978), p. 204.

[27] H. E. Fey (ed.), *The Ecumenical Advance: A History of the Ecumenical Movement*, vol. 2 (London: SCM Press, 1970), p. 245.

and theologians who made up the bulk included many distinguished church leaders of the country. The representatives of the Nederduitsch Hervormde Kerk, whose delegation, unlike the others, was all white, tended to keep apart. It was rumoured that they were in frequent consultation with political leaders, including Prime Minister Verwoerd, during the consultation. The NGK Cape and Transvaal Synod delegations, unlike the NHK, were at the centre of things, and whereas the NHK rejected the final statement out of hand, the NGK delegates were virtually unanimous in supporting it. One reason why the NGK supported the statement was that it was largely based on the preparatory documents they had produced for the consultation.

The concluding statement comprised three sections. Part One rejected all unjust discrimination. While it indicated that opinions varied on apartheid, it stated that the church had a duty 'to proclaim that the final criterion of all social and political action is the principles of Scripture regarding the realisation of all men of a life worthy of their God-given vocation'. In Part Two, far-reaching consensus was achieved:

> We recognise that all racial groups who permanently inhabit our country are a part of our total population, and we regard them as indigenous. Members of all these groups have an equal right to make their contribution towards the enrichment of the life of their country and to share in the ensuing responsibilities, rewards and privileges. No one who believes in Jesus Christ may be excluded from any church on the grounds of his colour or race. The spiritual unity among all men who are in Christ must find visible expression in acts of common worship and witness, and in fellowship and consultation on matters of common concern.[28]

The resolutions spoke of the need for consultation between race groups on all matters affecting them. Though some stressed the inadvisability of racially mixed marriages, the validity of such marriages was supported. Attention was drawn to the disastrous effects of migratory labour, the low wages paid to the black people, and the inequitable system of job reservation. Delegates asked for the direct representation of Coloureds

---

[28] Leslie A. Hewson (ed.), *Cottesloe Consultation: The Report of the Consultation* (Johannesburg, 1961), p. 74.

in the central Parliament. Part Three included concrete and specific resolutions on a variety of urgent matters: justice in trials, the position of the Asian community in South Africa, freedom of worship on a multi-racial basis, freedom to preach the gospel, and methods of future consultation and co-operation between the churches. The problems of past attempts at dialogue between the NGK and the other churches were discussed, and the consultation urged that churches consult one another before indulging in public criticism of each other.

It is not surprising, then, that in the closing stages of the consultation, Archbishop de Blank expressed his regret that he had sometimes spoken heatedly and through ignorance wrongly criticized the NGK for not making a public stand on racial issues. This was a clear retraction of his earlier demand for the NGK to be expelled from the WCC. In response, Dr A. J. van der Merwe said that the hand of friendship was gladly accepted. He said that his church had been painfully aware of the tension during the past few years which had damaged not only the fellowship and co-operation between the churches, but also the interests of God's kingdom.[29]

Cottesloe was held behind closed doors. But for outsiders who were interested in its proceedings, it soon became evident that something momentous was happening. Finally, the press was informed about the decisions. The delegates knew, of course, that whatever they had decided still required the ratification of their respective churches, but nonetheless they represented the top echelons of those churches and had good reason to anticipate such agreement. There was nothing in the resolutions that was new or unacceptable to the English-speaking churches. If anything, they did not go far enough. The NHK had clearly rejected them. Thus, the question was really: What would the NGK synods do about the decisions? Although these were based on the NGK preparatory documents, they questioned commonly held assumptions, were highly critical of some aspects of apartheid, and recommended that Coloureds should be enfranchised – a highly contentious and embarrassing matter for the government.

The response was dramatic. It came in the first instance, not from the synods, but from Prime Minister Verwoerd himself. He expressed his personal grave displeasure with the actions of the NGK delegation.

---

[29] Hewson (ed.), *Cottesloe Consultation*, pp. 81f.

There was also strong reaction from conservative groups within the church, notably Dr Koot Vorster, brother of the future Prime Minister, and Dr Andries Treurnicht, later to become a deputy minister in the Nationalist government, and then founder of the right-wing Conservative Party. In due course, the Cape and Transvaal Synods fell into line, thereby rejecting the role played by their own elected and distinguished representatives. In his autobiography, Visser 't Hooft comments:

> I have always wondered whether the majority of the delegates [i.e., to the synods] realized that they were not voting against positions imported by the World Council and imposed on their Churches, but against the convictions expressed by the best minds of their Churches and submitted at Cottesloe by their own trusted leaders.[30]

The NGK also decided to withdraw from membership in the WCC – there was no need for them to be expelled. De Blank had gotten what he originally wanted, but the integrity of the church and the struggle against racism had suffered a severe blow.

How, then, are we to assess the significance of Cottesloe? The Afrikaner author W. A. de Klerk puts it dramatically: 'The ghost of Cottesloe would return to haunt the Afrikaner's wayward theologizing. There was evidence that, in spite of the silencing, recantation, bowing of heads and deep cogitation, something remained. The Church could never quite be the same again.'[31] Visser 't Hooft's response to that question summed up the feelings of many outside the NGK who were disappointed by the official NGK rejection:

> The fact remains that this witness and the attitude which the World Council has taken with regard to race relations has encouraged many, particularly among the non-white Christians, who had begun to feel hopeless about the role of the Christian church. And it should be remembered in the churches of the World Council that not only in the present member churches in South Africa, but also in the churches which have left us, there are many men and women who are deeply

---

[30] W. A. Visser 't Hooft, *Memoirs* (London: SCM Press, 1973), p. 287.

[31] W. A. de Klerk, *The Puritans in Africa: A History of Afrikanerdom* (Harmondsworth: Penguin Books, 1975), p. 255.

conscious of belonging to the world community, gathered by the same Lord, whose task is to make the transcendent power of Christ tangible and visible in deeds of justice and fellowship through which the estrangement of the races can and must be overcome.[32]

Cottesloe itself represented a high point, the subsequent actions of the NGK synods the low point of relationships between the English-speaking churches and the NGK. To many, it now seemed as if the only way forward for co-operation between Christians of different churches was through personal participation in a new kind of ecumenical thrust not tied to denominational structures.

This was the conviction of at least one NGK participant at Cottesloe, Dr Beyers Naudé, who at that time was the acting moderator of the NGK in the Transvaal. His vision eventually gave rise to the Christian Institute of Southern Africa, an ecumenical organization for promoting dialogue between Afrikaans- and English-speaking Christians and for witnessing to justice and reconciliation between the races in South Africa. It also led to his being deprived of his ministerial status by his church, and eventually to his banning by the state. But the story of Naudé must wait. For the moment we must consider his church, and survey the situation up to the end of the 1970s to seek to discover why and how the NGK, which had so clearly rejected racial discrimination in principle, still supported government policy. What was the connection between the NGK and apartheid?

The Nederduitse Gereformeerde Kerk (NGK)

The NGK has had a great deal of influence in South Africa.[33] We have already seen how this came about, and how the NGK was integrally related with the Afrikaner nation, its culture, and its rise to power. Of course, not all its members are Afrikaners nor are all Afrikaners members of it, but the NGK with its million-and-a-half white members was, until 1994, quite clearly the dominant church in terms of its access

---

[32] Visser 't Hooft, *Memoirs*, p. 287.

[33] Readers will note that for this edition, this section which was written in the present tense in 1979, has – in the light of the dramatically changed context – been changed into the past tense where necessary.

to the policy makers of the nation. Included within its ranks were most of the members of Parliament and of the provincial councils. Its members virtually controlled many of the town councils throughout the land. The vast majority of people employed by the government in various capacities and institutions, including the police and the military, belonged to the NGK. It also had considerable influence over the nearly one million members of its black 'daughter churches'. Given this impressive position within society, and the access it had to the corridors of power at the national and local level, the NGK held one of the keys to the future of South Africa.

Relations between the NGK and the English-speaking churches have been plagued over the years by misunderstanding and misrepresentation. Indeed, any discussion such as ours runs this risk. While the risk has to be taken, it is necessary to be as objective as possible, bearing in mind that many of the criticisms that could be levelled at the NGK could be levelled against the other churches as well. Fortunately, the NGK has always stated its own position clearly. Its official stand on issues is contained in resolutions adopted by its General Synod meeting every four years, and interim statements are made by its executive when necessary.[34]

Prior to 1990, the position of the NGK on race and related issues was set forth fully in two major synodical documents. The first, *Human Relations in South Africa*, was adopted by the General Synod in 1966.[35] Its 52 pages of close print clearly set out the position of the NGK. The second, and the most definitive statement in the apartheid era, was the important document *Human Relations and the South African Scene in the Light of Scripture*, adopted by the General Synod in 1974.[36] This, in particular, is the basis for our discussion on the position of the NGK at that time, a discussion which, in the nature of the case, will have to be simplified a great deal, without, we trust, distorting the truth. In basing our discussion on this report, however, we must not lose sight of the fact that it reflected the carefully considered opinion of the synod. It is not necessarily how the person in the pew saw things. Synodical declarations are often far removed from the 'gut feelings' of the average church member.

---

[34] The official periodicals, *Die Kerkbode* and *NGK Africa News*, reflect the position of the church. English translation published by the NGK Information Bureau, 1966.

[35] English translation published by the NGK Information Bureau, 1966.

[36] English translation published by the NGK Publishers, Cape Town, 1975.

The position of the NGK in all its major pronouncements invariably begins with a statement of principle, and it is made clear that principles must arise from Scripture. In true Reformed Church style, the Word of God is the norm by which we test our opinions and our actions. That the Bible 'contains guiding principles for all spheres of life' is a constant refrain in the documents. Indeed, at least four years before Cottesloe, the NGK expressed the opinion that there is a 'danger in acquiescing in race relations which possibly do not accord with the Word of God'.[37] Similarly, J. C. G. Kotze wrote: 'The Scriptural principles must never be twisted to suit our practice.'[38] He, like others, is quite explicit in saying that Scripture and not 'traditional policy' is the court of appeal for the church and the Christian. So it is that human relations are considered by the NGK in the light of Scripture, and any critique must recognize this as the starting point.

The question then arises: How does the NGK interpret Scripture? Once again, the documents generally answer in considerable detail. The NGK is not fundamentalist in its approach to Scripture, though it is generally very conservative. Few within the Reformed tradition could take exception to the hermeneutical principles stated in *Human Relations and the South African Scene*, that is, principles which state not only how the Bible is to be interpreted but also how it is to be related to society. One of these principles states that 'the Church has a prophetic function in respect of the state and society when the Scriptural norms that should apply in all spheres of life are not respected'.[39]

Contrary to popular misconceptions, the NGK did not build its biblical case for its approach to race relations on such Old Testament episodes as 'the curse of Ham', nor did it transpose the 'people of God' motif from Israel onto the Afrikaner *volk*. But it did make a great deal of the creation narratives and the proto-history of Genesis 1–11. Two dominant themes emerge. The first is that 'the Scriptures teach and uphold the essential unity of mankind and the primordial relatedness and fundamental equality of all peoples'.[40] The second and subsidiary conviction is

---

[37] Cf. 'The Dutch Reformed Church and Non-Whites', Fact Paper 14, July 1956, pp. 11f.

[38] J. C. G. Kotze, *Principle and Practice in Race Relations* (Stellenbosch: CSA, 1962), p. 28.

[39] Kotze, *Principle and Practice*, p. 11.

[40] *Human Relations and the South African Scene*, p. 13.

that 'ethnic diversity is in its very origin in accordance with the will of God for this dispensation'. Babel is the consequence not just of God's judgment on sin, but also of his preserving mercy (cf. Acts 17:27), effecting the fulfilment of his saving purposes. Thus, while the unity of humankind is always the basic reality given in creation, there is also a given differentiation in creation. Furthermore, because of human sin, the unity of mankind has been seriously affected, and can only be restored through God's redeeming grace in Christ. The ultimate restoration of this unity will only occur at the final coming of the kingdom of God. This does not mean that the message of the kingdom has no immediate social significance. On the contrary, 'the church must exert itself to give concrete substance to the blessings of the gospel in the life and social structure of a people. On the other hand, the church should avoid the modern tendency to erase all distinctions among peoples . . .'[41] Moreover, in serving human relationships, the church must regard justice as 'a basic concept in the determination of such relationships', along with love, truth and peace.[42]

The theme of unity and diversity which is described initially in terms of Old Testament passages, is also developed on the basis of the New Testament:

> The New Testament upholds the equivalence of all people and nations . . . [It] maintains the unity and solidarity of the human race . . . [It] accepts and upholds the fact of the diversity of peoples . . . [It] accepts the diversity of peoples as a fact, but does not elevate it to the only or highest principle.[43]

Although the diversity of peoples is relative to their underlying unity, the synod's understanding of the theme of unity and diversity leads it to declare: 'In specific circumstances and under specific conditions the New Testament makes provision for the regulation on the basis of separate development of the co-existence of various peoples in one country.'[44] Having said this, the synod made it clear that the role of the

---

[41] *Human Relations and the South African Scene*, pp. 25f.
[42] *Human Relations and the South African Scene*, p. 26.
[43] *Human Relations and the South African Scene*, pp. 30f.
[44] *Human Relations and the South African Scene*, pp. 32f.

church is to ensure that diversity does not lead to estrangement; that love for the neighbour 'is the ethical norm for the regulation of relationships among peoples'; that such love must find expression in justice; and that the church must 'exhort its members, the authorities and subjects to uphold the ethical principles which must be applied in the regulation of inter-people relationships'. Within the church itself, human diversity exists but is sanctified, and thus 'the most serious attention must at all times be given to the New Testament concepts of the brotherhood in Christ and of the koinonia'.[45]

There is a great deal more that could be said, and certainly *Human Relations and the South African Scene* has much more to say than space permits us here. Christians of all traditions would agree with much of what it states. The report discusses the role of the church in society, the relationship between church and state, the questions of social justice, human rights, and social change, and it deals with many specifics such as migratory labour and racially mixed marriages.[46] However, enough has been said to provide a basis for fair assessment.

First of all, in these synodical documents the NGK rejected racial injustice and discrimination in principle. Equally clearly, the NGK accepted the policy of separate development.[47] For the outsider, this appears to be a major contradiction because apartheid and separate development are usually regarded as synonymous. Failure to understand this distinction drawn by the NGK between the blatant racism of apartheid and the anticipated blessings of separate development often led to considerable confusion in assessing the position of the church. For one thing, it led to false hopes, for whenever the NGK spoke out against racism many people presumed that this meant an attack on government policy. That does not follow, although it could be an attack – as it

---

[45] *Human Relations and the South African Scene*, p. 38

[46] *Human Relations and the South African Scene*, pp. 63–99.

[47] This position is reflected in all major NGK documents on the subject, at least since the NGK Congress held in Bloemfontein in 1950. Cf. The Minutes of the Cape Synod, 1961, pp. 271–2. It is certainly expressed in both the 1966 and 1974 reports on human relations. Indeed, even the NGK delegates at Cottesloe had no difficulty in affirming the Cottesloe resolutions and declaring in a concluding statement: 'We wish to confirm that, as stated in the preamble to the Consultation Statement, a policy of differentiation can be defended from the Christian point of view, that it provides the only realistic solution to the problems of race relations and is therefore in the best interests of the various population groups' (Hewson [ed.], *Cottesloe Consultation*, p. 80).

sometimes was – on the way in which policy is implemented. The position of the NGK is well stated in the final paragraph of the 1974 report:

> The Dutch Reformed Church is only too well aware of the serious problems in respect of inter-people, inter-racial and inter-human relationships in South Africa. It seeks to achieve the same ideals of social justice, human rights and self-determination for peoples and individuals, based on God's Word, as do other Christian churches. It is also convinced that it is imperative for the church to fulfil its prophetic calling, to be sympathetic, to give guidance according to Scripture and to intercede on behalf of man. If the Dutch Reformed Church does differ from other churches, the difference is not due to a different view of moral concepts and values or of Christian ethics, but to a different view of the situation in South Africa and the teachings of God's Word in this regard. There is no difference in ideals and objectives, but merely disagreement on the best methods of achieving these ideals.[48]

In this document, the policy of separate development is not contradicted by Scripture; indeed, the idea of diversity in the Bible lends some credence to the policy. At the same time, says the church, the policy must be 'applied in a fair and honourable way, without affecting or injuring the dignity of the person'.[49] So we find the Revd W. A. Landman, a leading minister of the NGK, referring in his *A Plea for Understanding* to the fact that his church has often been condemned for supporting something which 'could not possibly be tolerated by any Church or Christian worthy of the name'.[50] We are therefore faced with the question of whether separate development could be pursued according to the biblical norms of justice and love, that is, whether or not the policy is consistent with Scripture or, at least, not contradicted by it.

Before we consider this question, let us proceed with a second observation on the 1974 report. The black NGK theologian, Allan Boesak, heavily criticized the report as representing a 'downward spiral'.[51] While

---

[48] *Human Relations and the South African Scene*, p. 100.

[49] Cf. W. A. Landman, *A Plea for Understanding: A Reply to the Reformed Church in America* (Cape Town: NG Kerk-Uitgewers, 1968), p. 32.

[50] Landman, *Plea for Understanding*, p. 20.

[51] Allan A. Boesak, *Farewell to Innocence: A Social-Ethical Study of Black Theology and Black Power* (Maryknoll, NY: Orbis; Johannesburg: Ravan, 1977), p. 36.

we share many of Dr Boesak's criticisms, this one suggests far more movement than is warranted by the report. What we find in the report is much more static – in the most important areas there are no advances made on earlier positions adopted by the NGK, such as that of 1966. When one reflects on developments within the country and Christian thinking generally, including that within the NGK, this is surprising. It was certainly surprising for some Afrikaner Nationalist newspaper editors who expressed their disappointment that the General Synod had not been able to lead the way into the future. Instead of lighting up the road ahead, it had provided a cautious statement of past and present positions.

When we probe behind the report, however, and consider it in relation to the original draft presented to the synod, something of crucial significance emerges. The original report was far bolder in its prophetic stance and was much more consistent in its application of scriptural norms to socio-political realities. But the synod would not have it that way, with the result that the final report lost its teeth and cutting edge. Why? In some respects, we have here a repeat of the Cottesloe affair, where the clear and courageous thinking of some Dutch Reformed theologians and leaders was rejected for what appear to be politically pragmatic reasons. Three studies of the report, two by Dutch Reformed theologians, Professors J. Alex van Wyk and J. J. F. Durand, and the other by an English-speaking theologian, Dr Brian Johanson, tackle this issue head on.[52] Dr van Wyk suggests that concepts such as separate development were read into Scripture rather than out of it, and that the final result was, consciously or unconsciously, politically predetermined, supporting the status quo.

Dr Durand discusses the biblical hermeneutics of the report. After affirming the hermeneutical principles that are stated at the beginning of the report, he asks whether the document itself remains true to its own declared method. Durand's contention is 'that this does not happen, and that on one crucial point the document opts for the hermeneutical

---

[52] Alex van Wyk, 'Latente motiewe in die Verklaring van die N. G. Kerk oor: Ras, Volk en Nasie en Volkereverhoudinge in die Lig van die Skrif', *Ned. Geref. Teologiese Tydskrif*, vol. 17, no. 2 (March 1976); J. J. F. Durand, 'Bible and Race: The Problem of Hermeneutics', *Journal of Theology for Southern Africa*, no. 24 (September 1978); Brian Johanson, 'Race, Mission and Ecumenism: Reflections on the Landman Report', *Journal of Theology for Southern Africa*, no. 10 (March 1975).

method that it expressly rejected. This happens as soon as the document deals with one of the concepts that is basic for its theological content as a whole, i.e. the idea of a diversity of peoples.'[53] In fact, says Durand:

> the idea of ethnic diversity is completely stripped of its supposed salvation-historical framework and starts to function in itself as a God-given principle. The reason for this shift in argument is clear. The document is honest enough to realize that such a 'salvation-historical' application cannot be maintained on biblical grounds because that would mean that every phenomenon that runs counter to ethnic differentiation must be considered as a hindrance for the gospel and therefore as a sin against the purpose of God.[54]

The relative idea of differentiation between peoples, to which Scripture points and about which there can be little argument, has become 'an imperative for division between peoples'.[55] Thus, Dr Johanson asked the question:

> What is the ultimate, the real, criterion which influences the decisions and recommendations of this document? What is the value, the principle, the concern which determines what action should be taken, what attitude should be adopted? This issue is very important because this alone will explain why two groups of people, Christian people, working with the same Biblical data, with the same concerns for justice and peace, should come to almost opposite conclusions and solutions.[56]

Johanson's answer was a sharp one. The hidden value that emerges in the document is a 'concern for the "*volk*"', for the well-being of the Afrikaner community. In other words, a principle that cannot be derived from Scripture is injected into the discussion. We are face to face with the dilemma of the NGK. It did not claim to be a *volkskerk* like the NHK, but it found itself pushed in that direction time and again. The outsider cannot but wonder about the political pressures that were brought to bear on NGK decisions, whether at Cottesloe or the General

---

[53] Durand, 'Bible and Race', p. 4.

[54] Durand, 'Bible and Race', p. 6.

[55] Durand, 'Bible and Race', p. 8.

[56] Johanson, 'Race, Mission and Ecumenism', p. 60.

Synod. The survival of Afrikaner identity and power seemed to play such a determinative role. At all costs, the concept of separate development could not be surrendered – which meant that its theological basis had to be affirmed, for the future of the Afrikaner people was regarded as tied up with the success or failure of this policy.

For the moment, let us allow that separate development was defensible in principle. This is not out of keeping with at least some Christian thinking beyond the NGK. Dr John Philip, the LMS missionary of the nineteenth century, advocated something like this for the true well-being of the natives; some African leaders such as the Revd John L. Dube, a founding father of the African National Congress, early in the twentieth century made 'no protest against the principle of separation so far as it can be fairly and practically carried out';[57] and no less a person than J. H. Oldham, a leading figure in the ecumenical movement and in the founding of the WCC, acknowledged the plausibility of such a policy in his classic study on *Christianity and the Race Problem*, published in 1924.[58] So let us examine the policy of apartheid, or separate development as it was euphemistically called, to see whether it fitted in with what the NGK report says when it declared that 'the Christian must at all times seek to ensure that his political thinking and actions are based on justice and righteousness'.[59] In other words, let us see whether it could be morally justified in practice as the NGK maintained it was in principle.

One of the most articulate exponents of separate development, Dr Connie Mulder, a member of the Gereformeerde Kerk and a leading Cabinet Minister in the Vorster government, expressed the opinion in 1972 that the policy was 'in accordance with both the wording and the spirit of the United Nations Charter, when it speaks of the self-determination "of peoples", in that it respects the identity and dignity of the diverse peoples of the Republic and seeks to lead them each and all to a state in which they may competently manage their own affairs'.[60] The

---

[57] Thomas Karis and Gwendolen M. Carter (eds.), *From Protest to Challenge: A Documentary History of African Politics in South Africa, 1882–1964*, vol. 1 (Stanford: Hoover Institution Press, 1972), p. 85.

[58] J. H. Oldham, *Christianity and the Race Problem*, 8th edn (London: SCM Press, 1926), p. 192.

[59] *Human Relations and the South African Scene*, p. 72.

[60] C. P. Mulder, 'The Rationale of Separate Development', in Nic Rhoodie (ed.), *South African Dialogue* (Johannesburg: McGraw-Hill, 1972), p. 49.

argument went as follows: Instead of a melting-pot approach in which ethnic differences are submerged in one all-embracing national identity, ethnic plurality is stressed, and this provides the basis for political structures and social development. All of this is done in order to eliminate racial friction and ultimately to do away with racial discrimination. Thus government policy seeks to establish separate independent 'homeland' countries for each of the several African ethnic groups in the country, and to provide separate political structures through which Coloureds and Indians can express themselves independently of and yet alongside of the white community. It was recognized that all so-called petty-apartheid regulations that stressed the inferiority of black people, and all discriminatory practices such as segregated post offices and park benches, would have to go.

While it is contestable whether this distinction between petty-apartheid and grand apartheid could be maintained, either in principle or practice, in any event, the government, like the NGK, proclaimed that it was against racism while at the same time it pursued its declared policy of separate development. The role of the NGK in all this was to insist that the policy be implemented in a just manner. This was also the role of the Gereformeerde Kerk, a church that was often very critical of the government, not because it regarded the policy as unchristian and therefore wrong, but because the policy was not justly and properly pursued. The question, then, is whether it was possible to implement the policy 'in a fair and honourable way without affecting or injuring the dignity of the person'.[61]

Any political programme or policy that promises a better future, as did separate development, but requires considerable suffering in the present for the sake of that end, needs considerable moral justification. The question has to be faced: Who is doing the suffering, and for what end? Apart from the fact that political programmes are notorious for failing to deliver what they promise, does the promised future justify present human pain and cost?[62]

---

[61] See note 49.

[62] Cf. Peter Berger, *Pyramids of Sacrifice* (Harmondsworth: Penguin Books, 1977). Berger evaluates two so-called model developmental societies, capitalist Brazil and communist China, in terms of 'a calculus of pain and a calculus of meaning'. He finds both systems wanting. They dehumanize, even though they promise a better future. We have not attempted an exhaustive analysis and critique of apartheid and separate develop-

First, what did separate development promise? In spite of all that is said about the policy of helping blacks to regain and strengthen their ethnic identities, the policy was clearly designed in the first instance to safeguard white interests – identity, privileges, land, and resources. It promised blacks their own traditional homelands, but deprived them of South African citizenship. Moreover, it offered homelands that were totally disproportionate to the population. Eighty-seven per cent of the land was to belong to whites, and with them to Coloureds and Indians to some degree, whereas 13 per cent was to belong to blacks. And yet blacks outnumbered whites by five to one. Perhaps a theory of partition could have been justified, but not on such an unjust basis. Land and resources were by no means equitably allocated or distributed; traditional but very inadequate boundaries were maintained. The Native Land Act of 1913, and subsequent legislation in 1936, remained the basis for the policy. Meanwhile, the rights of the vast urban black population were gradually denied on the basis that these blacks were not citizens of South Africa but foreigners in the land of their birth. Seeing that black rights were few to begin with, this is not much of a promise for the future, even if the government improved the lot of urban blacks. Indeed, a major weakness in the policy of the government was its inability to deal with the urban black situation at all, which is part of the reason why it was in Soweto and other urban townships that protest erupted in 1976.

This failure of government policy must be emphasized, for it highlights the fact that the policy makers did not take seriously the industrial revolution that began in South Africa in the 1930s. Separate development was essentially a rural policy; it was totally inadequate for the demands of the rapid urbanization that took place after that period, as millions of blacks came to the cities in search of work. In fact, the policy intensified some of the problems, notably migratory labour, which was recognized by the NGK and other churches as a cancer in South African society. But the policy was also wanting in at least one major respect in the rural areas. It was unable to deal with the political future of those blacks who lived and worked on white-owned farms.

ment, but simply indicated some basic reasons why most churches in South Africa reject them. For a more detailed discussion, see, inter alia, Heribert Adam, *Modernizing Racial Domination: The Dynamics of South African Politics* (Berkeley: University of California Press, 1972). Adam includes a very useful bibliography. Chapter 4 of this book attempts to express some of the 'gut level' feelings of blacks regarding government policy.

It was estimated that approximately one-quarter of the African and Coloured populations were in this group.[63]

Second, what did separate development cost? In terms of human suffering it cost whites virtually nothing, except the support of the world community. However, it cost blacks a great deal. Whites stood to gain most, even though they lost some territory under their control, but blacks, who suffered the most for the sake of the policy, stood to gain far less than whites. The history of the implementation of separate development was full of human tragedy and pain. It required legislation and action that no amount of Christian casuistry can condone. Perhaps, though we doubt it, the policy *could* have been implemented in a way that would injure neither the dignity of people nor, indeed, their physical well-being. But this was not so. Nobody could really regard the Group Areas Act, and the racial classification procedures which lie behind it, as not violating the lives of people. We have only to think of the mass removals of people from places where they lived for generations, and their subsequent placement in areas unprepared for human habitation. Nobody could regard what happened to the Coloureds of District Six in Cape Town as 'fair', or what happened to Africans at Dimbaza or Limehill as 'honorable'. As Brian Johanson comments: 'It [i.e., the NGK] declares that it [i.e., separate development] can be morally justified from the Scriptures. But the Scriptural justification has not been shown. The tremendous social evils that the document [i.e., the 1974 report] itself reveals, which result from the attempt to enforce separate development, would condemn any such attempt to justify the social system from the Scriptures.'[64]

It could possibly have been argued that separate development brought some previously denied advantages to blacks in the homeland areas. For one thing, it provided some kind of political base. But any talk of advantages is offset by the fact that the system was not freely chosen by blacks. After all, such advantages as there were only conferred what is normally regarded in democratic countries as an inherent right of people. There were changes, but these highlight how bad things were in the past. Those black leaders who accepted the system were almost unanimous in holding that they had no other option. This does not

---

[63] Cf. F. A. Wilson, *Migrant Labour in South Africa* (Johannesburg: Spro-cas, 1972), ch. 8.

[64] Johanson, 'Race, Mission and Ecumenism', pp. 51–61.

mean that they regarded separate development as right or just. Separate development dictated what blacks should have.[65] It was not the result of sharing and consultation. This is true of all sections – African, Coloured, and Indian. For many black people, separate development was regarded as a sophisticated form of apartheid, certainly not as a means of overcoming racism. A significant indication of this attitude was the amount of internal security legislation that was required to prevent blacks from working for other alternatives. If separate development really promised something for blacks, why did they react so negatively against government policy in so many ways? In the light of all this, it is not surprising that the NGK advocacy of separate development on the basis of Christian love and justice was treated with considerable disbelief and scepticism by outside critics.

On the other hand, there was rigorous criticism by members of the NGK itself. There were many Dutch Reformed theologians and ministers who felt deeply hurt when their synods rejected Cottesloe. Earlier that year, nine Dutch Reformed theologians had published an attack on apartheid entitled *Delayed Action*. Professor Keet led the attack in the opening essay. White South Africa was doomed, he declared, if it hoped to overcome black nationalism by force. He wrote: 'Our Afrikaans Churches are rightly blamed for not being true to their prophetic calling with regard to the apartheid policy and its bitter fruits.'[66] The writer has vivid memories of hearing Professor Keet preach at the centenary of the founding of the Dutch Reformed seminary at Stellenbosch. Dr Keet spoke on theological developments over the past hundred years and their significance for Dutch Reformed theology. In no way could his own position be called anything but Calvinist theology of the highest order. He was no 'liberal'. Yet it was he, a father-figure in the NGK, who was the most fearless opponent of apartheid and the racism and injustice inherent in separate development. There were many others. When Beyers Naudé was forced to leave the ministry of the NGK, he had considerable support from many of his former colleagues in his critique of the church. In 1965, eight Dutch Reformed theologians published an open letter, 'A Call for Clarity in Confusion', in which they maintained that Dutch Reformed practice did not correspond to Dutch Reformed

---

[65] Cf. W. F. Nkomo, 'An African's View of Apartheid', in Rhoodie (ed.), *South African Dialogue*, p. 352.

[66] *Delayed Action* (Pretoria, 1961), p. 11.

theology and the confessions of the Reformed tradition, but was more determined by the interests of the Afrikaner than the Word of God.[67]

By the late 1970s, while there was this ongoing internal critique, the NGK had to face growing criticism from Reformed sources outside its own ranks. The NGK came under increasing fire from the Gereformeerde Kerken in Holland. This church, which stood within the neo-Calvinist tradition of Abraham Kuyper, has had the longest and closest fraternal ties with the NGK of any church outside the country. But differences on the race question finally led to a break in relations in April 1978. Though this rupture was finally precipitated by the support given by the Gereformeerde Kerken for the WCC Program to Combat Racism, this was but symptomatic of apparently irreconcilable theological and political viewpoints. In reflecting on this, the official newspaper, *NGK Africa News*, asked the question: 'Is it in reality merely a case of an ideology to which the DR Church obstinately clings or is it a deep seated Christian life-style which has crystallised in the crucible of practical co-existence over 300 years in South Africa?'[68] That is the crucial question. The answer given by the newspaper indicated once more the divergence between the NGK and most other churches on the subject: 'The brethren from the Netherlands are opposed to the system as such while the representatives of the DR Church proceed from the premise: the system is not necessarily inherently wrong – it should only be implemented honestly, reasonably and justly in respect of all concerned.'

What this would mean was spelled out in a penetrating statement, 'The Koinonia Declaration', prepared by a group of Gereformeerde Calvinists in 1977.[69] If separate development has to exist, it maintained,

---

[67] An unpublished mimeographed paper, 22 October 1965, signed by Ds. W. J. Villiers, Dr H. W. de Jager, Prof. I. H. Eybers, Prof. W. D. Jonker, Prof. J. A. Lombard, Dr H. J. P. van Rooyen, Dr A. J. Venter, and Mr A. C. Viljoen.

[68] March 1968, p. 7; cf. *NGK African News* (March 1977), p. 4.

[69] 'The Koinonia Declaration', dated 16 November 1977, was drawn up by some members of the Gereformeerde Kerk in Potchefstroom together with members of a Calvinist study group in Germiston, a town in the Transvaal. It was not an official church document, but a very thorough attempt to apply Calvinist principles to the political situation in South Africa. The declaration was warmly received by some English-speaking churches, becoming an official study document of the United Congregational Church. But it received a cool reception from the NGK and the Gereformeerde Kerk. The declaration was privately circulated, but was subsequently published, inter alia, in the *Christian Leader*, the newspaper of the Presbyterian and Congregational Churches, in March 1978, and the *Journal of Theology for Southern Africa*, September 1978.

then for it to be just requires that 'the consolidation of the Black Homelands be based upon economic viability and governability and not purely upon historical grounds . . . [that] the same economic opportunities, including property, business and labour rights, be extended to those individuals and families who are unable to prosper in a Black Homeland.' Furthermore, the government must 'take cognizance of the opinions of all responsible people (Black, White and Brown) living in South Africa and we particularly ask that all races and population groups of the country (including urban Blacks) will obtain an effective share in negotiations that concern their political future.' Much more is said, and much more is asked for, but for the writers, this was the very least that must be granted if government policy could ever have hoped to gain any semblance of moral approval.

However, while the political partition of South Africa on a just basis may sound fine in theory, and probably could have been fairly and humanely implemented earlier in the twentieth century, as John Dube, Oldham, and others acknowledged, by the early 1980s this was no longer possible. Writing soon after the National Party came to power, Professor Keet said: 'If the idea of total *apartheid* had arisen a hundred years ago, one might conceivably have regarded it as practicable, but at this point in our history it appears no other than the dream of Rip van Winkle.'[70]

Related to the critique of the Gereformeerde Kerken in Holland was that of the more conservative Reformed Ecumenical Synod which included those churches which strictly adhered to the Calvinist confessions of the Reformation. The NGK and the Gereformeerde Kerken in Holland, as well as the Christian Reformed Church in the United States, were dominant members of the RES but increasingly at odds with each other over apartheid.

Although the RES was cautious in its critique of the NGK, in the years following Sharpeville, this critique grew in sharpness and intensity. Without doubt, the black Reformed churches in South Africa, together with the Dutch Gereformeerde Kerken, were largely in the forefront of this challenge, but they were supported increasingly by other members such as the Christian Reformed Church in the United States. The fact of the matter is that in the period following the Soweto uprising in 1976, the NGK became more and more isolated in its defence of separate

---

[70] Keet, *Whither South Africa?*, p. 83.

development, even within the community of churches having the same credal and confessional basis.

For a church committed to the Reformed dictum that the church is only the church as it continues to be reformed by God's Word, critique is vital for its well-being and mission. True Calvinism is not conservative and reactionary, as it is often made out to be. There is a revolutionary dynamic implicit in that for which it stands.[71] But there can be no doubt that Calvinism, like all other theological traditions, can be misused for maintaining the status quo. Then it is no longer what it should be. In his perceptive study on 'The Decline of Calvinism', D. W. Howe shows how in eighteenth-century Europe and North America most 'educated Protestants were strongly occupied with the importance of preserving social order. Many of them seem to have felt that a quiet modification of the urgent demands of Calvinism offered the most promising possibility for attaining such order.'[72] But such modification always means that the cause of justice and righteousness must suffer.

As long ago as 1952, Dr Ben Marais expressed the dilemma of the whites in South Africa – 'to maintain ourselves, but not to do it in such a way that the non-whites and their aspirations will be the victims of our selfishness and self-interest'.[73] The promise of the NGK was that it would enable whites to rise above such selfishness and seek to practise the love, justice, and mercy to which the gospel of Jesus Christ calls us. More than any other church, the NGK was in a position to do that. But it had somehow to resolve the dilemma in which it was placed by the very fact that it was so closely related to Afrikaner history and culture. J. C. G. Kotze indicated the way for his church when he wrote shortly after Sharpeville:

> Self-preservation always has a tendency to drive people to selfinterest and acquiescence in injustice. Fear will easily drive us to do an injustice and then to justify it. But when our goal is centred in the Kingdom of God, and His principles are the standard of our life, we shall be saved from the deviating paths of death.[74]

---

[71] Cf. Andre Bieler, *The Social Humanism of Calvin* (Richmond, VA: John Knox Press, 1964); W. Fred Graham, *The Constructive Revolutionary: John Calvin and his Socio-Economic Impact* (Richmond, VA: John Knox Press, 1971).

[72] In *Comparative Studies in Society and History* (June 1972), p. 320.

[73] Marais, *Colour*, p. 70.

[74] Kotze, *Principle and Practice*, p. 29.

Overseas visitors to South Africa often expressed amazement at the extent of the NGK's ministry to blacks. Indeed, quite apart from the establishing of black churches, the NGK developed a far-reaching diaconal programme for the black communities throughout the country. This deserves greater recognition than it has received.[75] The NGK also worked for a more humane implementation of government policy. Without detracting from this, however, we discern that there was a strong tendency to use this ministry to justify support of the system. When this was done, it detracted from the ministry itself.

The NGK was not the only church in South Africa, and none of these churches could avoid its own responsibility to witness to God's kingdom in its particular situation. The other churches knew they could not expect of the NGK anything that they were not prepared to work for as well. Different as they may have been, they were all part of the church of Christ and needed each other in the struggle for justice and peace. This presupposed the need for some kind of dialogue and co-operation between the NGK and the English-speaking churches. Relationships were clearly strained over the years, and reached a breaking-point on several occasions in the 1970s. A spokesman for the NGK put it candidly:

> There can be no doubt about the desirability of dialogue between the Churches . . . [But] experience has shown in the past that on these two points – the lack of a common basis of belief and discussion on the one hand, and on the other a clash of basic policy standpoints – dialogue has been born and died.[76]

This was certainly true. Yet, the South African Council of Churches affirmed that in spite of differences, Christians in South Africa should 'have a common platform for the discussion of issues affecting the teaching and practice of the Christian faith in the context of the South African situation'.[77] It was clear that those critical of the NGK dared not

---

[75] A documentary account of this ministry has been published by Karl Breyer, *My Brother's Keeper* (Johannesburg: Dutch Reformed Church Publication, 1977).

[76] An editorial in *Die Kerkbode*, 19 September 1973.

[77] Part of a resolution on dialogue with the NGK adopted by the SACC National Conference, July 1975, published in *Ecunews* 23/75, appendix D; cf. *Ecunews*, 43/77, p. 1.

mute their criticisms – the interest of the gospel did not allow that. But the English-speaking churches also had to be open to critique. The Catholic Archbishop of Durban, Dennis Hurley, put the matter into perspective when he wrote: 'The Christian standard is a terrifying one. And even as we take it upon ourselves to suggest where our brothers of the Dutch Reformed Churches may have fallen short of it, we dare not judge and condemn, for in the same circumstances, would we have done better?'[78]

The English-speaking Churches

The designation 'English-speaking churches' is a somewhat clumsy and untheological description. However, in exploring the churches response to apartheid it seems impossible to avoid the phrase or find a satisfactory alternative. 'English-speaking churches' does not refer in any primary sense to some common doctrinal or liturgical commitment and practice, nor does it include all those churches in the country who use English as their main language of communication and worship. Rather, the designation refers to those churches of British origin that have grown together over the years as a result of the ecumenical movement and their common attitude towards the racial situation in general and apartheid in particular. They have not claimed this title for themselves. It was given to them by the mass media, politicians, other churches, and the populace in general. The English-speaking churches were regarded as those who opposed the racial policy of the Nationalist government.

In many ways, the appellation 'English-speaking churches' is inaccurate and unfortunate. Each of the denominations normally included – the Anglican, Presbyterian, Methodist, and Congregational – has its own independent and distinct tradition and ethos. They are all different. While it is necessary to lump them together in our analysis of the situation under apartheid, this does not mean that they were some kind of monolithic alternative to the NGK. At the same time, these churches have been deeply involved in the contemporary search for the unity of the church, and for many years have sought ways and means to express this given unity in Christ in concrete forms. At present they have

---

[78] In Rhoodie (ed.), *South African Dialogue*, p. 477.

intercommunion, share numerous joint projects, have a 'mutual recognition of ministry', and are working towards closer structural unity.[79]

'English-speaking churches' is also misleading because it may suggest that these churches are predominantly white, and culturally uniform. Nothing could be further from the truth. The majority of members in the English-speaking churches are black, and their mother-tongue is not English. For example, in the United Congregational Church at least eight languages are spoken, and probably as many members are at home in Afrikaans as in English. This language variety indicates something of the cultural plurality within the churches. English is the common language of communication beyond the local level, but racial and cultural diversity is part of the very fabric and significance of these churches.

There is a further problem. 'English-speaking churches' often suggested churches that were in opposition to the Afrikaans-speaking Dutch Reformed churches, or at least, churches opposed to the Afrikaans community. This impression is understandable. The English-speaking churches all came to South Africa during the upsurge of British imperialism, and they took sides by and large with the British government in the ensuing struggle for power in South Africa. The missionaries who were most critical of the social situation in the nineteenth century belonged to these churches, and were often regarded as the bitter enemies of the Afrikaners. Furthermore, these churches led the church attack on the apartheid policies of the Afrikaner Nationalist government. Thus, when government policies came in for attack by the English-speaking churches, this was often regarded as passing judgment on the integrity of the NGK and the Christianity of the Afrikaner. Historical legacies made it very difficult to avoid this impression. When and where the English-speaking churches were pro-British and anti-Afrikaner for purely cultural and political reasons, they certainly were guilty of denying the Christian faith, and need to recognize this fact. But following the Soweto uprising, in spite of much disagreement, there was very little anti-Afrikaner or anti-NGK sentiment. The churches tried to prevent their attacks on the ideology of apartheid from becoming anti-Afrikaner. Indeed, there were many Afrikaners in the English-speaking churches.

---

[79] The Church Unity Commission was established in 1967 by the Anglican, Congregational, Presbyterian, and Methodist Churches, to seek ways whereby these churches could form one church. Since then, considerable co-operation has developed. Cf. *Journal of Theology for Southern Africa*, no. 23 (June 1978).

Joost de Blank's outburst against the NGK angered many and embarrassed virtually all the leaders of the churches.

A final consideration regarding the title 'English-speaking churches' is its exclusive character. It should include the Baptists, but it generally does not, especially after the Baptist Union withdrew from the South African Council of Churches. It could include some of the Pentecostal churches, but their distinct character and lack of involvement in ecumenical groups and social issues excluded them. What of some other churches that are deeply committed to social witness and are ecumenically involved, in particular the Roman Catholic and the Evangelical Lutheran churches? In some respects, Catholics and Lutherans have been in the vanguard of Christian witness and action in South Africa. Yet, because they are not of British origin, we cannot properly refer to them as 'English-speaking'. These distinctions, then, must be kept in mind as we proceed.

Our discussion of the initial reaction of the churches to apartheid, and to the Cottesloe Consultation, has provided us with an insight into the basic attitude of the English-speaking churches to the race question in South Africa. When we consider the role of the South African Council of Churches in our next chapter, we will also be dealing with important aspects of the witness of the English-speaking churches, since during this period they made up the largest segment of membership in the council. Here we take a more general and critical look at the overall attitude and the witness of the English-speaking churches in the period between the advent of apartheid and the end of the 1970s.

After 1948, the synods, conferences, and assemblies of the churches protested against every piece of legislation they considered unjust. Innumerable resolutions were passed against everything designed to further apartheid and entrench discrimination. Countless deputations were sent to the Prime Minister and other ministers of state to express concern and raise objections. Programmes were initiated to try to deal with racism at the local congregational level. Pastoral letters were published, expressing the mind of the churches at the highest level. Indeed, there was no lack at all of official protest against apartheid, in principle and sometimes in practice.[80]

---

[80] Cf. Lesley Cawood, *The Churches and Race Relations in South Africa* (Johannesburg: Institute of Race Relations, 1964). Documentation can be found in the annual yearbooks of the churches, and in *Ecunews*, the weekly news bulletin of the SACC (no longer published).

The churches spoke out against race classification; the forced removals of population groups due to the Group Areas Act; the Immorality Act and Mixed Marriages Act, designed to preserve racial purity; the various education acts which created separate kinds of education along ethnic lines; job reservation, whereby certain occupations were reserved for one racial group, to the detriment of black people; the many security bills and acts which allowed banning and imprisonment without trial, the deportation of church workers and missionaries, and the extension of police powers beyond normally accepted democratic limits; the pass laws, which governed the movement of Africans, and which led to vast numbers of arrests and imprisonments over the years; the migratory labour system; and the farm prison system. The list is almost endless, since the racial policies of the government affected every aspect of social life in the country. Moreover, quite apart from legislation, the churches protested against state action, whether it was in connection with the removal of squatters, or the banning, detention, and imprisonment of particular people who were not brought to trial, or who were kept in solitary confinement for extended periods, or who died in prison. There must be few comparable instances in the history of the Christian church where such a sustained protest and battle has been waged over such a long period against state legislation and action. Naturally, this led to considerable tension between these churches and the state.

The conflict between the English-speaking churches and the apartheid state is an underlying theme throughout our discussion. The conflict had many dimensions. To begin with, the very nature of the policy of apartheid was anathema to these churches. And for them, there was little difference between apartheid and separate development. If the distinction was made, separate development was regarded as little more than a sophisticated form of apartheid. Since government policy was to separate and divide people on the basis of ethnicity, and since the churches understood part of their task as the reconciliation of groups and the implementation of social equality, conflict between church and state was often unavoidable. Further, the implementation of government policy directly affected many facets of the life of the churches in an adverse way. This included everything from the owning of property on a non-racial basis to the holding of residential conferences open to all races.[81]

---

[81] Cf. *Apartheid and the Church*, Spro-cas Church Commission Report (Johannesburg: Spro-cas, 1972), pp. 6ff.

Moreover, in pursuit of separate development, the state took over black church schools as well as many church hospitals and related institutions. This may be regarded as normal in modern states, but often, as in the case of the expropriation of the Federal Theological Seminary, it was done in ways that smacked of victimization of the churches.[82]

An important aspect of the church–state problem was the conviction embodied in the republic's constitution (1961) that South Africa was a Christian country. Religious persecution, as this is normally understood, did not exist. The state encouraged the propagation and teaching of the Christian faith, and respected the rights of religious minority groups. Moreover, government leaders were on record as saying that the prophetic witness of the church was part of the church's responsibility, and was important for the well-being of the state. All of this reflects the country's Calvinist heritage, as it was maintained by the NGK itself. For example, the 1974 report of the NGK specifically states that part of the task of the church is 'to preach the supremacy of Christ in all spheres of life, including that of the state . . . it must warn when injustice is being done in the implementation of national policy and the application of laws.'[83] However, two qualifications radically affected this position.

First, as the 1974 report indicates, Calvin's stress on the prophetic role of the church is tempered by Kuyper's teaching on the 'sovereignty of separate spheres'.[84] This means that the state is sovereign under God, and supported in its task by his 'common grace' given in creation. The church is likewise sovereign in her sphere, under the lordship of Christ, and it is her responsibility to proclaim God's 'special grace' to the world, and enable its members to fulfil their role as Christians in society. Thus, the church has no right to interfere in matters of government, but its members have a political vocation and responsibility as individuals. In other words, and here Kuyper differs from Calvin, the prophetic task of the church in society is not exercised by the church as church, but through its members in the world. These two positions can be reconciled, but when Kuyper's teaching is separated from Calvin's, you virtually end up with the Lutheran idea of the 'two kingdoms', the separation of the spiritual and the secular realms, an idea that is far removed from

---

[82] See Chapter 4, pp. 162f.

[83] Cf. *Human Relations and the South African Scene*, p. 69.

[84] Cf. *Human Relations and the South African Scene*, p. 70; see also *Human Relations in South Africa*, p. 39, and Kotze, *Principle and Practice*, p. 22.

Calvin. This is the direction in which the 1974 report moves. It states: 'The golden rule of sovereignty for each institution in its own sphere, of justice and of love, should be sufficient to preserve the state from revolutionary chaos and political absolutism and tyranny.'[85] Whether this is so is highly debatable, but this rule too often keeps the church silent when it should speak. Indeed, it prevents the church from speaking concretely and specifically for fear that in doing so it might trespass on the 'sovereign sphere' of the state. Without doubt, the apartheid government's own understanding of the political role of the church was that of Kuyper – hence the insistence that the church stick to its own spiritual task and let the government get on with its secular vocation.

Second, the prophetic task of the NGK was qualified in terms of separate development. The church, as we pointed out above, 'must warn when injustice is being done *in the implementation of national policy . . .*' When all is said and done, there was little difference between the position of the NGK and the English-speaking churches on the political responsibility of the church in principle, though ironically the latter took a more Calvinist position than the former. But the English-speaking churches saw their prophetic task in a different light because they fundamentally rejected national policy as unjust in itself.[86] Over the years, the English-speaking churches were relatively free to criticize the government, even to criticize the fundamentals of separate development. They also had reasonable access to those in authority. Yet, no matter how free they were to speak out, or how cordially their deputations were received by state officials, little was achieved because of the basically different understanding of, and attitude towards, separate development. NGK criticism was heeded by the state, but it did not really affect the status quo. The critique of the English-speaking churches was disregarded, and sometimes led to conflict and confrontation.

Tension between the English-speaking churches and the apartheid state, which normally meant an uneasy coexistence, intensified when words became deeds. The 1970s and '80s saw regular government action against church people – pastors, missionaries, leaders, and those involved in Christian agencies and projects. The reason was obvious. If the

---

[85] *Human Relations and the South African Scene*, p. 70.
[86] See John W. de Gruchy, 'The Relationship between the State and some Churches in South Africa, 1968–1975', *Journal of Church and State*, vol. 19, no. 3 (Autumn 1977).

churches were against government policy, then it followed that church workers would become involved in programmes that went against what the government regarded as the well-being of the state. Hence there was a spate of deportations of missionaries, and banning, detaining, and imprisoning of South Africans involved in this way.[87] In this connection it is appropriate to mention the celebrated trial of the Very Revd Gonville ffrench-Beytagh, a former Anglican Dean of Johannesburg. Dean ffrench-Beytagh was charged by the state of engaging in 'terroristic activities'. On 15 October 1971, he was found guilty in the Transvaal Supreme Court, and sentenced to five years' imprisonment. Later, in February 1972, the Appellate Division of the Supreme Court rescinded this verdict, and the Dean was acquitted. But the whole trial indicated the extent to which the security police kept watch over the activities of people, especially of well-known clerical critics of the government.[88]

In reacting against Christians in this way, the state denied that it was acting against the churches. It insisted that its target was individuals or quasi-religious organizations who use the cloak of religion to disguise subversive activities. The churches responded in various ways. But in responding, they generally affirmed their corporate nature, holding that action against individuals who seek to obey Christ is action against the church. They also called on the government to give reasons for its actions. These were seldom forthcoming. The churches also insisted that their words and deeds were motivated by Christian obedience and not politically pragmatic considerations, and that their witness was open to, not hidden from, public scrutiny. But how could one handle the government argument that it knew more about people and institutions than was in the public interest to declare, and that its actions were always the result of such inside information?

Government propaganda, especially the charge of being unpatriotic, certainly sowed seeds of bewilderment, and helped spawn opposition to the witness of the churches among their own members. This was exacerbated by a lack of clear biblical teaching on the part of the churches

---

[87] A full list of names would be too lengthy to include here, even if it were available. *Pro Veritate* carried documentation before it was banned. The Revd Ben Ngidi, a former chairman of the United Congregational Church, was in prison without trial or reason given for almost a year. This is one example among many.

[88] Cf. *The State vs. the Dean of Johannesburg* (Johannesburg: S.A. Institute of Race Relations, 1972).

regarding their social witness. And, of course, many white members accepted government policy as right and necessary anyway. It would be wrong then, to give the impression that, in this conflict between the English-speaking churches and the state, the churches' members stood united. Indeed, the churches' struggle against apartheid and racism was compromised in a variety of ways. First, there was a gap between synodical resolutions and congregational resolve and action. Second, there was something of a credibility gap between the stand of the churches and discriminatory practices in their own life. Third, the churches by and large failed to educate their constituencies in the meaning of Christian social responsibility. Let us elaborate on these points.

A major dilemma of the English-speaking churches was the chasm that existed between the prophetic utterances of the church courts and the attitudes and actions of local congregations and members. In writing about the Anglicans shortly after Cottesloe, Hinchliff remarked: 'It is probably true to say that when members of the government accuse the bishops and clergy of the Province of interfering in politics, many of the laity silently agree with the accusation and wish that their own consciences and the secular authorities might both be allowed to rest in peace.'[89] How are we to explain this credibility gap? In the first place we need to recognize that it is only half-true to say that there was this wide gap between synods and congregations. It is half-true because the majority of the members and congregations are black not white, and this majority was fully supportive of their churches' stand against apartheid. The gap was really between the synods and leadership on the one hand, and some white congregations and many white members on the other. This does not deny that there was white support. The churches would have been rent asunder early on if there was not general support from their membership, although one suspects that one reason why schism did not happen is simply the knowledge from past experience that resolutions are seldom implemented anyway. A major failure of the leaders of the churches was their overconfidence in the power of resolutions. There is a tendency to believe that if the right word is uttered, the task is achieved. Thus, there was a plethora of pronouncements, but a lack of grass-roots teaching and a paucity of deeds. Reflecting on resolu-

---

[89] Hinchliff, *Anglican Church*, p. 240.

tions of the Presbyterian Church (PCSA), the Revd Robert Orr told the General Assembly in 1963:

> In previous years your committee (Church and Nation) has tried, in its own stumbling fashion, to indicate some of the positive things Christians may do, considering all the circumstances. We have also done our best to study legislation and make clear its implications for the Christian. To the best of our knowledge, these statements and recommendations, piously noted by this Assembly, have had less effect than the rattling of tin cans tied to a cat's tail. In fact, we are worried that they may have had a negative effect, that they may have soothed the conscience of the Church members, who can point to them and say 'There you are – that is what my Church thinks' and then go back to their reading of the Sunday paper.[90]

While the prophetic witness of the English-speaking churches was gravely impaired by this gap between the leadership and many white members, it was equally affected by discriminatory practices within the life of the churches themselves. Although blacks increasingly took on leadership roles, many remained sceptical about the seriousness of the churches in combating racism. They pointed to a wide range of discriminatory practices that existed over the years, and which were only being slowly and painfully removed. Writing in *Pro Veritate* in the early 1960s, Hinchliff remarked that 'Anglicans are sometimes rather smug, sometimes rather angry, because our Church leaders are outspoken in their attacks on the Government. What they do not realise is that other (African) members of the Church feel that the practice of the Church lags a long way behind what its leaders say.' This gap between word and deed was exploited by the government as blatant hypocrisy. Many a deputation to the state floundered on the mere fact that the churches' own lives were not beyond reproach. Indeed, on occasion the state exercised a prophetic ministry to the churches. For example, the churches soon learned that they could not justly criticize wage discrimination between whites and blacks in society or in state employ because there was similar discrimination in the churches. Earlier we quoted Archbishop Hurley's query as to whether the other churches in the same

---

[90] Quoted in Cawood, *Churches and Race Relations*, p. 95.

position would have done better than the NGK. His conclusion deserves quotation:

> In the light of the behaviour of the other Churches in South Africa, we would not. For these Churches, too, have been hamstrung by their inability to break out of theory into practice. They have not suffered from an inadequate theory. They have just suffered from a paralysing incapacity to translate the right theory into practice.[91]

Following the Soweto uprising in 1976, the English-speaking churches became more aware of the gaps between resolutions and resolve, between word and deed, and sought ways of overcoming the inherent problems. But it remained true that white members were usually opposed to change or else apathetic. It seems that the problem lay at a deeper level than simply the question of race relations. It was wrapped up in political uncertainties and fears for the future. There was also considerable reticence to oppose the government. There was a basic uneasiness, a sense of insecurity; and a lack of a sense of purpose was very evident. The problem had to do with what might be called a crisis of faith, commitment, and hope. And this had to do with the peculiar situation of the white, English-speaking community and a failure on the part of the churches to meet the crisis in a creative way.

The dilemma of white, English-speaking South Africans under apartheid, quite apart from the church, is vividly shown by the difficulty one had in trying to define them. This was demonstrated at a conference on 'English-speaking South Africans Today' held in 1974 in Grahamstown. A broad definition would include all South Africans for whom English is the language of daily discourse, irrespective of their ethnic origin. But, as many people of very different ethnic backgrounds speak English, this is not very helpful. Moreover, the British home connection no longer means a great deal. There is no distinguishing cultural life, and much of what there is, is mediocre, a pale shadow of something else. As Guy Butler said in his introductory lecture at the Grahamstown conference:

> The group is small, split among many religious denominations, secular by temperament, with very few cultural organizations; without a

---

[91] Cf. note 78.

political party which makes it its business to look after its interests; with virtually no say in the education of its young, except when rich enough to send them to private schools; a socially mobile group, sprinkled over a large country, and alas, a predominantly white-collar group cut off from the sobering realities of manual labour and honest poverty.

And further, commented Butler:

Behind the facade of our impressive material success, what do we find? A great deal of cynicism and shoulder-shrugging, bitterness and resentment at Afrikaner power; disillusionment at Britain's diminished world-stature; fear of, and guilt towards our [sic] blacks; and a habit of buck-passing and scapegoat hunting.[92]

What we had, in fact, was a minority (English-speaking) within a minority (white) community with little historical awareness, and an individualism that had lost the ruggedness of settlers and pioneers, with a morality that was either very secular and materialistic or pietist and escapist. By the early 1980s an English-speaking white identity crisis was rampant, although it was recognized that their contribution did not need to be something of the past. The traditional strengths of the English-speaking community – pragmatism, tolerance towards other commitments and ideas, and a sense of fair play – while by no means theirs alone, were considered important. But they were inadequate for the crisis, and no match against other strong ideological options. It was this situation that called for a rediscovery of prophetic elements within the tradition of the English-speaking churches, a tradition that was often maintained by people who became despondent about the apathy of the churches and left them in order to join the struggle for human rights.

English-speaking South Africa has produced notable poets and writers, historians and social scientists, and leaders in many other disciplines and fields, but there were very few who had the ability and charisma to provide the theological insight and leadership that was adequate for the struggle against apartheid. It seems that authors such as

---

[92] André de Villiers (ed.), *English-Speaking South Africa Today* (Cape Town: Oxford University Press, 1976), pp. 11f.

Olive Schreiner, Alan Paton, and Nadine Gordimer engaged in far more profound reflection on the historical experience and challenges than all the churches and theologians put together. Writing in the midst of that situation, we ventured this opinion:

> What is essential today is, of course, more than reflection and analysis, but this is still of primary importance for the life and witness of the English-speaking churches. Neither rampant liberalism nor doctrinaire fundamentalism is adequate for the task at hand, nor are they of the essence, by any means, of the traditions of the English-speaking churches. For one thing, both are far too individualistic. On the contrary, the rich Catholic and evangelical and Nonconformist heritage of the English-speaking churches is full of tremendous potential for spiritual renewal and mission in the final decades of twentieth-century South Africa.[93]

Roman Catholics and Lutherans

It may seem strange that Catholics and Lutherans should be placed together in our discussion of the church response to apartheid up to the end of the 1970s. There is at least one good reason for this. Neither the Roman Catholic Church nor the various Lutheran synods were in the forefront of the struggle against racism in South Africa until a relatively late period. At least, it may be more accurate to say that they were not as visible in this regard as the English-speaking churches. There have been good historical reasons for this.

Traditionally, the Roman Catholic Church has been in a peculiar situation in South Africa because of the strong position of the Protestant and especially the Dutch Reformed churches. Catholics were prohibited from public worship until 1804, and were only allowed their first bishop in 1837. For many years after that, obstacles were placed in the way of Catholic missions to the indigenous peoples of the land, and there was a clearly acknowledged anti-Roman Catholic bias in the policies of the Afrikaner Nationalist government, particularly with regard to immigration. This latter bias did slowly change as more and more immigrants

---

[93] John W. de Gruchy, *The Church Struggle Against Apartheid*, 2nd edn (Grand Rapids: Eerdmans; Cape Town: David Philip, 1986), p. 96.

from traditionally Catholic countries settled in South Africa. But the cry of 'Roomse-gevaar' (Roman danger) would evoke considerable emotion from some people in the white Afrikaner community. This anti-Catholic sentiment produced a cautious attitude within the church, and the hierarchy was far more diplomatic in its relation to the state than the English-speaking churches were. Perhaps such diplomacy is more traditionally characteristic of Roman Catholics, but it resulted in more caution than is normally the case.

Caution, however, did not mean indifference to the racial situation in the country. Before 1950, the Catholic bishops made few pronouncements on the subject, but after that, and particularly after Vatican II, the church took a clear and often bold stand on the issues. Just as the English-speaking churches reacted strongly to the apartheid policy after the National party victory in 1948, so Catholic bishops spoke out in similar terms. In September of that year, Bishop Hennemann addressed the churches of his diocese on the subject. In the course of his pastoral letter he said:

> In recent years it [i.e., segregation] has reappeared in the guise and under the name of 'apartheid'. A beginning has already been made to put into practice this noxious, unchristian and destructive policy . . . To make matters worse, all this is done in the name of Christian civilization . . . 'Christian civilization' is, we are asked to believe, one and the same thing as 'white civilization'. The truth is, there is no such thing as 'white civilization', and there never was. If it is 'white' exclusively, it is not Christian, and if it is Christian, it is not 'white'. The false doctrine of 'white civilization', if pursued to its logical conclusions, will open wide the doors of South Africa to the world's most formidable enemy today – Communism.[94]

The first joint pastoral letter of the Catholic bishops was issued in 1952, the tercentenary of white colonization of the Cape, on the subject of race. This was followed by seven letters solely on matters of racial harmony and social justice. An excerpt from a recent commentary on the stand taken by the bishops over these years reads:

> The content of the Joint Pastorals can be summed up as applying to our own circumstances the Gospel teaching of the universality of love

---

[94] Cf. The Churches' Judgment on Apartheid, p. 15.

and justice and the 'code' of human rights which protect man's dignity, freedom and well-being . . . From the beginning they stated that the concession of these rights to all in the country in the same manner was a necessity of justice, and refused to be distracted from this when the theory of partitioning South Africa into separate states was brought up. The reason for this was and is that the majority of those who do the work of the Republic are black, and to refuse them citizen rights is injustice and inhumanity. As the inevitable rigidity of law grew, and harshness in its enforcement, they protested in 1964 against the law depriving Africans resident in the country hundreds of years of permanent residence rights, and four times in 1974–75 against methods used in administering security laws and treatment of church institutions witnessing against injustice.[95]

The stand taken by the leadership of the Roman Catholic Church was very similar to that of the English-speaking churches. It is not surprising, then, that after Vatican II, the Catholic Church developed its relationship with the other churches to a marked extent and became an observer of the Council of Churches. While the Roman Catholic Church remained sensitive to its peculiar position in the country, it did not let this prevent it from speaking prophetically to the situation. In some instances, such as the integration of church schools, it led the way with some success. It is also noteworthy that Catholic analyses of the situation paid considerable attention to labour and other economic factors. A key and comprehensive statement by the bishops was *A Call to Conscience Addressed to Catholics by their Bishops*, issued in 1972, and further statements were issued in 1977 on a variety of matters arising out of the political and social situation.

The problem of the Catholic Church was the same as that of the English-speaking churches. Although the church had a black membership at that stage of over one million, there was considerable reluctance on the part of its 350,000 white members to follow the lead of their bishops. Archbishop Dennis Hurley of Durban was a constant critic of this failure within his own diocese and the church at large, and over the years he attempted in various and creative ways to bridge the gap. But

---

[95] Finbar Synnott, O. P., *Justice and Reconciliation in South Africa*, a report of the Southern African Catholic Bishops' Conference (Pretoria, n.d.), p. 11.

the sharpest critique came from black priests. This resulted in considerable tension within the church, and led on a number of occasions to confrontation situations. In some respects, black Catholic priests took a more militant line within their church than was true in most other denominations.[96]

With regard to the Lutheran denomination, there were German-speaking Lutherans among the early settlers at the Cape in the seventeenth century, and the white Lutheran community grew as successive groups of German and later Scandinavian settlers came to South Africa. From the middle of the nineteenth century, a number of continental and American Lutheran missionary societies began work among the African peoples, mainly in Natal and the Transvaal. This eventually led to the formation of various synods composed of black Lutherans, which have been independent of each other and also largely separated from contact and certainly fellowship with the white Lutheran synods.[97]

In 1966, the various Lutheran churches and synods throughout South Africa and Namibia (South West Africa) joined together to form the Federation of Evangelical Lutheran Churches in Southern Africa (FELC-SA). This new organization for Lutherans, and also Moravians, did much to bring the various Lutheran communities closer to each other and closer to the other churches in South Africa. This was particularly true of relationships between the black synods and the churches belonging to the South African Council of Churches. During the early 1970s, an attempt was made to unite white and black Lutherans in one church. However, due to white reticence, four black synods finally went their own way and formed the Evangelical Lutheran Church of South Africa in 1975. Although the black Lutherans were highly critical of the race situation in the country, a great deal of their struggle was centred on the unity of the Lutheran Church. This struggle for unity was extremely difficult because of the conservative position adopted by most German-speaking Lutheran congregations. In 1975, FELCSA unanimously

---

[96] Early in the 1970s this led to such tension at St Peter's Seminary, Hammanskraal, that the rector was forced to resign. A black priests' movement was established to remove discrimination from the life of the church. Cf. Drake Koka, 'Open Letter on Day of Consecration', sent to Bishop P. J. Buthelezi on 22 October 1972, on behalf of the Black Justice and Peace Vigilantes Committee. It is notable that in 1968 Bishop Buthelezi became the first black Catholic archbishop in South Africa.

[97] Cf. Hans W. Florin, *Lutherans in South Africa* (Durban: Lutheran Publishing House).

adopted an *Appeal to Lutheran Christians in Southern Africa*, in which the following was stated:

> The confessional basis of the Lutheran churches obliges every Lutheran Christian, the individual church bodies as well as FELCSA, to withstand unanimously alien principles which threaten to under-mine their faith and to destroy their unity in their doctrine, in their witness and in their practice . . . The most dangerous of these alien principles are the following:

> 1. An emphasis on the loyalty to the ethnic group which induces Lutheran Christians to worship in a Lutheran church dependent on birth or race or ethnic affinities which insist that the Lutheran churches in Southern Africa remain divided into separate churches according to ethnic principles;
> 2. The belief that the unity of the Church is only a spiritual unity which need not be manifested;
> 3. The belief that the structures of society and the political and economic system of our country are to be shaped according to natural laws only, inherent in creation or merely according to considerations of practical expediency, without being exposed to the criterion of God's love as revealed in the biblical message.

Later in the same document FELCSA addressed the political situation more directly: 'To us the political system now prevailing in the Republic of South Africa appears to be based on a number of errors and misap-prehensions. We are convinced that this whole system needs to be radically reconsidered and reappraised in the light of the biblical revela-tion and of the general experiences of mankind.' The statement also held that 'the political system in force in South Africa, with its discrimination against some sectors of the population, its acceptance of the break-up of many families, its concentration of power in the hands of one race only, and the limitations it imposes on freedom, cannot be reconciled with the gospel of the grace of God in Jesus Christ'.[98]

---

[98] On Lutheran thinking in South Africa in the 1970s and 1980s see, inter alia, the publications of the Lutheran Missiological Institute, Umpumulo, Natal. The Institute was held annually under the auspices of FELCSA to examine the socio-political situation

Like the English-speaking churches, as well as like some within the NGK, the black Lutherans and FELCSA saw the direct connection between the unity of the church and the social situation in South Africa. This ecclesiological dimension to the church struggle was of the utmost importance. To regard the unity of the church largely in spiritual and 'invisible' terms would be to misunderstand the teaching of the New Testament, and in the end to compromise the witness of the church as it struggles against racism and other forces that divide and separate people on the grounds of culture and ethnicity.

---

in South Africa. See, for example, K. Nürnberger (ed.), *Affluence, Poverty and the Word of God* (Durban: Lutheran Publishing House, 1978). J. Lukas de Vries, *Mission and Colonialism in Namibia* (Johannesburg: Ravan, 1978), is a discussion of the issues by a black Lutheran theologian and Namibian church leader. While de Vries concentrated on Namibian issues, his position reflected that of many black Lutherans in South Africa.

3

The Growing Conflict

A Confessing Movement

World-wide observers of the church struggle in South Africa are probably very familiar with the name of Dr Beyers Naudé, and the work of the Christian Institute of Southern Africa, which he directed until both he and the Institute were banned in October 1977. While the witness of the CI was by no means the sum total of Christian testimony and action against racism in South Africa, the story of the struggle of the church to confess Christ as Lord, over against the claims of race, cannot be told with any completeness if the struggle of the CI is omitted from its rightful place on centre stage. And the story of the CI is also the story of Naudé, of his change, of his charismatic leadership, and of the community of people who rallied around the cause he represented.

Naudé was a distinguished minister in the Transvaal Synod of the NGK. He was also a member of the Broederbond. His roots lay deep within Afrikaner tradition and culture, and especially within the piety of evangelical Calvinism as he experienced it in the early, formative years of his life in the Cape and at the Dutch Reformed theological seminary at Stellenbosch. At the time of the Cottesloe Consultation, to which he was a delegate, he was acting moderator of the Transvaal Synod. Although there were other factors which influenced the direction of Dr Naudé's life, it was Sharpeville and then the failure of his church to stand by the resolutions of Cottesloe that finally led him to take a stand contrary to that officially adopted by the NGK.

Post-Sharpeville South Africa was a society in crisis. Nothing quite like it had happened before to disturb the apparent tranquillity of white South Africa and the confidence of foreign investors. Nothing comparable was to take place again until Soweto erupted in protest in 1976, and evoked support from nations and peoples throughout the world. Thus, the early 1960s were critical years for the church as well as society in South Africa. The question was simply: Could Christians in South Africa, irrespective of confession or race, transcend apartheid and find each other in the service of justice and reconciliation in the name of Christ?

In spite of official opposition from his own church, but with support from some ministers and members within it, in 1962 Naudé launched a journal entitled *Pro Veritate*. The following year, when the Christian Institute was founded by him and some English-speaking church leaders, he accepted the position of director. The founders of the CI hoped that the Institute would enable members of all races of the Afrikaans and other churches to share together in bearing witness to the unity of the church and the lordship of Christ over society. Its first attempt to do this was through the formation of Bible study groups throughout the country, many of them led by Dutch Reformed ministers. Through its study guides and *Pro Veritate*, the CI provided material to challenge and guide Christian understanding and action. It also sought to expose South African Christians to developments taking place in the church in Europe and North America by providing study fellowships and arranging for scholarships. The emphasis in these original years was one of changing the awareness and understanding of white Christians who had never questioned the status quo, through a rediscovery of the biblical message.

The new work and witness of Naudé and the CI was unacceptable to the NGK from the outset. The church went so far as to declare that it would not allow Naudé to remain a minister if he accepted the position of director in the CI. Thus, Naudé faced a costly decision – whether to continue to work for change through his church and congregation, as some friends advised, since he was in a strong position to do so, or to resign as a minister and work through the Institute in a more direct and radical way. It was an agonizing decision to make. Naudé appreciated the counsel of friends who urged him to remain a minister in the NGK, but finally decided to the contrary. He did not wish to lose his ministerial status, but he believed God was calling him to fulfil a new kind of ministry. Indeed, as he explained to his congregation in his farewell sermon, it was a matter of obedience to God rather than human authority.[1] The

---

[1] International Commission of Jurists, Geneva (eds), *The Trial of Beyers Naudé* (London: Search Press; Johannesburg: Ravan, 1975), pp. 68f.

kind of witness the CI was designed to make was a divine imperative he could not resist.

A similar decision faced other Dutch Reformed ministers who had joined the CI in support of their colleague. Some of them resigned from the NGK in protest and a few became ministers of other denominations. Catholic Archbishop Hurley, a strong supporter of the CI from its inception, describes the story of the Institute in terms of radical conversion:

> Those who experienced the conversion referred to here were dedicated Christians of the Dutch Reformed faith. Fellow believers would not normally think of them as needing conversion. Yet they went through a painful transformation and emerged as men keenly aware of the demands of love in race-ridden South Africa.[2]

In 1965 the General Synod of the NGK resolved that all members of the church should resign from the CI. The congregation in Parktown, Johannesburg, to which Naudé and his family now belonged, and of which Naudé was an elder, stood by these members in support, rejecting the decision of the synod as contrary to the gospel. But the going was very difficult. The CI, and Naudé in particular, were regarded as driving a wedge down the middle of Afrikaner society. And in a very real sense, the accusation was correct. In accepting the leadership of the CI, Naudé had in effect rejected the determinative role of the *volk* in the life of the NGK. For him, confessing Christ meant rejecting the culture-Christianity of those who supported apartheid. An eventual result of this alienation from Afrikanerdom was an important change in the CI itself. Having failed to influence the NGK and Afrikaans-speaking Christians to any real or positive extent, Naudé turned more and more for support to English-speaking Christians. Here he gained some encouragement, but Naudé soon discovered that white English-speaking support was not much greater than Afrikaner support when it came to fundamental social change. As a result, he grew increasingly disenchanted with most whites and attempted to become more directly involved with blacks in their struggle.

While the English-speaking churches supported the CI, their relation-

---

[2] D. E. Hurley, OMI, 'The Christian Institute', *South African Outlook* (November 1977), p. 163.

ship to it was seldom more than tentative and lukewarm. Many church leaders and members were committed to the CI and supportive of Naudé; if this were not so, the CI would have collapsed early on. But there was also unease. The CI was a fellowship of individuals answerable only to itself, and in no way responsible to the churches. The CI was widely and heavily financed by overseas church agencies. This meant that it was able to develop a large staff, drawn largely from the ministerial ranks of the churches, and to embark on far-reaching programmes. The CI regarded these programmes as supplements to the work of the churches; the churches often saw them as a threat to what they were doing – and they probably felt guilty that they were not doing all that they should. There was also an element of distrust. In order for the CI to gain and maintain overseas support, subconsciously or not, it had to project the image that it was a more significant witness against apartheid than the churches. This was not very difficult to do, but it tended to distort what the churches had done and were doing, and to minimize their potential role in the situation. These kinds of tensions are not new to Christian history, but they did compromise both the CI and the churches in their mutual struggle against apartheid.

Yet, the undoubted significance of the CI for the churches was that it provoked and challenged them in a way that had never occurred before. The growing radicalism of the CI was regarded with some trepidation, but the English-speaking churches could not dissociate themselves from the basic principles and confession for which the CI stood. And so, time and again, the CI set the agenda and forced the pace for the churches. Naudé's prophetic discernment, supported later by others such as Dr Theo Kotze, Director of the CI in Cape Town, probed deeply into the ills of South African society and challenged the churches to action.

The CI did more than prod the churches. It attempted to create a 'confessing movement', something akin to the Confessing Church that arose in Germany during the Hitler regime, but something more adapted to the situation in South Africa.[3] Indeed, the CI was profoundly influenced by the German church struggle in its basic orientation to the state and to the churches, and in its understanding of the lordship of

---

[3] See Beyers Naudé, 'Die Tyd vir 'n "Belydende Kerk" is Daar', *Pro Veritate*, vol. 4, no. 6 (July 1965). Subsequent articles on the same theme by Dr Naudé can be found in *Pro Veritate*, vol. 4, nos. 7 and 8.

Christ. But despite much discussion and considerable support for the idea, a Confessing Church as such never materialized. One reason for this was that the German model was both impractical and inappropriate for South Africa, where the churches are so different in ethos, tradition, and self-understanding from those in Germany.[4] A more important reason was that a 'confessing element' existed within the churches, and though many were disillusioned with their own denomination's witness, they nevertheless saw the need to work as members of their churches rather than create something new. After all, whatever the churches might do in practice, the English-speaking churches, the Catholic and Lutheran churches, were all committed in principle to the struggle against apartheid. What the CI did do, however, was to provide resources and an ad hoc supportive community for those who were at the cutting edge of the churches' witness. And this proved an immense strength to those involved.

It is beyond the scope of these pages to describe all the functions fulfilled by the CI before it was banned. But two are of special importance for our discussion. First, the CI was instrumental in bringing many of the African initiated churches into relationship with each other and the wider church in South Africa and beyond. Until the mid-1960s, the 'mainline' churches were sceptical of these independent churches. They shared the same kind of attitude typified by Sundkler's initial assessment of them as a bridge from Christianity back into heathendom. This opinion was shared by blacks and whites alike in the major denominations. The independent churches were equally sceptical of the other churches, for the same reasons that they had originally broken away. But they did feel the need for some kind of association, especially for theological education and training. Thus, they turned to the CI for help, and found a ready welcome. Supported by massive grants from Germany and

---

[4] See E. Bethge, 'A Confessing Church in South Africa? Conclusions from a Visit', in John W. de Gruchy (ed.), *Bonhoeffer: Exile and Martyr* (London: Collins, 1975; New York: Seabury, 1976). Although the title of our book may remind readers of the church struggle in Germany during the Third Reich, we have not attempted to relate our discussion to that situation. That there are illuminating parallels we do not wish to deny, but simply to equate the two distorts reality and clouds the issues. Cf. H. Adam, *Modernizing Racial Domination: The Dynamics of South African Politics* (California: University of California Press, 1972), esp. ch. 3. An attempt to draw out the similarities will be found in 'An Open Letter Concerning Nationalism, National Socialism and Christianity', supplement to *Pro Veritate*, July 1971.

Holland, the CI enabled the African Independent Churches Association (AICA) to come into being. Through AICA a new era dawned for the independent churches as they became more closely associated with other Christian communities in the country. The fledgling association was not without its internal problems, and after a few years it broke its ties with the CI. Later it became related to the South African Council of Churches (SACC). But whatever the failures of AICA or the CI, what they achieved together was a pioneering step of considerable consequence for the church in South Africa. Not only did it help the independent churches find a wider ecumenical fellowship and become a more integral part of the total life of the church and its witness, but it also made the other churches aware of the contribution and challenge of this rapidly growing tradition.

Second, the CI played a determinative role in the Study Project on Christianity in an Apartheid Society (Spro-cas I), and the action-oriented follow-up programme, Spro-cas II. Spro-cas was a result of the *Message to the People of South Africa*, published by the South African Council of Churches in 1968. Later we shall examine the *Message* and Spro-cas in more detail, but some preliminary remarks are required here in order to understand the development of the CI. The *Message* was a decisive rejection of apartheid and separate development as contrary to the Christian faith in principle. Spro-cas I was an attempt by the SACC and the CI to work out alternatives to apartheid in South African society. It was run by an executive appointed by the SACC and the Institute. By 1972 the project was complete, and a new phase began. Previously the emphasis had been on study, but now it shifted to action and implementation. This new programme, Spro-cas II, was dominated by the CI, though also supported by the SACC. It represented a decisive turning-point in the work and witness of the CI. From this stage onwards, the Institute rapidly attempted to become more clearly involved in the struggle of blacks who had rejected any co-operation with the system of separate development. As part of this involvement, the CI was also beginning to offer a radical critique of the economic structures of South African society.

In a perceptive article entitled 'The Christian Institute and the Resurgence of African Nationalism', Peter Walshe has described this change in the stance of the CI as a parting of company with 'the old liberal illusion that change could be effected solely by education and moral appeals directed at the privileged'. While Walshe tends to over-state the role that the CI played in the development of black conscious-ness, it is still basically true that the Institute, as he puts it,

> began to encourage the resurgence of black consciousness as a source of renewed dignity and potential for the poor. This involved the judg-ment that black initiatives would be crucial in pressing for change; that whites could and should no longer expect to control, such initia-tives; that the Institute, by increasing its black membership and witnessing to the essential human community above colour, could assist in the emergence of a new generation of black leaders.[5]

It is a massive understatement to say that the CI was never popular with the government. But however irksome it was in its critique of apartheid, the crunch only really came when the CI became involved in the black consciousness movement. In 1972 the apartheid govern-ment instituted the Schlebusch Parliamentary Commission of Inquiry to investigate the activities of the Christian Institute, the University Christian Movement (UCM), the National Union of South African Students (NUSAS), and the South African Institute of Race Relations. In the course of its labours, it also investigated the Wilgespruit Ecumenical Centre at Roodepoort, near Johannesburg, which had a long history of providing a multiracial programme related to church and society issues. In 1975, now under the chairmanship of another Nationalist Member of Parliament, Mr Le Grange, the Commission of Inquiry presented its findings to Parliament. As a consequence, the work of Wilgespruit and NUSAS was heavily censured, and both the CI and UCM were declared 'affected organizations'. As the UCM had already disbanded, it was only the CI that was affected. Being an 'affected organization' meant that it was no longer able to receive financial aid from sources outside the country, the government rationale being that it was involved in political action rather than bona fide Christian work.

Before continuing the story, it is important to recall that the Schlebusch/Le Grange Commission was a highly contentious matter,

---

[5] Peter Walshe, 'Church versus State in South Africa: The Christian Institute and the Resurgence of African Nationalism', *Journal of Church and State*, vol. 19, no. 3 (Autumn 1977), p. 462.

strongly opposed in principle by the churches belonging to the South African Council of Churches, as well as by some opposition politicians and other community leaders. It was also opposed by those organizations being investigated; in fact, the CI leadership refused en bloc to give evidence to it, though this was an offence punishable by law. Eventually, the refusal to testify led to a series of court cases, one of which was the trial of Naudé himself.

The full story of the trial of Naudé has been told elsewhere.[6] It is certainly one of the most significant trials of any church leader in the history of the church in South Africa. Here was a former dignitary of the NGK, a former member of the Broederbond, on trial for refusing to give evidence to a state commission of inquiry. The penalty was not very serious (50 rand or one month in prison), but the issue was: Does the state have the right to investigate people and institutions in secrecy beyond the normal processes of the law, especially when the investigation is conducted by party politicians appointed by a government clearly opposed to those being investigated? Impartiality was impossible under the circumstances. Naudé regarded the giving of evidence which could – as it already had in the case of people involved in NUSAS and Wilgespruit – lead to banning and deportation, as contrary to the gospel. No Christian, he maintained, could participate in a trial that could implicate others if it were so conducted that those implicated would be unable to refute any false evidence that might be forthcoming. He made it clear in his defence before the magistrate that this opposition was not a matter of scoring political points, but of evangelical conviction. Indeed, the whole of Naudé's statement before the court is a model of Christian witness, as clear as it was bold. But eventually he was found guilty. Having elected to go to prison for the month, Naudé was released soon after, when a friend paid the fine on his behalf, much against Naudé's wishes. Naudé was not a martyr. But many would echo the words of Lord Ramsey, the former Archbishop of Canterbury, who shortly after the trial wrote: 'When I think of the men who have shown me what it means to be a Christian my thoughts will always go quickly to Naudé.'[7]

Now that the CI was an 'affected organization', it was forced to cut

---

[6] See *The Trial of Beyers Naudé.*

[7] In his preface to *The Trial of Beyers Naudé.*

back on its programmes and staff. At the same time, it managed to increase its financial support from within the country to a considerable extent. But the focus of the CI was concentrated in the prophetic witness of men like Naudé and Kotze. By the time of the Soweto uprising in June 1976, the CI was already deeply committed to black initiatives, and it became involved in providing guidance and support for those in the forefront of the black protests.

This involvement, especially the support given to black leaders, and the publicizing of allegations of police torture and brutality,[8] including protest at the death of Steve Biko in prison, eventually led to the mass bannings on 19 October 1977. The CI was declared illegal, many of its black staff were detained by the police, and the senior white staff, Beyers Naudé, Theo Kotze, Brian Brown, Cedric Mayson, and former Spro-cas Director Peter Randall were all banned. So was *Pro Veritate*. The Revd David Russell, an Anglican priest working among migrant workers, especially among the squatter communities in Cape Town, was also banned, and placed under house arrest during weekends. Russell worked closely with the CI, particularly in publicizing injustices and enabling blacks to fight for their legal rights through the courts.[9]

The end was sudden and total, though not unexpected. It was more than symbolic that it should have occurred on the same day that Percy Qoboza, editor of the mass-circulation black newspaper *The World*, was detained and his paper banned, the day newspaper editor Donald Woods was banned, and the day many black organizations working for social change were made illegal and their leaders arrested. By now the CI was fully identified with the black cause symbolized by leaders such as the dead Steve Biko. After 16 years of courageous and often lonely witness, the CI was no more. Within a few hours, its once busy offices were empty and silent. One of the most articulate Christian witnesses to non-violent but radical social change was now out of action.

---

[8] During the last four years of its existence, the CI regularly published details of political arrests, bannings, etc., in its *CI Newsletter*.

[9] 'Banning' meant that action whereby a person, while not imprisoned, was virtually excluded from public life. Bannings prevented the affected persons from teaching, publishing, and speaking in public. They could not meet with more than one person at a time, except their immediate family; they could not leave their magisterial district; they could not enter educational or publishing premises. On occasions, banned clergymen preached, some regularly, but all charges against them for doing so were dropped by the state.

How are we to assess the significance of the Institute in the church struggle in South Africa? Peter Walshe has suggested at least two major contributions.[10] First, he says that the CI 'functioned as part of a vital matrix for the dissemination of ideas at a time when African political organisations had been systematically repressed'. Second, he points to the CI as 'another example of contemporary renewal', particularly in challenging exploitative structures in society on behalf of the poor. The CI, he writes, 'can be seen as ethico-prophetic in opposition to the bourgeois cultic ethos of white-dominated churches. It can be described as helping to articulate an indigenous South African liberation theology that has its primary impulse in the struggle for identity taking place in the black community.'

It would be asking too much of any institution to be without faults. Certainly the CI had its fair share. Perhaps we might simply say that it was weakest where it was strongest. It was very dependent upon overseas support, especially finance. This meant the constant need to design programmes that would capture the imagination of donor agencies. Inevitably this meant taking responsibility for many tasks and programmes which, however important, were tangential rather than central to the task of the CI. One rather crippling result of this was the considerable drain on the energies and resources of Naudé and others. Another was the tendency for the CI to become too centralized, even bureaucratic, thereby losing some of its dynamic as a confessing movement. (In many ways, being declared an 'affected organization' proved to be liberating rather than inhibiting.) A further problem was the lack of participant support at the grass-roots level. The CI had undoubted moral support within the black community, and some encouragement from sections of the white community, but relatively few supporters were involved in its programmes. Indeed, the impact of the CI was totally disproportionate to the size of its membership. But what it lacked in numbers it made up for in vision and courage. Then, of course, the CI was in many ways Beyers Naudé. Without his presence and leadership, it would never have been launched or sustained through the many years of its existence. This was central to its strength. It could be argued that it was also an inevitable weakness, for without Naudé the CI would have lost its charismatic centre.

---

[10] Walshe, 'Church Versus State', pp. 477f.

All of this was recognized by Naudé, Theo Kotze, and others within the leadership of the CI. It was, and still is, not easy to challenge the status quo in the radical manner eventually adopted by the CI. Many of the problems and the failures of the Institute were directly caused by the difficult conditions under which it had to operate. Through its insights, it bore witness to the radical implications of the kingdom of God for society. But a variety of circumstances prevented its being sustained as an ongoing institution. This fact is nothing new. Church history is full of instances where prophetic movements have arisen to challenge both the church and society in ways similar to that of the CI. Such movements have invariably been short-lived or else surrendered their original character. It is difficult to sustain a radical movement even in relatively open societies, let alone in situations where the state feels directly threatened by its presence.

Reflecting on this for a moment, we are inevitably brought face to face with the dilemma of the church. The church is called to bear witness to the kingdom of God in the world. That is its reason for existence. This kingdom is the antithesis of the kingdoms of this world – it constantly brings them under judgment. This being so, a faithful church will always find itself in a position of tension with society. At the same time, the church cannot escape being a social institution if it is to exist in the world. Jürgen Moltmann reminds us that a church which is simply a community of people founded on a relatively ad hoc basis 'cannot disturb the official doings of this society and certainly cannot alter them – indeed, it is hardly any longer even a real partner for the social institutions.'[11] Being an institution is not the problem – that can be both a blessing and a curse. The question is always: What kind of institution? The church loses its soul if it allows itself to become part of the system, to be used by society for its own interests, or to be neutralized in favour of the status quo. The church as an institution is called to be faithful to the kingdom of God, to be the 'salt', 'light', and 'leaven' of the world. For this reason the church desperately needs the presence of prophetic movements like the CI, for these movements provide the critique that forces the church to a new assessment of itself. Such movements are part of God's way of renewing his church in every generation and situation. After all, the members of the CI were not outside the church, but also

---

[11] Jürgen Moltmann, *Theology of Hope* (London: SCM Press, 1967), p. 321.

members of the church. The protest comes from within, and the protest and critique continued even though the doors of the CI were closed.

In the light of the CI experience, Peter Walshe raised three questions for Christian witness in the context of apartheid.[12] First, he asked if it is sufficient for the churches to work at educating their constituency in moral issues without dealing with economic justice. Second,

> in pursuing the scriptural demands for social justice, can Christians place themselves at the cutting edge of social evolution, activating protests and working with secular movements for justice, all the while seeking to arouse compassion and to limit the inevitable element of violence inherent in radical social change as it threatens the power of defensive established elites?

And finally, 'can hope and a new directional morality be affirmed while maintaining an essential element of humility which recognises man's persisting venality and so avoids triumphalism?' These were vital questions that had to be faced by the churches, who could no longer depend upon the CI to take the risk of prophetic leadership. The churches now had the full responsibility laid on themselves. They might act and speak in a different way, but they could not avoid the questions, nor could they with integrity depart from the biblical principles to which they are committed.

A Message to the People of South Africa

Long before the birth of the CI, the churches and missionary societies in South Africa were related to each other through the Christian Council. The Council had served a very useful purpose over the years in enabling the member institutions to grapple with the issues facing South African society. A number of the conferences we have considered were the result of Christian Council initiative. By the time of Cottesloe, however, the Council was a relatively ineffectual body, unprepared for the tasks that were about to come its way. It was not taken too seriously by its member churches or those in authority. It was virtually unknown to the public. In

---

[12] Walshe, 'Church Versus State', pp. 478f.

short, it was ill-suited and ill-equipped to serve the churches in a time of crisis. Partly for this reason, the CI took on many of the responsibilities that the Council should have shouldered in the early 1960s.

This relative ineffectiveness was recognized by church leaders for whom the Council was regarded as a potentially important agent of church co-operation and witness. Thus, shortly after Cottesloe, the Christian Council began to expand its programme under the Revd Basil Brown, its first full-time General Secretary. In 1966 the Council moved its head office from Cape Town to Johannesburg and, under the leadership of Bishop Bill Burnett, rapidly widened the scope of its work. In 1968 it changed its name to the South African Council of Churches (SACC) to emphasize the fact that it was established by the churches to facilitate inter-church co-operation. It was not intended to be an autonomous institution. In this respect, it was by constitution very different from the CI. During the 1970s, the SACC expanded greatly, with a wide range of programmes, a large budget, and growing participation from the black Christian community. Much of this growth was due to the dynamic leadership and vision of a Methodist layman, Mr John Rees, who became General Secretary in 1970.

Although the SACC is widely known in South Africa today because of its opposition to the racial policies of the apartheid state, its work and witness during the 1970s included much more than public pronouncements of a political nature. Its wider work was often forgotten because it seemed less newsworthy to the media. This resulted in an unbalanced view of the SACC in the popular mind, as though its sole vocation was to criticize the government. A great deal of its ministry on behalf of the churches was out of the public eye. Through its Division of Inter-Church Aid, the SACC was deeply involved in a wide variety of development and community projects throughout the country, and sought to help in emergency-aid situations. This work took the largest slice of its annual budget. Related to this was its concern about such problems as migratory labour, an issue that received serious attention from most churches, including the NGK during those years. One of the most dire consequences of migratory labour, about which the churches warned at the time and which has had such a serious impact on contemporary society, was the break-up of family life and the destruction of the social fabric that supported African life whether in the cities or the countryside. The SACC sponsored a definitive study of the problem, undertaken by economist Dr Francis Wilson in the early 1970s.[13] Its scholarship programme provided both academic and technical scholarships to many black students, particularly in the rural areas. Its Dependants Conference cared for the dependants of political prisoners. And, quite apart from this, the SACC fulfilled the more obvious ecumenical tasks – study programmes, communications, and assistance in the total search for the union of the churches in life and witness.[14] In the words of its constitution, it sought 'to co-ordinate the work and witness of Churches and Missionary Societies and other Christian Organisations in South Africa in order more effectively to carry out the Church's mission in the world'.[15] Part of this co-ordination involved supporting and working alongside local councils of churches which grew up in many centres throughout the country.

The whole story of the SACC cannot be told here, even though much of it was part of the total struggle of the church to be the church of Christ in South Africa. We need to look more specifically at what launched it into public prominence in the late 1960s and made it, along with the CI, an instrument of prophetic leadership.

In 1966 the World Council of Churches held its highly influential Geneva Conference on Church and Society. It was this conference that set the agenda for considerable theological debate and social action within its member churches during the next ten years. It also paved the way for the Programme to Combat Racism in 1970, a most contentious and traumatic event for its South African member churches. Geneva confronted the churches with the cry of millions of people, particularly

---

[13] *Migrant Labour in South Africa* (Johannesburg: SACC, 1972). This volume is also recommended in the NGK 1974 report on *Human Relations and the South African Scene*; see p. 75.

[14] The SACC has published a monthly newspaper, *Kairos*, since 1968. Prior to that, the *Christian Council Quarterly* was its official mouthpiece. *Ecunews*, a weekly news service, was started in June 1971.

[15] 'The Constitution of the SACC', Article 2(b), published in E. Strassberger, *Ecumenism in South Africa: 1936–1960* (Johannesburg: SACC, 1974), pp. 270ff. The membership of the SACC is extensive. Inter alia, it includes all the English-speaking churches. While none of the white Afrikaans churches is a member, the N. G. Kerk in Afrika is, and the Sendingkerk is an observer. The African Independent Church Association has recently joined, and the Roman Catholic Church has been an observer since Vatican II. The Baptist Union withdrew as an observer in 1975, having been a member up until 1973. 'A Statement of Theological Principles' was adopted by the SACC in 1977; see *Kairos*, vol. 9, no. 8 (September 1977).

in the so-called Third World, for a just world. It was at Geneva that the question of Christian participation in the revolutionary struggles of our day was first raised at such a high level for the Christian church.[16]

There were many delegates at Geneva who were unprepared to accept the more extreme radical position adopted by some spokesmen. But few delegates were untouched by the new demands that were being made on the churches with respect to their calling to witness to the biblical demand for social justice and peace. Bishop Burnett and Beyers Naudé were among those affected. Thus, following the Geneva Conference, regional consultations were held throughout South Africa, sponsored by the SACC and the CI, to explore the significance of the Geneva recommendations within the South African context.[17] Though the impact of these consultations was limited, they raised far-reaching questions for Christians in South Africa, and offered fresh insights for those seeking answers.

In the same years as the Geneva Conference, the SACC established a theological commission 'to consider what obedience to God requires of the Church in her witness to her unity in Christ in South Africa'. It was this commission that set about preparing the *Message to the People of South Africa*,[18] which, when published in 1968, would launch the SACC into national headlines and usher in a new phase in the saga of growing conflict with the state.

The *Message* was first aired at a 'Conference on Pseudo-Gospels'[19] convened by the SACC in May 1968. But it was in August that the *Message* was sent to all clergy, English and Afrikaans, throughout South Africa. At a news conference it became a public document. Seldom has a theological document brought such immediate reaction from so many sections of the populace, including the Prime Minister, Mr John Vorster, himself. In a speech a few weeks after the publication of the *Message*, Mr Vorster, in a clear reference to it, warned against people 'who wish to disrupt the order in South Africa under the cloak of religion'.[20]

---

[16] Cf. *Christians in the Technical and Social Revolutions of our Time*, the official report of the World Conference on Church and Society, 1966 (Geneva: WCC, 1967).

[17] Cf. *Church and Society*, a report on a national conference sponsored by the SACC and CI, February 1968.

[18] Cf. John W. de Gruchy and W. B. de Villiers (eds.), *The Message in Perspective* (Johannesburg: SACC, 1969).

[19] Cf. *Pseudo-Gospels in South Africa*, a report published in Johannesburg, 1968.

[20] *Pseudo-Gospels*, p. 35.

Expressing his own respect for the proclamation of the Word of God, he went on to warn clerics who were planning to 'do the kind of thing here in South Africa that Martin Luther King did in America' to 'cut it out, cut it out immediately for the cloak you carry will not protect you if you try to do this in South Africa'. In a long open letter to the Prime Minister, a number of church leaders, including the president of the SACC, Archbishop Selby-Taylor, Bishop Burnett, and Beyers Naudé, set forth the reasons for criticizing government policy and expressed sorrow that the Prime Minister had reacted with a threat. They wrote:

> With all due respect, though with the greatest firmness, we must assure you that as long as attempts are made to justify the policy of apartheid by appeal to God's Word, we will persist in denying their validity; and as long as it is alleged that the application of this policy conforms to the norms of Christian ethics, we will persist in denying its validity.[21]

In his reply to this open letter, Mr Vorster wrote:

> It is your right, of course, to demean your pulpits into becoming political platforms to attack the Government and the National Party, but then you must not be touchy when I and others react to your political speeches in the way I have done. It does not surprise me that you attack separate development. All liberalists and leftists do likewise. It is with the utmost despisal, however, that I reject the insolence you display in attacking my Church as you do. This also applies to other Churches, ministers of the Gospel and confessing members of other Churches who do in fact believe in separate development . . . I again want to make a serious appeal to you to return to the essence of your preaching and to proclaim to your congregations the Word of God and the Gospel of Christ.[22]

Nothing portrays the basic dilemma of the church struggle in South Africa better than this correspondence in response to the *Message*. The church leaders appealed to the Word of God, as did the Prime Minister. The conflict concerns two fundamentally different ways of interpreting the biblical message. That is part of its tragic sadness. What was it, then, that the *Message* declared?

---

[21] *Pseudo-Gospels*, p. 31.
[22] *Pseudo-Gospels*, p. 34.

To begin with, it should be noted that, unlike the Barmen Declaration of the German Confessing Church, to which some have likened it, the *Message* was a six-page document which some critics, with justification, called 'too wordy'. The *Message* attempted to show how apartheid and separate development are contrary to the gospel of Jesus Christ. Taking as its starting-point the conviction that, in Christ, God has reconciled the world to himself and therefore made reconciliation between people both possible and essential to the Christian faith, the *Message* proceeded to draw out the implications of this atoning work of Christ in terms of South African society. It first of all made clear that 'excluding barriers of ancestry, race, nationality, language and culture have no rightful place in the inclusive brotherhood of Christian disciples'. But the main burden of the *Message* was that this unity within the church could not be divorced from what was happening in society itself: 'A thorough policy of racial separation must ultimately require that the Church should cease to be the Church'. In other words, apartheid and separate development attacked the church at its centre; they denied the work of Christ. The *Message* declared:

> There are alarming signs that this doctrine of separation has become, for many, a false faith, a novel gospel which offers happiness and peace for the community and for the individual. It holds out to men a security built not on Christ but on the theory of separation and the preservation of racial identity. It presents separate development of our race groups as a way for the people of South Africa to save themselves. Such a claim inevitably conflicts with the Christian gospel, which offers salvation, both social and individual, through faith in Christ alone.

The task of the church was to demonstrate the reality of this reconciling work of God in its own life. Thus, Christians 'are under an obligation to live in accordance with the Christian understanding of man and of community, even if this be contrary to some of the customs and laws of this country'.

The *Message* aroused the feelings of white South Africa in a dramatic way because it went for the jugular vein in the body politic. For days, some English-newspaper editors came out in strong support of the SACC and its *Message*. Equally strongly, Afrikaans newspapers deplored it. Six hundred ministers formally signed the *Message*, indicating their commitment to what it proclaimed. But the SACC also received letters of criticism and condemnation. In the meantime, the member churches had to consider the *Message* at their annual synods, assemblies, and conferences. With few exceptions, the churches were warmly support- ive. Some of them expressed minor criticisms of points, but none, with the exception of the Baptist Union, rejected it.

The Baptists gave the *Message* considerable attention. They did not reject the concern of the *Message*, for they too condemned racism as contrary to the gospel. But they believed that the *Message* was theologi- cally questionable.[23] It confused humanity's eternal salvation with the salvation of political issues. Separate development, they maintained, is not a rival gospel, even though it may be an unjust political policy. Salvation through grace alone cannot be made contingent upon sup- porting or rejecting a political philosophy: 'The views and attitudes of an individual in racial matters do not enter into the realm of his being justified by faith.' This Baptist critique raised central issues in a clear and concise way, issues that are fundamental to the question of Christian confession in the world.

The difference between the Baptists and those who subscribed to the *Message* was largely a difference in understanding the nature of apartheid or separate development. For the drafters of the *Message*, apartheid was not just a political policy, but an ideological substitute for the gospel. It represented a total way of life based on racial identity. It determined all human relations, even marriage, in a way that contra- dicted Christian belief. As such, it denied in a fundamental sense Christian anthropology, and ultimately the doctrine of God. In other words, apartheid was more than a pragmatic programme, it was a heresy. And heresies do have a bearing on humanity's salvation.

But the Baptist response raised two other issues as well. It posed the question, on the one hand, of the meaning of salvation, and, on the other, of the relation between faith and obedience. Salvation is not merely a matter of individual redemption after death; according to the gospel, eternal life begins now. It is a way of life. It is participation in the kingdom of God. Moreover, while it is personal, it is not individualistic. The great prophetic tradition of Israel continually warned the nation not to trust in any political programme, but to do, and therefore trust in, the

---

23 De Gruchy and de Villiers (eds), *The Message*, pp. 39f.

will of God. Otherwise, judgment and disaster would befall the nation. The nation, too, could only be saved, as it were, by faith and obedience. This brings us to the final issue: Can it be said that the 'views and attitudes' of people, on any issue, 'do not enter into the realm of his being justified by faith'? To say this is to consign faith to a world of unreality, as though faith existed in a vacuum. Ethics cannot finally be separated from doctrine. This does not mean that moral effort saves us, but that faith must not become a metaphysical abstraction. Dietrich Bonhoeffer dealt with this question in a profound way in his *The Cost of Discipleship*, when he wrote: 'Only he who believes is obedient, and only he who is obedient believes.'[24]

The *Message* had some serious consequences. It made dialogue between the English-speaking churches and the NGK extremely difficult, for in effect the SACC statement condemned those who were prepared to justify separate development on theological grounds. The Baptists did not attempt this, but the NGK did. The *Message* also ushered in a new and more intense phase in the relationship between the state and the churches belonging to the SACC, and, of course, between the state and the Council itself. But the *Message* also raised basic questions about the life and witness of the churches and individuals who had responded positively to it. When were confessing words going to become deeds? Separate development having been rejected, what alternative consonant with Christianity could be pursued? It is one thing to speak out and criticize, it is another to respond positively amid the harsh realities of day-to-day South Africa. Perhaps it is better to remain silent if there is no answer to these questions.

Following the publication of the *Message*, some of those committed to its stand formed themselves into 'obedience to God' groups. This took place as part of the growing interest in forming a Confessing Church in South Africa, a concern that was then being debated and discussed within the Christian Institute. Many of those involved in the 'obedience to God' movement were members of the CI who regarded the *Message* as a confession of faith for the South African situation. While this 'obedience to God' movement never managed to grow beyond a relatively small circle of predominantly white Christians centred in the Transvaal, its leaders did a great deal to stimulate thinking about the implications of

[24] Dietrich Bonhoeffer, *The Cost of Discipleship* (London: SCM Press, 1963), p. 69.

the *Message*, particularly for the life of the churches. In one declaration they stated:

> The Church has no right to address and accost the state except if
> a) it has been preceded by a sincere confession by her of the guilt of the Church and of Christians in South Africa in neglecting to discover and combat effectively ignorance, indifference, prejudice, lack of compassion, even active opposition in racial attitudes and affairs;
> b) she is willing and eager continually to put her own house in order and to take all steps through preaching, teaching and practice to be in deed the community of the redeemed.[25]

This declaration spoke directly to the credibility gap in the life of those churches which had condemned apartheid as a government policy, but whose own life was a denial of their confession. It was this concern that lay behind the production of a report jointly prepared by the SACC and the CI, *Apartheid and the Church*.[26]

Apartheid and the Church was part of a much larger programme than simply relating the *Message* to the churches. After the *Message* was published, the leaders of the SACC and CI were faced with the questions: So what? What does all this mean amid the realities of South African society? Having uttered a prophetic critique of separate development, what alternative is there that could receive the support of those who believed in the *Message*? It was questions like these that led to the formation of the Study Project on Christianity in Apartheid Society (Spro-cas) under the directorship of Mr Peter Randall. The project embraced a wide variety of people from many different disciplines: academics, politicians, lawyers, clergy, teachers, theologians. Working in six different commissions – economics, education, law, society, politics, and the church – these people met regularly over a period of two years, preparing reports on the meaning of the *Message* for each of these spheres of national life.[27] It is

---

[25] Mimeographed document, 1969.

[26] See *Apartheid and the Church*, Spro-cas Church Commission Report (Johannesburg: Spro-cas, 1972).

[27] The Spro-cas reports, edited by Peter Randall and published in Johannesburg by the SACC and CI, were: *Education Beyond Apartheid*, 1971; *Towards Social Change*, 1971; *Power, Privilege and Poverty*, 1972; *Apartheid and the Church*, 1972; *Law, Justice and Society*, 1972; *South Africa's Political Alternatives*, 1973. A co-ordinated report, *A Taste of Power: The Final Spro-cas Report* (Johannesburg: Spro-cas, 1973), was written by Mr Randall.

still difficult to assess the full impact of the reports, which were detailed and thorough not only in their analyses but also in their recommendations. But there is little doubt that they contributed to, and initiated a great deal in, the growing debate on the future of South African society.

Of particular importance for our reflections on the church and the SACC in their struggles against apartheid was the report of the church commission. *Apartheid and the Church* described how apartheid affects the life of the church through external legislative controls and through 'internal ideological captivity', fear, prejudice, despair, conformism, legalism, authoritarianism, and wordiness. It showed how denominationalism, segregation, discrimination, and paternalism all undermine the witness of the church. It called upon the churches to move beyond ecclesiastical self-concern, pragmatic pietism, and clericalism, and to become faithful to the demands of the kingdom of God. In so doing, it made very specific recommendations on many matters affecting the life of the churches, including the equalization of salaries for ministers irrespective of race by 1975, the need to refuse any racial classification if required by the state for the purposes of owning property and so forth, and the demonstration that persons of all races are welcome as members and worshippers within every congregation. Other recommendations touched on the question of church investments, the need for a simplicity of lifestyle, the call for symbolic acts against racial discrimination, and the question of conscientious objection. This was the first time that this last-mentioned issue was raised in recent church history in South Africa, particularly in the context of the struggle against racism. Within a few years it was to become one of the most emotive points of contention in the growing conflict between the churches and the state.

The importance of a document such as *Apartheid and the Church* must not be overemphasized. It certainly reflected the thinking of many leaders, ministers, members, and theologians within the member churches of the SACC, but in itself all that could be hoped for was that it should contribute to the debate, challenging and enabling the churches to become more faithful. In retrospect, it is sobering as we reflect on the many strong and articulate statements and resolutions that have emanated from the churches to see how little they achieved. There is a danger that confidence for renewal be placed in commissions and reports rather than in what God is seeking to do. This does not invalidate such reports or confessions of faith, but it reminds us that simply because certain things have been said or written, does not necessarily mean that they have happened or will happen.

During the years following the publication of the *Message* and *Apartheid and the Church*, the life and work of the SACC grew rapidly. We have already mentioned some of the more important aspects of its programme. At the same time, however, it was entering a new phase in its existence. This new phase may be described in terms of three highly significant developments. The first was the impact of the World Council of Churches' Programme to Combat Racism on the churches in South Africa; the second was the debate about violence and non-violence, highlighted by the stand taken by the SACC on conscientious objection at its national conference in 1974; and the third, and most important, was the increasingly dominant role played by black Christians in the life of what were increasingly referred to as the mainline denominations. Much of what follows in this and the following two chapters has to do with these issues. But before we turn to them, let us reflect a little on the significance of the SACC in the church struggle in South Africa in the decade following its founding (1968–78).

In criticism it could be said that some of the weaknesses of the SACC were similar to those of the CI, particularly the extent to which the SACC was dependent upon overseas funding. In a basic sense, this reflects more on the lack of support by the churches than on the SACC itself; it also reflects the tremendous needs that the SACC tried to serve, needs often created by apartheid, and for which overseas funding was essential. At the same time, it must be remembered that the mission of the church in South Africa had been extensively supported by overseas donors for more than 150 years. This, then, was nothing new or exceptional. So it is not simply a question of failure and blame, but a question of how to generate support within the churches in South Africa for the kinds of programmes the SACC had implemented. This question has bothered the leadership of the SACC a great deal over the years. A related problem was the relationship between the SACC and its member churches. On the one hand, the SACC existed only because the churches created it; on the other hand, the SACC had an ongoing life of its own. This dialectical relationship to the churches inevitably led to tension between the SACC and its members, even though the leadership of the Council sought to avoid this. But given the nature of the SACC, the diversity of its membership, and the disparity in the roles fulfilled in its life by its member churches, it was unavoidable that the SACC's policies and programmes were often more acceptable to some than to others. In order for the Council to do its work, it had to stay close to the churches, but it also had to pioneer and break fresh ground if it was to avoid becoming just another bureaucratic ecclesiastical organization. The tension between prophetic movement and social institution was agonizingly real. In its earlier days, the SACC tended to be more ecclesiastical in the narrow sense; in the 1970s, it began to develop a momentum of its own, though still in relationship with the churches.

Gradually at first, but with increasing speed, the SACC changed during the 1970s from being a white-dominated institution, to becoming much more widely representative of the black Christian community. This was reflected not only in the changes that took place in the staff, culminating in the appointment of Bishop Desmond Tutu as General Secretary in March 1978, but also in the national executive. Past presidents, the Revd E. E. Mahabane of the Methodist Church, the Revd A. W. Habelgaarn of the Moravian Church, the Revd John Thorne, a Congregationalist, and Ds. Sam P. Buti, of the NGK in Africa, were all leaders from within the black community.

This transformation was of considerable significance and consequence for the SACC. It meant that through the Council, black leaders within the churches were able to discover each other and so share their concerns, but it also meant that white church leaders came to know the feelings of blacks in a new and united way. It meant that the policy and programmes of the SACC began to reflect black Christian opinion, thereby making it more suspect in the eyes of the authorities and more removed from much white opinion in the member churches. And thus it meant that the SACC found itself at the centre of the church struggle. Often regarded as not radical enough by overseas ecumenical bodies and some blacks, and always regarded as too radical by the South African authorities and most whites, the SACC was a crucial catalyst in setting the agenda and tackling the issues facing the churches under apartheid.

The Programme to Combat Racism

South African churches have been closely associated with the modern ecumenical movement since its earliest beginnings in this century.

Along with the English-speaking churches, the NGK Synods of the Cape and Transvaal were founding members of the World Council of Churches in Amsterdam in 1948. Although the NGK withdrew from the WCC in 1961 after Cottesloe, it continued as a member of the World Alliance of Reformed Churches and the Reformed Ecumenical Synod. The English-speaking churches, together with the Moravian, the Tsonga Presbyterian, the Bantu Presbyterian, and the United Evangelical Lutheran Churches, are members of the WCC, and each has ecumenical links with its own world-wide confessional bodies and missionary councils. Since the founding of the All Africa Conference of Churches (AACC) in 1958, those churches belonging to the WCC have also belonged to the AACC. It is difficult to overestimate the significance of these longstanding and extensive ecumenical relationships for the struggle of the church in South Africa.

The ecumenical connection, however, had a rather particular dimension. Since the first WCC Assembly, which was held the same year that the National party came to power, South Africa's racial policies were high on the agenda of ecumenical debate and concern. With clear reference to South Africa, the Evanston Assembly of the WCC in 1954 declared that 'any form of segregation based on race, colour, or ethnic origin is contrary to the gospel'.[28] This world-wide Christian concern about apartheid grew rapidly during the 1960s, especially after Sharpeville and Cottesloe. Ecumenical agencies, mission boards, and confessional bodies all had direct contact with South Africa through their related organizations in the country, through the reports of missionaries and staff members, and through increasing contact with black and white South African exiles living in Europe and North America. Indeed, there was no lack of information, a great deal of contact, and an awareness of black opinion – all of which were and remain determinative for much ecumenical decision-making.

For the period 1948–66, international ecumenical interest in South Africa was expressed in resolution after resolution, and while the resolutions became increasingly sharp, relationships remained warm and cordial. Indeed, even though the NGK had withdrawn from the WCC in 1961, it continued to have informal links with the world body. But a

---

[28] Cf. Harold G. Fey (ed.), *The Ecumenical Advance: A History of the Ecumenical Movement* (London: SCM Press, 1970), pp. 11, 244f.

rather dramatic change began to occur after the Geneva Conference in 1966, and especially the Fourth Assembly of the WCC held at Uppsala in 1968. The Uppsala Assembly set in motion plans to establish a programme for the elimination of racism throughout the world. A subsequent Consultation on Racism held at Notting Hill, London in 1969 proposed the formation of a Programme to Combat Racism (PCR). This proposal was endorsed by the Central Committee of the WCC meeting at Canterbury that same year. Clearly, the WCC was no longer willing simply to talk about the evils of racism. Plans were being formulated to engage it head on, not just in the life of the churches, but especially at the political, economic, and social levels. This meant working for the liberation of racially oppressed people in the broadest sense.

South African Church leaders, especially those involved in the SACC and the CI, were increasingly aware of this more militant mood, particularly of the WCC, but also as it affected other ecumenical and confessional communities to which they were related. In August 1969, the executive of the SACC responded to the proposals of the Notting Hill Consultation. In the main, it was a critical response. It was critical not because the SACC had any desire or reason to defend apartheid, nor because the WCC had decided to move beyond resolutions to deeds, but because of the means proposed to combat racism. The SACC acknowledged that 'our social order in South Africa is already to a considerable extent based on the use of violence' and that 'the conclusion reached by the World Council of Churches Consultation on Racism in London, that force may be resorted to by Christians in order to dislodge entrenched injustice, has been reached, at least in part, on account of the failure of the churches'. But, the SACC also commented, 'We are disturbed by the way in which the Churches and the World Council in section 6 are called upon to initiate the use of means usually associated with the civil power in the struggle against racism. These are the weapons of the world rather than the Church.'[29] The appeal of the SACC executive to the Central Committee of the WCC was presented personally by the General Secretary, Bishop Bill Burnett. But it had little effect. The PCR was approved and began its work in January

---

[29] 'Comments by the South African Council of Churches' Executive on the Statement of the WCC Consultation on Racism', a mimeographed letter, 6 August 1969.

1970.[30] However, the real bombshell had yet to be dropped on the still largely unsuspecting South African member churches of the World Council.

In September 1970, Dr Eugene Carson Blake, then the General Secretary of the WCC, visited church leaders in South Africa. Not only did he meet with leaders of member churches and the SACC, he also had a cordial discussion with NGK leaders about the possibility of renewed fellowship between their churches and the WCC. He was invited to return for further discussion. Within a week, the scene changed dramatically. On his return to Europe, Dr Blake attended the executive meeting of the WCC held at Arnoldshain in West Germany, where it was resolved at the request of the PCR to give financial aid to antiracist liberation movements fighting in southern Africa against white minority governments. Nothing apparently had been said by Dr Blake to prepare the South African churches for this resolution. The first time they learned about it was when the decision was splashed across the headlines of the daily newspapers. Neither the church leaders nor the SACC had information at its disposal to answer questions, correct distortions in the media, or respond to the threat by the Prime Minister, Mr Vorster, of government action against the South African member churches of the WCC. Mr Vorster told them to get out of the WCC or face penalties for staying in.

The fact that the financial grants made by the WCC were for 'humanitarian purposes consonant with the aims and policies' of the world body, was lost on the South African public. The way the news had been released, with very little attempt to make sure that it would be correctly and fully communicated to the media in South Africa – as it could have been through the member churches or SACC – meant that the WCC was now identified by most whites as a 'terrorist organization' under

---

[30] On the PCR, see 'An Ecumenical Programme to Combat Racism', *Ecumenical Review*, vol. 21, no. 4 (October 1969), pp. 348f.; 'Programme to Combat Racism', *Ecumenical Review*, vol. 23, no. 2 (April 1971), pp. 173f.; 'Programme to Combat Racism: 1970–1973', *Ecumenical Review*, vol. 25, no. 4 (October 1973), pp. 513f.; and Wolfram Weisse, *Sudafrika and das Antirassismusprogramm* (Frankfurt: Peter Lang, 1975). The only South African on the PCR Committee was Dr Alex Boraine. He withdrew early on when his pleas against the grants to liberation movements went unheeded. His position was stated in his presidential address to the Methodist Conference in 1971, 'The Church and Society', in which he called for 'revolutionary non-violence'.

communist control. There was very little the churches could do to alter this first impression, and it persisted throughout the apartheid era.

Of course, irrespective of the impression created by the media that the WCC was supplying guns instead of Bibles to the world, the fact remained that the WCC had committed itself to the liberation movements and their struggle. It appeared to be a sign that the leaders of the WCC had given up hope on the churches' own struggle for change through working for justice and reconciliation (although they continued to give support to many church-related projects). It also meant that the WCC had identified itself with those engaged in warfare against South Africa, and therefore had taken sides in a way that placed its member churches in the country in an unenviable position. The churches could not escape either the threat of the Prime Minister or the challenge of the WCC. Even if the leaders wanted to avoid the issue, opposition within the ranks of their own churches to the WCC meant that they had to face it head on.

As already indicated, the SACC in its statement to the Canterbury meeting of the WCC Central Committee had clearly acknowledged that the social order in South Africa was to a large degree based on force and even violence. This, however, led the SACC not to an espousal of counter-violence to change the situation, but to a rejection of violence in principle, whether in support of the status quo or in fighting to change it.

In the rather heady days following the PCR recommendation to aid liberation movements, and its approval by the WCC, the leaders of the South African member churches held a series of meetings to reach a common agreement. In so doing, they strongly affirmed the position taken by the SACC. Though none of them stood in the pacifist tradition, they unanimously committed themselves, and eventually their churches, to a non-violent stance with regard both to defending and to attacking apartheid. This stance was to have considerable consequences a few years later when the military situation in southern Africa deteriorated, and South Africa was drawn into combat. But that was still in the future. In the meantime, while the South African churches expressed their critique of the grants to liberation movements, they also expressed their support for much of the rest of the work of the Programme to Combat Racism. This support needs to be underlined. The churches were unanimous in affirming the programme. The only significant point of difference was on the grants made by the Special Fund to liberation movements using violence to achieve their ends. In rejecting the support, whether implicit or explicit, of violence as a way to solve racism, they were not opting for the status quo. They had long been committed to change that, at least in theory.

For the moment, however, the churches had to deal with the threat of the Prime Minister, and the growing opposition of their own membership to continued participation in the WCC. For many whites within the churches, the issue was crystal clear. The WCC had provided Christian legitimation for organizations committed to the violent overthrow of South Africa. By implication, member churches that supported such a programme were anti-South African and had opted for a revolutionary course in fighting apartheid. Withdrawal of membership was the only option available. This was not just the opinion of those who might have had sympathies for the government, but also of many within the churches who had no desire to defend apartheid, but who felt that a principle was now at stake on which there could be no compromise. Furthermore, some believed that churches might gain credibility at home for their struggle against racism if they refused to be associated with foreign interference. A less worthy motive expressed was that withdrawal would have certain financial and membership benefits.

The national synods and assemblies of the member churches towards the end of 1970 were very tense. All eyes were on the General Assembly of the Presbyterian Church of Southern Africa, which met first. This church, though multiracial, had a majority of white members, had large congregations in Rhodesia (Zimbabwe), and was generally more conservative than the other English-speaking churches.[31] It came close to withdrawal. But the majority at the General Assembly voted to remain in the WCC, and the church responded to the Prime Minister's threats by reminding him 'that its [the church's] only Lord and Master is Jesus Christ, that it may not serve other masters, and that its task is not necessarily to support the politics of the Government in power but to be faithful to the Gospel of its Lord and to seek justice for the afflicted and liberty for those who are oppressed'.[32] There was a remarkable degree of consensus in the responses made by the member churches:

---

[31] The white-majority PCSA united with the black Reformed Presbyterian Church to become the Uniting Presbyterian Church of Southern Africa in 2002.

[32] *Pro Veritate*, vol. 9, no. 6 (October 1970), p. 7. This was a special issue on the PCR, containing, inter alia, South African church resolutions and responses.

1. All decided to retain their membership in the World Council.
2. All criticized the World Council for the implicit support of violence by making their grants to the liberation movements.
3. All strongly criticized racism in South Africa.
4. All desired consultation with the WCC.
5. Most decided not to send any funds to the WCC as a sign of protest.

An editorial in *Kairos*, a monthly periodical of the SACC, summed it up:

> In making these decisions, the Churches have obviously refused to be forced into irresponsible action. They have been aware that they will be falsely accused of being unpatriotic and even agents of violence, and that they would perhaps lose members as a result. They have also been aware that their decisions would not please the more radical groups, both within and beyond our borders. But they have spoken what they believe to be the truth in the situation and have revealed a responsible maturity. People may not like where they stand – but they can do no other.[33]

In response to the WCC issue, the South African government made it illegal for any funds to be sent from the country to the World Council. It also made it virtually impossible for people identified with the WCC to visit South Africa, thereby ending a long tradition of such direct contact within the country. It could also be argued that from this time the government took a harder line on the SACC as well as on the member churches of the WCC.

One of the decisions of the member churches of the WCC in South Africa was to request a consultation with the World Council on the subject of the grants to liberation movements made from their Special Fund. In order for this to take place in South Africa, the permission of the Prime Minister was required. This was obtained by a delegation of church leaders who met with Mr Vorster in March 1971. Negotiations immediately began with the General Secretary of the WCC, Dr Blake. In a letter to Dr Blake, Mr John Rees, who was acting on behalf of the South African church leaders, issued the invitation 'to come to South Africa in

---

[33] John W. de Gruchy in *Kairos*, vol. 2, no. 9 (November 1970), p. 1.

order that we may discuss with you the reasons and theology behind the grants which you have given to certain organisations operating in Southern Africa and, further, to offer your delegation the opportunity to learn first hand the feelings of the member churches in South Africa about the decision'.[34]

It was deemed wise that correspondence between the various parties be shared in order that there be no room for misunderstanding at any point. Thus, correspondence from the planning committee in South Africa to the General Secretary of the World Council was also submitted to the Prime Minister. And copies of Mr Vorster's letters to the South African committee were forwarded to Dr Blake.[35] This meant that considerable care had to be taken in clarifying and stating the issues – a difficult task.

Perhaps the consultation was doomed from the start. One of the church leaders who had visited Mr Vorster to obtain his permission for the meeting, had spoken of a 'confrontation' between the churches and the WCC. And this is what the Prime Minister insisted should be the case. He wanted the South African churches to confront the WCC on the grants they had made 'to terrorists in Southern Africa' on the basis of the reactions of the member churches 'in terms of their respective resolutions against this abhorrent decision'.[36] The WCC, on the other hand, while it obviously found this unacceptable, also regarded the wording of the original invitation as too vague. The members of the WCC wanted a more detailed agenda in order to prevent any misconstruing of their reasons for visiting South Africa. They were coming to explain, not to backtrack on their position. They proposed that the Programme to Combat Racism and the Special Fund be discussed in terms of the history and the whole life and work of the WCC.[37] This was certainly acceptable to the South African leaders. How else could the grants be understood and debated? But the more detailed the prepared agenda, the more difficult it

---

[34] Letter of 9 March 1971, published in *Pro Veritate*, vol. 10, no. 3 (July 1971), p. 14.

[35] *Pro Veritate*, vol. 10, no. 3, contains all the correspondence on the proposed consultation. The correspondence of the planning committee of the South African member churches was written by Mr Rees and the Revds Alex Boraine and John de Gruchy.

[36] Letter of 8 May 1971, to the Revd John de Gruchy; cf. letter of 16 March 1971, from the Prime Minister to Mr J. C. Rees.

[37] Letters of Dr Blake to Mr Rees, 2 April 1971, and 26 May 1971.

was to ensure that the consultation would take place at all. They knew that any departure from the agenda as stated in the original request would mean an end to the consultation as far as the Prime Minister was concerned. As it was, his wording of the agenda was already very different from that of the South African churches.

In the end, the consultation floundered, not on the agenda as such, though that was certainly the major issue, but on additional conditions laid down by the Prime Minister in a letter to the convener of the South African delegation, Dr Alex Boraine, in May. Mr Vorster stated that he was 'not prepared to allow the visiting delegates to go further than the International Hotel at Jan Smuts Airport and to stay longer than the actual duration of the confrontation'.[38] This was totally unacceptable to the WCC; it was also unacceptable to the South African church leaders. It meant the end of the consultation before it had even begun.[39]

It is instructive to look back and reflect on this abortive attempt in the light of the Cottesloe Consultation held ten years before. First, the reason for Cottesloe was the deteriorating race situation in South Africa demonstrated by Sharpeville. After Sharpeville, many black political leaders left South Africa, and the eventual result of this exile was the growth of external forces seeking the overthrow of white South Africa. Cottesloe attempted to find just ways of resolving racial conflict and so prevent the escalation of violence. Ten years later, the situation had changed dramatically. The liberation armed struggle was gathering momentum throughout southern Africa, chiefly against the Portuguese in Mozambique and Angola, and the white UDI government in Rhodesia, but inevitably aimed at South Africa as well. Second, whereas in 1960 the WCC leaders still believed that the NGK and the other churches could play a major role in changing the direction of South Africa, by 1970 they had begun to despair regarding the churches. For them, the liberation movements were legitimate expressions of political revolt, and while their methods might be questioned, the rightness of their cause was not. This did not mean that the WCC had completely written off the churches in South Africa as agents of social change, nor that they had espoused violence as the means to achieve that change, but

---

[38] Letter of 26 May 1971, to the Revd Alex Boraine.
[39] For the WCC reaction to the cancellation of the consultation, see *Ecumenical Review*, 23, no. 3 (July 1971), pp. 320f.

that they did not foresee change coming except through pressure from beyond the country. Moreover, the liberation armies included many members of South African churches, and these required humanitarian aid.

Third, whereas the real stumbling block to Cottesloe had been the attitude and demands of Archbishop de Blank, ten years later neither he nor the NGK was in the picture. The real tussle lay directly between the WCC and the Prime Minister, with the other member churches caught in the middle. Dr Verwoerd had only come into action after Cottesloe, when he stepped in to prevent its resolutions from being accepted by the NGK synods. Mr Vorster acted from the outset, and eventually made the proposed consultation impossible. Perhaps he wanted to avoid another Cottesloe. In the end, the South African churches had very little power to do anything about the impasse. But in a final letter to the Prime Minister in June, Dr Boraine stated the feelings of the churches:

> I must point out that our understanding of our meeting with the World Council of Churches is not a meeting between people in opposite camps but Christian leaders who belong to the world-wide family of Christ, who share the concern for the problem of racism but who differ on the methods whereby this problem can be faced and overcome.[40]

The years between 1960 and 1971, with Cottesloe at the beginning and the proposed PCR Consultation at the end, were critical for the church in South Africa as well as for South Africa as a whole. This was scarcely understood by white South Africans, since from the second half of the decade there was considerable economic growth in the country, and the diplomatic activities of South Africa seemed to be paying off in some parts of Africa such as Malawi. But dramatic changes were taking place nonetheless – changes within the black community in South Africa that would eventually surface in the black consciousness movement; changes in the black struggle for power in southern Africa which eventually led to the withdrawal of Portugal from her colonies and the advent of Marxist states; and changes in world opinion, reflected in the decision of the WCC to support liberation movements. The WCC was certainly ahead

---

[40] Letter to Mr J. Vorster, 11 June 1971.

of Western countries, but the chart of the future was being plotted. These dramatic changes were acutely felt in the member churches of the WCC in South Africa. As the issues were debated, usually with great emotion, if not always with comparable clarity, the churches rapidly became aware of how urgent and critical everything was becoming for both themselves and the country. Synods were a kind of barometer, forecasting coming storms. Earlier winds of change would be insignificant in comparison to the approaching hurricane.

The full impact of the WCC grants upon the life of the churches in South Africa is still difficult to determine. The grants did not end in 1970. They were continued and increased every year until the end of apartheid. Thus, the debate about the WCC was kept alive in the churches and in public. Perhaps it is possible to make some tentative observations about the impact of all this on the churches themselves.

First, the WCC action tested the fellowship and commitment of the churches. In one synod in 1970, during a heated moment in the debate on membership in the WCC, a white pastor spoke out against continued membership on the grounds that his son was at that time in the army defending the borders of South Africa against attacks by terrorists funded and supported by the WCC. In response, a black pastor spoke for continued membership because his nephew was fighting on the other side of the border as a member of the liberation army. It is difficult to imagine a greater test of fellowship within one church than this radically different and highly emotive pair of responses to the same issue. It was nothing short of a miracle that the churches did not fall apart at the seams. At times it seemed as if they would. But fellowship, if not consensus, was somehow maintained. Nevertheless, the white members of the churches were divided down the middle, and this division seriously affected other aspects of the life and witness of the churches.

Second, for black Christians, without whose participation some of the churches might have withdrawn from the WCC, the issue was not primarily membership in the world body. Membership was important because it meant contact with Christians throughout the world. But membership meant more than that. It meant continued commitment by their churches in the struggle against racism in South Africa. If the WCC action did anything, it raised this question for the churches: How real was their commitment to this struggle?

Third, and arising out of this question, the WCC action, whatever it was intended to achieve, awakened the South African churches to the fact that time for non-violent change was running out. The liberation movements in southern Africa were not only achieving some success, but were gaining influential international support. The real issue was not so much what the WCC was doing, but what the churches in South Africa were doing to prevent disaster. God was not calling the churches to emulate the WCC, but to renew their commitment to him, and to be more faithful to his purposes. In other words, the WCC action could be regarded as a call to repentance and action on the part of the South African churches. Whatever else the WCC might have achieved, this was certainly of significance in the long run. From now on, a new note of determination could be detected in the churches. But events were not going to make that determination any easier to translate into action.

The Conscientious Objection Debate

The Annual Conference of the SACC was held in 1974 at St Peter's Catholic Seminary in the black area of Hammanskraal, north of Pretoria. Hammanskraal was a name unfamiliar to most South African church people at the time. But for those who were in any way involved in the churches' attempt to relate to the events that were happening in southern Africa, Hammanskraal soon became known as the place where the SACC first made its far-reaching proposals on conscientious objection, and so launched a debate as intense and demanding as those associated with the *Message* and the Programme to Combat Racism.

The historical context of the debate is important, as is the fact that it took place at Hammanskraal. The seminary at Hammanskraal provided an opportunity for the delegates to share a common life in a way that had never been the case before at a national conference of the SACC. This sense of community made white delegates more aware of black concerns than might otherwise have been the case. But Hammanskraal was also a centre known for polarization between black and white. A number of other conferences, not of the SACC, had come to grief here on this issue, and the seminary itself had been the scene of black revolt against the white authorities in the Roman Catholic Church. More important than the place, however, was the time. The national conference was held shortly after the war in Mozambique had concluded, with Marxist

Frelimo in power. Thus, many younger blacks in South Africa were full of expectation, anticipating the beginning of the end of apartheid. The conference was also held during the period in which the Angolan Civil War was most intense. South African troops were increasingly involved in the fighting there, a fact unknown to many of the country's population. It was also held at a time when guerrilla warfare was escalating both in Rhodesia (Zimbabwe) and South-West Africa (Namibia). South Africa was arming herself as she never had before, certainly not since the end of the Second World War. Military training and service was being intensified, and the defence budget was growing beyond all recognition.

In this tense situation the SACC National Conference met at Hammanskraal. Whites were aware that in spite of many resolutions and programmes, little had been achieved to resolve the urgent problems arising out of apartheid, and the escalation of violence was now a major concern. Black delegates were aware both of the rising mood of discontent among their fellows and of the sense of expectation in the air. They were aware of black polarization, symbolized by Hammanskraal itself, and felt the need for the SACC to take a stand on the issue of nonviolence that would indicate serious commitment to a Christian solution to the escalation of events that might soon engage southern Africa in a holocaust. There was the feeling that while the position adopted by the churches on the grants to liberation movements was correct, insofar as violence was rejected as a solution, the churches had not really come to grips with the growing militarism of South Africa. Yet, both issues hung together. This provides the background to the challenge to SACC members which required a response as costly for whites as resolutions had normally been for blacks. The response came in the form of resolutions on conscientious objection.

The CO debate at Hammanskraal was sparked by a series of statements and resolutions prepared by a white Presbyterian theologian, Douglas Bax, who had long reflected on the question of conscientious objection. He had contributed to the report of the Study Project on Christianity and Society (Spro-cas), *Apartheid and the Church*, where the question of conscientious objection was tentatively raised in relation to the church struggle in South Africa. But the statement he presented to the Council was not the product of detailed study; it was certainly not the result of some commission's work. It was an attempt to confess Christ as Lord in a way that related directly to the situation at large, and to the growing anguish of black fellow Christians.[41] It was a serious response to the declared position of the churches that violence could not be supported in defence of the status quo. Mr Bax's proposals, seconded by Dr Beyers Naudé, started a debate which, like the *Message* and the Programme to Combat Racism grants, not only made headlines but evoked the wrath of the government.

The SACC Resolution on Conscientious Objection was a very revealing document.[42] In spite of its hurried preparation, it opened up major issues facing the churches, and so requires careful attention. In the Preamble to the resolution, the whole question of peace in South Africa is rooted in justice, and justice is seen in relation to the will of God to 'set at liberty those who are oppressed' (Luke 4:18). The Preamble maintains that 'the Republic of South Africa is at present a fundamentally unjust and discriminatory society', and thus must be regarded as responsible for the threat to peace. Since 'the military forces of our country are being prepared to defend this unjust and discriminatory society', the question must be asked: Can it be right for Christians to participate in the military?

The Preamble develops a second theme in its argument. The Christian is called to 'obey God rather than men', especially 'in those areas where the government fails to fulfil its calling to be "God's servant for good" rather than for evil and oppression' (Acts 5:29; Romans 13:4). The Christian dare not regard military service as an unquestioned duty simply because it is demanded by the state. Indeed, Christian tradition, both Catholic and Reformed, 'has regarded the taking up of arms as justifiable, if at all, only in order to fight a "just war"', and this would exclude the 'defence of a basically unjust and discriminatory society'. A third thrust in the argument of the Preamble raises the question of Christian integrity and consistency in opposing the use of violence. If the violence of 'terrorists or freedom fighters' is to be condemned, can Christians defend institutionalized violence? Moreover, if one says that Afrikaners were justified in the use of violence in their struggle against British imperialism, or that the British were justified in the use of violence to further their aims, 'it is hypocritical to deny that the same applies to the black people in their struggle today'.

---

[41] Cf. D. Bax, 'Hammanskraal . . . A Vital Christian Witness to Fundamental Change', a letter in response to criticism, *Pro Veritate* (April 1975), pp. 12f.

[42] The full text was published in *Ecunews* (5 August 1974), p. 6.

The Preamble, after much heated debate, was accepted, clause by clause, by a majority at the conference. There then followed a series of resolutions, all of which were adopted by the Council meeting. One of the resolutions asked the churches of the SACC to consider whether or not the South African situation required Christian discipleship to be expressed in the form of conscientious objection to military service. Another raised questions about military chaplains, and the churches were asked to 'reconsider the basis on which they are appointed and to investigate the state of pastoral care available to the communicants at present in exile or under arms beyond our borders and to seek ways and means of ensuring that such pastoral care may be properly exercised'.

It is not difficult to imagine the impact all this had in the country within the days following the meetings at Hammanskraal. The opponents of the SACC pointed out that the churches who now spoke about conscientious objection were the same as those who supported the WCC grants to 'terrorists'. The fact that the CO statement explicitly indicated that violence was deplored as a means to solve problems, and clearly did not therefore justify the black use of violence, was lost from sight. Most people did not really want to know the full position of the churches, which was submerged beneath a plethora of press publicity and propaganda. Government reaction was as strong as it was inevitable. The Minister of Defence, Mr P. W. Botha, intimated that he would introduce the Defence Further Amendment Bill in Parliament. This new bill provided for a fine of up to 10,000 rand or ten years' imprisonment, or both, for anyone attempting to persuade any person to avoid military service. Existing legislation, Mr Botha said, was inadequate to take action against persons or organizations guilty of this 'reprehensible conduct'.[43] This meant that not only was conscientious objection unacceptable to the state, but any positive discussion of it was also illegal. All of which confirmed what the distinguished American moral philosopher, John Rawls had written a few years before: 'Conscientious refusal based upon the principles of justice between peoples as they apply to particular conflicts . . . is an affront to the government's pretensions, and when it becomes widespread, the continuation of an unjust war may prove impossible.'[44]

---

[43] Cf. *Ecunews* (21 August 1974), p. 4.
[44] John Rawls, *A Theory of Justice* (Oxford: Oxford University Press, 1972), p. 382.

The bill aroused strong opposition from a variety of quarters, including the opposition parties in Parliament, the member churches of the SACC, and some Dutch Reformed theologians. For a few days, Parliament itself indulged in heated theological debate, as the views of Paul, Tertullian, Aquinas, Kuyper, and Karl Barth were tossed to and fro. Dr Alex Boraine, a former president of the Methodist Church and now a Progressive party member of Parliament, led the attack sympathetic to the SACC Resolution. He made it clear that if the bill was passed, many would have no alternative but to break the law.[45] Similar statements were forthcoming from other church leaders, including Archbishop Dennis Hurley, and the newly elected Archbishop of Cape Town, the former General Secretary of the SACC, Bill Burnett. By this time, Archbishop Burnett was deeply committed to the 'charismatic renewal' then growing apace in his church. In his enthronement sermon before a massive congregation in St George's Cathedral in August 1974, a congregation that included the state President and military chiefs, Burnett called for a new Pentecost and expressed the hope that the SACC Resolution, which he supported, would help the church to 'grasp the significance of the fact that some Black South Africans, many of whom are Christians, are outside our country seeking to change our power structure by force . . .'[46] The connection between charismatic renewal and non-violence had found a powerful advocate. It is not surprising, then, that the synods of the churches that year also came out in general support of the Hammanskraal Statement and Resolution, as it was by then known. This was not done without heated debate. But the churches were clear in their rejection of any cheap call to patriotism behind which a multitude of unchristian attitudes and commitments were hidden. Eventually the bill was passed by Parliament, but it was slightly modified, possibly because of NGK influence, to read:

> Any person who uses any language or does any act or thing with intent to recommend, to encourage, aid, incite, instigate, suggest or to otherwise cause any other person . . . to refuse or fail to render any such service to which such other person . . . is liable or may become

---

[45] On the Parliamentary debates, cf. *Hansard* (1976), cols. 798–828; 1450–86; 6749–66; and 6809–86. See also *Kairos*, vol. 6, nos. 10 and 11 (November/December 1974), p. 11, for the views of the SACC on the Defence Further Amendment Bill.

[46] *Seek* (September 1974), p. 8. Cf. *Ecunews* (5 August 1974), p. 6.

liable in terms of this Act, shall be guilty of an offence and liable on conviction to a fine not exceeding five thousand rand or to imprisonment for a period not exceeding six years or to both such fine and such imprisonment.[47]

These were strong sentences indeed, sufficient to deter most who might have had a desire to influence others.

The conscientious objection debate needs to be put into perspective. First, it should be understood that there was virtually no pacifist tradition in South Africa. There were Quakers at the Cape in the early 1800s, and the Society of Friends had a number of meeting-houses, but the number was very small. The only other religious body that had opposed participation in the military was the Jehovah's Witnesses, who had strongly resisted at considerable cost. But theirs was a particular situation, which resulted in special treatment by the state. There were also members of the Fellowship of Reconciliation, but they too were very few. Thus, the Hammanskraal Statement was not the product of peace churches; in fact, it was not a pacifist statement. Fundamental to its logic is the 'just war' theory, a theory dependent upon situational analysis, and one which no thorough-going pacifist would use to defend or promote his position.

The debate at Hammanskraal and in the ensuing months revealed that the churches, to say nothing of the public, were ill-prepared for it. They had categorically rejected violence as a means either to prevent or to promote change, but they had not worked through the implications of the former. Now they were forced to do precisely this. The wonder is that they were able to deal with it as well as they did. Whatever else may be said about the debate, there is no doubt, especially in the light of subsequent developments, that it awoke the churches to an issue they had never really faced, but one which became tremendously important.

Second, conscientious objection was a highly emotive issue that raised the whole question of patriotism in the sharpest possible way, and its apparent pacifism was embarrassing for many opponents of apartheid who fought in the war against Hitler. Indeed, the SACC Statement went far beyond anything that the Confessing Church in Germany even thought of doing during the Hitler regime. The question was raised

---

[47] Section 121(c) of the Defence Act, as amended on 20 November 1974.

by Dietrich Bonhoeffer, but was deemed too embarrassing for the Confessing Church to handle. This was one reason why he left Germany in 1939 for the United States. Thus, it is understandable that many in the churches, some who had fought against Hitler in the Second World War, found the Hammanskraal Resolution exceedingly difficult to accept. It is not difficult to imagine, then, how the bulk of the white population felt.

Third, the Hammanskraal Statement advocated a 'situational pacifism'. As Douglas Bax subsequently indicated: 'The Hammanskraal resolution does not proceed from a perfectionist, pacifist point of view but from the point of view that seems to take seriously the ethical approach which is called selective pacifism'.[48] The position adopted depends on how unjust a particular situation is regarded. But this was a very difficult position to adopt with any consistency. Granted that South Africa was an unjust society, could this not have been said about most other countries as well? If it was a matter of degree, by what criteria can we determine that a society has become sufficiently unjust to make conscientious objection a Christian obligation? And who, in the context of a divided church, was to decide when this was the case?

Fourth, not only had the churches done little thinking on the question of conscientious objection prior to Hammanskraal, they had also given virtually no attention to the actual legislation on military service currently existing in the country and affecting the lives of many young people. This made it very difficult for them to respond to the Defence Further Amendment Bill when this was published in Parliament. Fortunately, the situation quickly improved, and considerable reflection and some research enabled the churches to deal with the issues. The perceptive analysis by Dr James Moulder in a brief to the Episcopal Synod of the Church of the Province is worth noting.[49] According to Dr Moulder, at that time South African law allowed a conscientious objector 'to be a conscientious non-combatant; that is, it allows him to be exempted from combat training in the South African Defence Force. But it does not allow him to be a *conscientious non-militarist*: that is, it does not allow him to be exempted from every kind of military service

---

[48] Bax, 'Hammanskraal', p. 14.

[49] Conscientious Objection in South Africa, a summary of South African law and a considered opinion by Dr James Moulder, 1977. Mimeographed. Cf. the more detailed discussion by Dr Moulder, 'The Defense Act and Conscientious Objection', in *Philosophical Papers* (Rhodes University), vol. 7, no. 1 (May 1978), pp. 25–50.

whatsoever.' In this respect, South African law was virtually the same as that which pertained in most Western countries, although the penalty of three years' imprisonment for conscientious objection was severe. It was Moulder's contention that the authorities were relatively liberal in their interpretation of the law with regard to those who wished to be conscientious non-combatants. Religious reasons for not bearing arms were generally accepted. But there was no alternative to military service in a non-combatant role, unless there were medical or similar reasons involved.

The Hammanskraal Statement did not ask the churches to adopt a pacifist position but to consider whether or not in the South African situation conscientious objection and military chaplaincies should not be rethought. The results were reasonably positive. The churches supported the SACC Resolution by asking the state to reconsider the position of the conscientious objector. The state did not comply with this request; in fact, it increased the penalties for both advocating and adopting the position. But the churches were united in maintaining that conscientious objection was a valid Christian option. Among the many church resolutions which might be quoted, the Catholic bishops' statement of February 1977, reads:

> We defend the right of every individual to follow his own conscience, the right therefore to conscientious objection both on the grounds of universal pacifism and on the grounds that he seriously believes the war to be unjust. In this, as in every other matter, the individual is obliged to make a moral judgment in terms of the facts at his disposal after trying to ascertain these facts to the best of his ability. While we recognise that the conscientious objector will have to suffer the consequences of his own decision and the penalties imposed by the State, we uphold his right to do this and we urge the State to make provision for alternative forms of non-military national service as is done in other countries in the world.[50]

This statement expresses well the mind of the other churches belonging to the SACC.

The churches also took a fresh and serious look at the military chaplaincy. The debates in the synods during 1976 and 1977 were as

---

[50] *Ecunews*, 5/77 (11 February 1977), p. 11.

heated on this matter as any on the Programme to Combat Racism. Apart from the question of providing pastoral care for members of the churches, the question of patriotism loomed large. On the whole, black members were against and white members for continued chaplaincies, but the issue was not primarily the rightness of having chaplains in the military. Rather, it was the one-sided nature of such ministry. The chaplaincy's identification with the South African army made it virtually impossible for it to minister to opposing forces. The consensus of the non-Dutch Reformed churches was that military chaplains should be appointed, but that, as the Episcopal Synod said, 'The Church must minister pastorally both to men in the SADF [South African Defence Force] and to those opposing them.'[51] In the words of a resolution of the Assembly of the United Congregational Church, 'The Church must ensure that those on both sides of the operational front lines . . . receive the ministry of Christ'.[52] These concerns of the churches received a sympathetic hearing from the Chaplain General of the South African Defence Force.[53] The churches believed that the command of Jesus to love both neighbour and enemy, which is not conducive to blind patriotic obedience, remained the command of the Lord of the church for Christians in South Africa.

In this chapter several important themes and issues have emerged. The problem of church and state had, by the end of the 1970s, become more acute than before, as seen in the banning of the Christian Institute, the reaction of the government to the SACC and its member churches following the publication of the *Message*, and its response to the WCC Programme to Combat Racism and to the Hammanskraal Statement on Conscientious Objection. As we have seen, the Prime Minister was personally involved on a number of occasions. The question of the church's involvement in social change was also raised, especially by Spro-cas and related programmes. Related to this were further questions concerning the economic order of society, problems of labour, human rights, and a host of similar thorny issues. All of these directly affected

---

[51] *Ecunews*, 14/77 (April 1977), p. 1. The Anglicans expressed total support of the Roman Catholic bishops by adopting the Catholic resolution. On the Catholic stand, cf. *Ecunews* 5/77 and 4 September 1974.

[52] *Ecunews*, 38/77 (26 October 1977), p. 5.

[53] Cf. *Kairos*, vol. 9, nos. 9 and 10 (November 1977).

the lives of people, and people are the concern of the church. Moreover at this stage, South Africans found themselves in a situation of growing violent confrontation both within and outside the country. The Programme to Combat Racism and the question of conscientious objection forced the churches to a new and urgent consideration of violence and non-violence.

Another theme, less explicitly dealt with in this chapter, but present throughout, was the renewal of black protest and struggle within the churches, within the country, and through external anti-apartheid organizations. Related to this was the gradual change in white consciousness as the whole situation in southern Africa went through remarkable and swift change. It is to these latter issues of black protest and white awareness that we must now turn, so as to prepare for understanding the dramatic events of the church struggle in the 1980s.

4

Black Renaissance, Protest, and Challenge

Black Consciousness and Theology

Black protest in South Africa died down in the wake of Sharpeville, with the banning of the African National Congress and the Pan African Congress, due largely to the growing strength of state internal security measures. Many within the black community, especially of the generation that had borne the brunt of the early years of apartheid and struggle, despaired of meaningful change. Albert Luthuli was banned, Robert Sobukwe and Nelson Mandela, together with other leaders, were imprisoned on Robben Island, and many others went overseas into exile or into the shadowy world of the political underground in South Africa itself.

By the mid-1960s, however, there were some black community leaders who were reluctantly and cautiously prepared to consider the only option that now seemed open to them – working through the system of separate development. Some avowed apartheid critics, such as Chief Mangosuthu Buthelezi of Kwazulu, finally accepted that they had no other alternative but to take at least part of what was being offered to them by the government. Often they did this with the declared intention of exploiting the system as much as possible for the sake of their people, and ultimately as a means of destroying the very policy of apartheid itself. They were unequivocal about the fact that their working through the system was not intended as a compromise with apartheid. As most of these homeland leaders were devout members of their respective churches, this espousal of separate development, however critical, implied that at some point in the future, church opposition to government policy would be affected.

About the same time as the reluctant acceptance of separate development was gaining ground within some black quarters, another movement was beginning to emerge, mainly among younger urban blacks who categorically rejected the role of the black homeland leaders. Ironically, this new generation was largely the product of separate development, unlike their parents, unlike the members of the African National Congress and the Pan African Congress, and unlike the homeland leaders. The recently founded black ethnic universities of Zululand, the North, Durban-Westville, and the western Cape, together with Fort Hare, were producing a new generation of leaders reared in terms of government policy. One result of this separate education was that these new leaders had little meaningful contact with white people. As a result, they were suspicious of all whites – Nationalists, because of apartheid, liberals, because they appeared only theoretically concerned about the black struggle. Thus, this rising generation of blacks became increasingly committed to the politics of polarization as the first necessary step in destroying the fabric of apartheid: 'Black man, you're on your own!'

If they felt on their own in South Africa, however, they did not feel out of touch with what was happening in the rest of the world, especially in Africa and North America. The idea of negritude, so powerfully expressed by such African leaders as Leopold Senghor, joined the black cry for political freedom with the song of personal discovery. In Africa, the 1960s saw the culmination of decolonization and independence throughout most of the continent. Where colonial authorities were reluctant to hand over power, black liberation movements and guerrilla armies were formed to win independence by force. By the end of the decade, these movements were gaining in momentum, world-wide support, and effectiveness, and were beginning to make headway in southern Africa itself. In the United States, the 1960s witnessed the civil rights struggle. While this was not a fight against colonial oppression, it was a confrontation with white racism that finally paid off. Like the struggle for *uhuru* in Africa, it was also part of the growing consciousness among black people everywhere that their rights had been trampled on for too long, and that there was nothing inferior about their own culture and identity.

Black South Africans did not have to be told by outsiders that their own rights and dignity had been crushed by racism, nor that their culture was thought to be second-class to that of whites. But they had to be made more aware of what their identity meant, and of their potential for changing the situation in which they lived. Black consciousness aimed at doing precisely this.

Its youthful leaders grew increasingly aware of what had happened within their own community since Sharpeville, and were determined that they were not going either to opt out of the struggle or to espouse separate development. Moreover, they were very much the product of a rapidly changing urban environment. Whereas many of their elders were born in the rural areas, with all that that meant in terms of cultural and kinship ties, this younger generation by and large was born and brought up in townships such as Soweto, Umlazi, New Brighton, and Langa. Cultural roots remained important, but the process of detribal-ization had made its impact. The binding factor in this new situation was not tribal identity but black awareness of the dehumanizing power of apartheid. Separate development might promise something in the distant, rural homelands, but it held out little hope for urban blacks. Thus, black consciousness, formulated and guided by student leaders such as Steve Biko, sought to raise the level of awareness within the black community – awareness of their situation and identity as blacks, and of their potential to change their lot.

Within a remarkably short time, the black consciousness movement injected a potent dynamism into South African social and political life. It provided a bridge across ethnic divisions within the black community, binding in one all African, Coloured, and Indian students who rejected separate development, and who were striving for alternative ways of combating apartheid. And while it started off mainly as a youth move-ment, it soon gained adherents across the generation gap. But this success inevitably meant that the movement had to face the full impact of government action, and eventually the elimination of much of its leadership. However, this did not happen until after black consciousness had already made a tremendous impact upon both South African society in general, as well as the churches, and upon the black community in particular.

The churches, especially those associated with the SACC, could not avoid being affected by this black renaissance. Eventually even the NGK, and especially its black 'daughter' churches, did not escape its impact. In the first place, many of the black students and their leaders, like the homeland leaders, were members of these churches. Some were even seminarians. In the second place, the awakening of black consciousness and the struggle for political rights were rooted in Christian convictions. Blacks were taking seriously the gospel they had heard preached concerning God's love and grace for all, irrespective of race or colour, and concerning his purposes of justice. Black consciousness was a spiritual reawakening which drew its resources from Christianity, but also discovered new meaning in African culture, which, for many, was closer to Christianity than European culture. Speaking about this, Manas Buthelezi, a Lutheran theologian, declared:

In a very real and special sense this decade marks the beginning of a 'Black Renaissance'. Never before now have black people been so successful in retrieving the image of their blackness from the dung-heap of colour prejudice and a maze of statutes that make it difficult for the black man to be proud of his colour. Never before now have black people derived inspiration and strength, not in possessing military might, wealth or constitutional power – for all these are denied them – but in delving into the immeasurable resources of the liberating gospel and exploiting that which God has implanted in their souls.[1]

A third reason for church involvement in black consciousness was the existence of black theology, which gained considerable prominence through the University Christian Movement (UCM) in the late 1960s.

Before discussing the significance of black theology it is necessary to clarify the terms black consciousness, black power, and black theology. Dr Allan Boesak has helpfully summed up their meaning as follows:

Black Consciousness may be described as the awareness of black people that their humanity is constituted by their blackness. It means that black people are no longer ashamed that they are black, that they have a black history and a black culture distinct from the history and culture of white people. It means that blacks are determined to be judged no longer by, and to adhere no longer to white values. It is an attitude, away of life. Viewed thus, Black Consciousness is an integral part of Black Power. But Black Power is also a clear critique of and a force for fundamental change in systems and patterns in society

---

[1] Manas Buthelezi, 'The Challenge of Black Theology', an unpublished, mimeographed paper.

which oppress or which give rise to the oppression of black people. Black Theology is the reflection of black Christians on the situation in which they live and on their struggle for liberation.[2]

There is, then, an integral relationship between black consciousness, power, and theology. Yet, they can and must be distinguished. Black theologians vary in the way they handle this relationship, but it is no different from the traditional problem of Christ and culture. Their respective positions reflect the different ways this problem has been resolved by Christians throughout the centuries.

The earliest articulation of black theology under that title was primarily the work of the African-American theologian James Cone.[3] By the end of the 1960s, Cone's original expositions of the subject were widely known to black theological students in South Africa, stimulating their own search for an authentic theology and Christianity related to their personal experience. The Federal Theological Seminary of the Anglican, Congregational, Methodist, and Presbyterian Churches, situated then in Alice near the University of Fort Hare, as well as the Lutheran seminary in Mapumulo, Natal, and the Catholic seminary at Hammanskraal, were all places where black theology was debated, and sometimes taught.

Though influenced by James Cone and others, black students of theology were not content to import theologies from elsewhere. They sought to develop a theology that spoke directly to their own condition. In this they found special help and support from the UCM and its General Secretary, Dr Basil Moore, a white Methodist minister. A special Black Theology Project was soon established in the UCM, and this became the major focus of the movement. The UCM was formed by the English-speaking churches in 1966, shortly after the Student Christian Association (SCA) changed its constitution and divided into separate ethnic organizations. At the same time, the SCA adopted a conservative evangelical statement of belief which excluded some members of the churches from holding office. For these reasons, especially the first, the English-speaking churches decided to launch their own student movement in the universities.

---

[2] Allan A. Boesak, *Farewell to Innocence: A Social-Ethical Study of Black Theology and Black Power* (Maryknoll, NY: Orbis; Johannesburg: Ravan, 1977), p. 1.

[3] See James H. Cone, *Black Theology and Black Power* (Maryknoll, NY: Orbis, 1969).

The story of the UCM is full of controversy. Within a short time, it had adopted a radical theological position at once removed from conservative evangelicalism and its supporting churches. Apart from some of the leaders, not many students went along with this avant-garde theology, or with some of its expressions in liturgy and lifestyle. Certainly the supporting churches felt uneasy about much of it. There was more support for the UCM in its attempt to bridge the racial gap between students, for this, after all, was the major reason for rejecting the reorganization of the SCA. But the radical approach adopted soon brought the UCM to the harassing attention of the government, and eventually led to its being investigated by the Schlebusch/Le Grange Commission of Inquiry in 1972. By then, however, the movement had already disbanded.

By the end of the 1960s, the UCM was largely a black students' movement. Most white students had withdrawn from active participation because of the emphasis placed upon black consciousness and black theology within the movement. The mood among black students was very much one of polarization. The National Union of South African Students (NUSAS), a liberal multiracial organization, split down the middle in 1969 when black students under the leadership of Steve Biko moved out to form SASO, the South African Students' Organization. Biko's personal pilgrimage was typical of many black students. His role as a leader began in the black Student Christian Movement at the University of Natal's medical school. A committed Christian, Biko grew disillusioned with both the churches and liberalism as agents of change, but he was deeply influenced by the Christian tradition and the development of black theology. Indeed, it was at a UCM Conference that Biko and others first conceived of the need to form SASO, of which he then became president.

During 1971 the UCM conducted, in various parts of the country, a series of seminars on black theology, which resulted in the publication of the first South African book on the subject, *Essays in Black Theology.*[4] The seminars succeeded in bringing black theology to the attention of the public and the churches. One reason for this was that the distinguished Bishop of Zululand, Alphaeus Zulu, was arrested during one of

---

[4] Johannesburg, 1972. For the American edition, see Basil Moore (ed.), *The Challenge of Black Theology in South Africa* (Atlanta: John Knox Press, 1973).

the seminars on a technical pass-law offence. Another reason was the banning of *Essays in Black Theology*, as well as the subsequent banning of leaders within the UCM and the Black Theology Project, including Basil Moore and the director of the project, Sabelo Ntwasa. But no matter how many people and publications were banned – and essays on the subject soon proliferated – nothing could prevent the development of black theology.[5] Seldom had a new theological movement achieved such publicity. From then on, it simply could not be pushed under church carpets, escape the vigilance of the authorities, or fail to influence the black community.

Whatever its immediate cause, in an important sense black theology in South Africa began with the revolt of black Christians at the turn of the century, a revolt which found institutional expression in the African Independent Churches, or as they are commonly known today, African Initiated Churches. Black theology is rooted in the ongoing search by black Christians for authentic expressions of Christianity in Africa. For this reason, it is wrong to suggest that there is a fundamental difference between African Christian theology and black theology.[6] The latter is one expression of the former. As such, it is in continuity with it, while also breaking fresh ground in the search for Christian witness and thought. This new development was demanded by changes in the existential experience of blacks in South Africa. In this way it is inseparable from black consciousness.

The integral connection between African and black theologies in this formative period in South Africa distinguished them from much African theology in other parts of the continent, and from most African-American theology. Black theology as a theology of liberation did not seem to be of particular relevance in decolonized Africa. There the search was for an indigenous theology relevant to African culture. African theologies of indigenization, on the other hand, were not at that time of great importance for black theology in the USA, because there

---

[5] Essays on black theology by a wide range of South African authors have appeared in *Pro Veritate, South African Outlook*, and the *Journal of Theology for Southern Africa*.

[6] *Missionalia*, the *Ned. Geref. Teologiese Tydskrif*, and the *Journal of Theology for Southern Africa*. There are extensive bibliographies in Ilse Todt (ed.), *Theologie im Konfliktfeld Süd Afrika: Dialog mit Manas Buthelezi* (Stuttgart: Ernst Klett, 1976), and Boesak, *Farewell*. Cf. Manas Buthelezi, 'An African or a Black Theology?', in Moore (ed.), *Challenge*.

the problem was regarded as the need for liberation from white domination. In South Africa both concerns came together. Black theology, like the implicit theology of the African Initiated Churches, was a theology of indigenization, but it was decidedly more than that. It was primarily a theology of contextualization. Indigenization describes the attempt to ensure that Christianity becomes rooted in African culture. Culture here refers to language, music, and lifestyle. Contextualization, however, is more embracing. A contextual theology has to wrestle with the socio-political and economic situation. It is this which provides the context for the life and mission of the church. In the emergence of black theology in South Africa in the 1970s, these two streams came together – the concern for cultural indigenization and the struggle for liberation from socio-political bondage.

An interesting and helpful illustration of this relationship between indigenization and contextualization in black theology is seen in the concept of communalism. In traditional African society, personal identity has always been social, with a strong emphasis on the kinship system. Kinship ties played an important role in the emergence of the African initiated churches, providing a sense of belonging so fundamental to African society especially given the break up by migratory labour of the traditional supportive social structures. Black theology likewise saw the importance of the kinship system and relates it to the biblical concept of 'corporate personality'. This concept was made explicit in a paper given at one of the black theology seminars in 1971, when Bonganjalo Goba compared the biblical and the African ideas:

> What we discover in the concept as it manifests itself in Israel and Africa is the unique idea of solidarity, a social consciousness that rejects and transcends individualism. Apart from this, one discovers a unique sense of a dynamic community, a caring concern that seeks to embrace all, a love that suffers selflessly for others.[7]

Under the growing impact of colonization, urbanization, and racial discrimination, African communalism and solidarity suffered severely in South Africa. It was Goba's concern and contention that black

---

[7] Bonganjalo Goba, 'Ancient Israel and Africa', in Moore (ed.), *Challenge*, p. 29; cf. D. Tutu, 'Some African Insights and the Old Testament', in Hans-Jürgen Becken (ed.), *Relevant Theology for Africa* (Durban: Lutheran Publishing House, 1973).

theology would help to restore this fundamental biblical and African idea within contemporary society. This is very important for understanding black theology, for black solidarity is of its essence. It rejects any attempt to divide the black community along ethnic or denominational lines.

How, then, was black theology understood by those black theologians who were helping to shape it in South Africa in the 1970s? Manas Buthelezi answers: It is a theology that 'comes out of an attempt to characterise by means of a word or phrase the reflection upon the reality of God and his Word which grows out of that experience of life in which the category of blackness has some existential decisiveness'.[8] The use of the word 'black' to qualify theology was not intended as racialism in reverse, nor even to suggest a new theology. 'Because the word black', writes Khoso Mgojo, 'has been given such a negative connotation there is a further assumption that Black Theology cannot be good theology. Interestingly enough, our interrogators do not question the legitimacy of British, German, American and Afrikaner theologies as valid expressions of Christian theology although they are identified with specific cultures and national entities.'[9] Black theology is 'an attempt by black Christians to grasp and think through the central claims of the Christian faith in the light of black experience'.[10]

In order to understand this emphasis on 'blackness', white people had to realize how much black people were dehumanized because of their skin colour which was the key, but not the only factor, in determining racial identity according to the apartheid ideologists. Although the term 'non-white' had gone out of vogue, when black theology originated, 'non-white' was still the main way of describing black people. Hence blacks felt the need to stress 'blackness'. Manas Buthelezi put it perceptively when he said:

The fact that Africans, Indians and Coloureds have been collectively referred to as 'non-whites' in official terminology suggests that they have the identity of non-persons who exist only as negative shadows

---

[8] Buthelezi, 'African or Black', p. 29.
[9] Elliot Mgojo, 'Prolegomenon to the Study of Black Theology', *Journal of Theology for Southern Africa*, no. 21 (December 1973), p. 27.
[10] Mgojo, 'Prolegomenon', p. 28.

of whites. In a theological sense this means that they were created in the image of the white man and not of God. I am aware of the fact that many people never think of the theological significance of calling us non-whites. The practical consequence of this 'non-white theology' has been the belief that 'non-whites' can be satisfied with the 'shadows' of things the white men take for granted when it comes to their needs. Hence 'non-whites' have not had a meaningful share in the substance of the power and wealth of the land and they were treated to the shadow of the substance. There was therefore a need for the substitution of a 'non-white' theology with a 'black theology' or a theology of the image of God in order to put the question of human identity in a proper theological perspective.[11]

This emphasis on 'black' has often been misunderstood and misrepresented by critics of black theology. Although some black theologians, especially in North America, have made 'blackness' into some kind of basic criterion for Christian faith and action, this is certainly not true of black theology in South Africa. Allan Boesak made this quite clear in his criticism of James Cone. For Boesak, as for most others, 'black' has to do with the existential situation, not with the criterion of theology: 'The black situation is the situation within which reflection and action takes place, but it is the Word of God which illuminates the reflection and guides the action.'[12] It is vital to understand this, for otherwise it is impossible to appreciate the evangelical conviction and motivation that characterized the emergence of black theology in South Africa.

Similarly, it is important to clarify the connection between black theology and liberation theology, since most of the formative black theologians expressly made this connection. Liberation theology, though associated initially with Latin American theology, soon became an umbrella term which included several other theologies including black theology in South Africa. There was, in fact, no definitive liberation theology, only theologies that resulted from reflection on Christian witness in the struggle for justice in a variety of contexts. This was one reason why, despite having much in common, there were also

---

[11] 'The Relevance of Black Theology', published in a mimeographed booklet by the Christian Academy of Southern Africa (Johannesburg, 1974).

[12] Boesak, *Farewell*, p. 12.

differences between liberation theologies. Unlike liberation theologians in Latin America, for example, black theologians in South Africa seldom used Marxist analysis, preferring to work from a black consciousness perspective. Nonetheless there was a clear connection between them. 'For us', wrote Ephraim Mosothoane, 'liberation as a theological theme represents a central element in today's theological contextualisation'.[13] Desmond Tutu expressed his understanding of black theology as a liberation theology in this way:

> I count Black Theology in the category of liberation theologies. I would hope that my White fellow Christian theologians would recognise the bona fides of Black and therefore liberation theology, since I don't want us to break fellowship or cease our dialogue. I desire this earnestly. But I want to say this with great deliberation and circumspection. I will not wait for White approbation before I engage in Black or liberation theology, nor will I desist from being so engaged while I try to convince my White fellow Christian about the validity of Black or liberation theology, for I believe that the Black or liberation theology exponent is engaged in too serious an enterprise to afford that kind of luxury. He is engaged in gut-level issues, in issues of life and death. This sounds melodramatic, but, you see, in the face of an oppressive White racism, it is not a merely academic issue for my Black people when they ask 'God, on whose side are you?' 'God, are you Black or White?' 'Is it possible to be Black and Christian at the same time?' These are urgent questions, and I must apply whatever theological sensitivity and ability I have trying to provide some answers to them under the Gospel. Indeed I will subject my efforts to the criticism of fellow Christians and will attempt to pay heed to their strictures; but I will not be held back because they withhold their approval. For one thing, it is an evangelical task that is laid on me to ensure that the Black consciousness movement should succeed, and I will not be deterred by governmental disapproval or action. Because, for me, it is a crucial matter that Black consciousness succeeds as a theological and evangelical factor because I believe fervently that no reconciliation is possible in South Africa, except reconciliation

---

[13] Ephraim Mosothoane, 'The Liberation of Peoples in the New Testament', *Missionalia*, vol. 5, no. 2 (August 1977), p. 70.

between real persons. Black consciousness merely seeks to awaken the Black person to a realisation of his worth as a child of God, with the privileges and responsibilities that are the concomitants of that exalted status.[14]

Black theology, then, was understood to be a theology of liberation both in its basic methodology and its content. While, in the words of Manas Buthelezi, black theology was 'nothing but a methodological technique of theologizing',[15] this technique inevitably affected what theology said, that is, its content. Theology as Buthelezi and others understood it could not be separated from what they believed God was presently doing in history, and therefore from the task of the church in the world today. Black theology was not and is not a theoretical exercise trying to get at philosophical truths. It was reflection on 'doing the truth', that is, on 'praxis', in obedience to the gospel amid the realities of contemporary suffering, racism, oppression, and everything else that denies the lordship of Christ.

As we seek to explore and appreciate this emerging black theology in the 1970s, we can note that like all dynamic theologies that attempt to relate the Word of God to the human situation, it had both a negative, critical thrust and a positive, constructive dimension. It was a theology of protest against apartheid, but it was also one of liberating reconstruction. Writing in 1978 we described this first critical thrust in this way:

The gospel provides the black theologian with the tools for critique. It dissects the dehumanizing power of apartheid, and brings a word of judgment upon the structures which embody this power. It challenges white domination in the church, liberal elitism, cheap reconciliation, economic injustice, and pseudomultiracialism. In short, it protests against the destruction of the Christian faith because of racism, especially as this manifests itself in social structures. Black theologians in South Africa are deeply conscious of the fact that Christianity is on trial in the black community because it has too often been experienced

---

[14] Desmond Tutu, 'God Intervening in Human Affairs', *Missionalia*, vol. 5, no. 2 (August 1977), p. 115.
[15] 'Toward Indigenous Theology in South Africa', in Sergio Torres and Virginia Fabella (eds.), *The Emergent Gospel* (Maryknoll, NY: Orbis, 1978), p. 74; cf. Moore (ed.), *Challenge*, p. 34.

as a white person's religion and a means of black subjugation. Christianity has to be liberated from every form of racial bondage if it is to speak meaningfully to blacks of today and tomorrow.[16]

Manas Buthelezi spelled this out with great effect at the South African Congress on Mission and Evangelism in 1973. Speaking on the subject of evangelism in the South African context, he proposed the following six theses (albeit in the sexist terminology of the time):

1. The future of the Christian faith in this country will largely depend on how the Gospel proves itself relevant to the existential problems of the Black man. This is so not only because the blacks form the majority in the South African population, but also because Christendom in this country is predominantly black. Almost all the churches have more blacks than whites in national member-ship. This means that the whites currently wield ecclesiastical power out of proportion with their numerical strength.

2. The whites in as far as they have incarnated their spiritual genius in the South African economic and political institutions have sabotaged and eroded the power of Christian love. While profes-sing to be traditional custodians and last bulwarks in Africa of all that goes under the name of Christian values, the Whites have unilaterally and systematically rejected the black man as someone to whom they can relate with any degree of personal intimacy in daily life and normal ecclesiastical situation. They have virtually rejected the black man as a brother. Love can never be said to exist where normal fellowship is banned. Christian love is one of the most misunderstood Christian concepts in South Africa. This has created credibility problems not only for white men as messengers of the Gospel, but also for the Gospel itself. The days for the white man to tell the black man about the love of God are rapidly decreasing as the flood of daily events increases the credibility gap.

3. For the sake of the survival of the Christian faith it is urgently necessary that the black man must step in to save the situation. He should now cease playing the passive role of the white man's victim. It is now time for the black man to evangelize and humanize the

[16] See John W. de Gruchy, *The Church Struggle in South Africa*, 2nd edn (Grand Rapids: Eerdmans; Cape Town: David Philip, 1986), p. 161.

white man. The realization of this will not depend on the white man's approval, but solely on the black man's love for the white man. From the black man's side this will mean the retrieval of Christian love from the limitations of the white man's economic and political institutions.

4. For this to be a reality it is imperative for the black man to reflect upon the Gospel out of his experience as a black man in order to discover its power as a liberating factor for him as well as for the white man. The black man needs to be liberated from the white man's rejection so that the white man's rejection may cease to be a decisive factor in the process of the black man's discovery of his human worth and potential. He needs to see his own blackness as a gift of God instead of the biological scourge which the white man's institutions have made it to be. The white man will be liberated from the urge to reject the black man in that his rejection will be rendered irrelevant and inconsequential.

5. The black theologian must therefore discover a theological framework within which he can understand the will and love of God in Jesus Christ outside the limitations of the white man's institutions. He is the only one best equipped to interpret the Gospel out of the depths of the groanings and aspirations of his fellow black people.

6. The future of evangelism in South Africa is therefore tied to the quest for a theology that grows out of the black man's experience. It will be from this theological vantage point that the black man will contribute his own understanding of Christian love and its implications in evangelism.[17]

These theses probe deeply into the sickness of apartheid society and the way in which the dominant white Christian culture too often became captive to the system. They declare that the bondage of black people was concomitant with the bondage of white people to a social, political, and economic system contrary to the gospel. The theses stress that blacks, who make up the bulk of the churches, have heard the gospel of Christ's liberating power. Therefore, the theses call on blacks to claim their freedom in Christ, both for their own sakes and for the sake of the future

---

[17] 'Six Theses: Theological Problems of Evangelism in the South African Context', *Journal of Theology for Southern Africa*, no. 3 (June 1973), p. 55.

of the gospel in South Africa. This, in turn, would enable whites to hear again the good news of their own liberation. Of course, black theologians were aware that liberation has to do with more than socio-political bondage. It is

> fundamentally liberation from sin to which we are all (oppressed and oppressors alike) in bondage; it means a readiness to forgive, and a refusal to be consumed by hate, a refusal to conform to worldly standards; it means reminding the oppressed that we do have a common humanity which has, as Paul declares, made us all fall short of the Glory of God; and that this means we should not forget that the oppressed of today become the oppressors of tomorrow.[18]

Protest against injustice and racism was only the first word of this emerging black theology, and though it was the most dominant emphasis in the early years, it was really only the clearing of the ground for the positive message of liberation and renewal. In the second place, then, black theology in the 1970s spoke of black freedom and the recovery of black dignity and solidarity, primarily within the Christian community, but also within the black community as a whole. Like other liberation theologians, the exponents of black theology regarded the exodus as the paradigmatic event in God's dealings with the world, an event which finds its culmination and fulfilment in the gospel of the resurrection of Jesus Christ from the dead. According to these events, it is clearly God's purpose to set people free from bondage, and to make 'all things new'. While this purpose cannot be realized in any ultimate sense in this life and present history, it is not unrelated to the here and now. The ministry and message of Jesus made it abundantly clear that the gospel intends life to be lived to the full. Jesus came to make people whole in every facet of their lives, as individuals and in society.

Boesak referred to the persistent temptation to spiritualize Christianity. Reflecting on Jesus' sermon in the synagogue at Nazareth, he remarked on the fact that most Western commentators had so spiritualized what Jesus said, that they destroyed what he meant:

> The spiritualization we have indicated not only compartmentalizes life, but also leads to a distortion of the gospel message which then

---

[18] Tutu, 'God Intervening', p. 111.

serves to sanction unjust structures and relations. It forces Jesus and his message into a western, white mould, degrades him to a servant of mere self-interest, identifies him with oppression. It makes the gospel an instrument of injustice instead of the expectation of the poor.[19]

Drawing on the Old Testament concept of jubilee as an interpretative clue for the ministry of Jesus, Boesak said: 'There is not a single aspect of the life of Israel that is not confronted with the demand for liberation. This is what Black Theology calls the "wholeness of life" and "total liberation". This is the scope within which the gospel should be understood, proclaimed and lived.'[20]

Critics of black theology were quick to label it as a heresy, 'another gospel'. Certainly, as we shall indicate, black theology was by no means beyond criticism, but we must pause before we use the label 'heresy' too readily. That some theologies so distort the gospel that they become destructive of Christian faith is beyond doubt, but, as Manas Buthelezi reminded us, the New Testament itself distinguishes between 'salutary and destructive' heresies. Addressing a major theological conference of the Church Unity Commission in South Africa, Buthelezi referred to the fact that 'heresy', strictly speaking, means 'to choose', that is, to take a position. In this sense, since all theology takes sides and is inevitably inadequate to its subject, it is all one-sided in some respect, and therefore open to the charge of heresy. The question is whether or not a particular theology points towards or away from Jesus Christ. Buthelezi remarked:

For our purpose, this means that mutual acceptance involves taking seriously each other's heresies and incorporating them as legitimate subjects for our ecumenical discussion. This is to say, in other words, that we should use as points of departure not only the 16th century insights but also what is being articulated today, e.g. the insights of black theology or liberation theology. Then when our children sing the hymn 'Faith of our Fathers living Still', they will also think of the contribution of South African blacks.[21]

---

[19] Boesak, *Farewell*, p. 23.

[20] Boesak, *Farewell*, p. 26.

[21] Manas Buthelezi, 'Mutual Acceptance from a Black Perspective', *Journal of Theology for Southern Africa*, no. 23 (June 1978), p. 74.

The fact is that in the face of the apartheid system, for many black Christians at the time, as Boesak put it, 'Black theology is not only "part of the gospel", or "consistent with" the gospel, it is the gospel of Jesus Christ.'[22] In other words, there was no sense here of destroying Christian faith, but of restoring it. For the black theologian, the false gospel was that which dehumanized people because of their race. The true gospel judged this distortion of Christianity and sets people free to be the 'children of God'.

Perhaps the most important point on which black theologians in South Africa appeared to differ was on how they were to relate their theology to political issues in the situation.[23] Boesak, as we saw, maintained an integral relationship between black theology, black consciousness, and black power. For him they were inseparable entities. Others were more cautious. Without denying the political implications of black theology, Khoso Mgojo said he did not want it to become 'a mere instrument of propaganda for certain political ends'.[24] But Boesak agreed with that too, for he, like the others, was as aware of the dangers of ideological captivity from the black side as he was of the dangers from the white. Buthelezi put it sharply:

> To interpret the quest for a Black Theology purely in terms of the awakening of black nationalism or the consolidation of Black Power forces us to trifle with one of the most fundamental issues in modern Christianity. We know that this not uncommon appraisal of the phenomenon of the quest for a Black Theology is often expressed in pejorative phrases calculated to call in question the theological integrity of the quest itself.[25]

Buthelezi was clearly not saying that Christian faith is unconcerned about politics. As we have already seen, black theology arose out of black reflection on the biblical message from within the socio-political context. It involved no dualistic spiritualization of the gospel. But for

---

[22] Boesak, *Farewell*, p. 9.

[23] This is the major issue discussed by Boesak in his *Farewell to Innocence*, and 'Civil Religion and the Black Community', *Journal of Theology for Southern Africa*, no. 19 (June 1977).

[24] Mgojo, 'Prolegomenon'.

[25] In Moore (ed.), *Challenge*, p. 29.

black theology it was the Christian faith that determined how to relate to the socio-political situation, not the situation that determines the faith.

Ironically, black theology was, in principle, not that much different from Calvinism as expressed by many NGK theologians. In fact, for Boesak, as a Reformed theologian, black theology was Reformed theology arising out of the context of black Christianity. As black theologians indicated, Calvinism had played precisely the same role in the historical struggles of the Afrikaner as black theology played in that of the black community. 'It is the same message of the Bible', writes Manas Buthelezi, 'which inspired the spirit of the Afrikaner . . . which is motivating us to sing the song of Black Theology.'[26] There would be something wrong with black Christianity if it did not relate to the needs and hopes of black people. But the crucial question for black theology was one that was raised by Professor Keet for the Afrikaner, and by theologians such as Boesak for blacks: Is it politics and culture that determines theology and practice, or is it the other way around? Is the Word of God the norm, or is culture and ideology?

Reflecting on the similarity between Afrikaner religion and black theology, Dutch Reformed theologian David Bosch asked:

Theology must be contextual, that is true, but may it ever be exclusive? We have to ask in all seriousness whether the category 'people' or 'nation' may be the object of the church's concern for liberation. 'People' as cultural and ethnic entity is not a theological category and wherever it is made into such a category (as an 'ordinance of creation' or 'God-given distinctive entity') it cannot but lead to mutual exclusiveness which endangers the life of the church as the new community.[27]

The focus of redemption in the Scriptures is the people of God. Can we then make use of the Christian gospel as a tool in the liberation of an ethnic group? Dr Bosch's position was attacked by both Afrikaner and black theologians, the former in defence of separate development, the latter in advocating the role of Christianity in the cultural and political

---

[26] Buthelezi, 'Challenge of Black Theology'.
[27] D. J. Bosch, 'The Church and the Liberation of Peoples', *Missionalia*, vol. 5, no. 2 (August 1977), p. 334.

struggles of the black community. But, as we noted then, Bosch's warning needs to be taken seriously. The real danger in any alliance between faith and ideology, Christ and culture, is that the gospel becomes exclusive in a false sense, and the nature of the church as the body of Christ becomes radically distorted. This does not mean that 'the people' or culture is unimportant, but that they are relative and not determinative for the Christian faith. It is at this point that Allan Boesak expressed a basic disagreement with James Cone. Unlike some forms of Latin American liberation theology, both Boesak and Cone regarded the covenant relationship between God and his people as essential to the biblical message of liberation, but whereas Cone virtually confined the covenant community to blacks, Boesak expressly did not. He rejected any notion of a black Christian nationalism.[28]

As we have now shown, black theology in South Africa was neither beyond criticism, nor was it without inner tensions. Its leading exponents were not uncritical of their efforts,[29] but they were convinced that black theology was a valid and necessary expression of the Christian faith in apartheid South Africa. They were also increasingly aware, along with others, that their understanding of the gospel had implications beyond the black community itself. Before commenting on that, however, it is well to remember that this emerging black theology was not an academic exercise. It was a direct challenge to the system of apartheid and separate development. As such, it involved a costly commitment on the part of those involved in it. Dr Buthelezi said that 'What is significant about it is that its appearance has aroused anything from positive interest to alarm even outside the theological arena, especially among politicians. This proves beyond doubt its timely relevance . . .'[30] One symbol of this relevance and its cost was the story of the Federal Theological Seminary in Alice, which was expropriated by the government in 1974.

The Federal Theological Seminary (FedSem) was established in 1961 by the English-speaking churches for the training of their black candidates for ordination. While the churches were against segregated seminaries in principle, South African law gave them little option if such a

---

[28] Cf. Boesak, *Farewell*, pp. 125ff.; 'Civil Religion and the Black Community', pp. 35f.

[29] The earliest critique 'from within' came from Bishop Alphaeus Zulu; see his 'Whither Black Theology?', *Pro Veritate*, vol. 11, no. 11 (March 1973), pp. 11f.

[30] Buthelezi, 'Relevance', p. 1.

seminary was to be residential. FedSem was built on a large tract of land donated by the Church of Scotland adjacent to the black University of Fort Hare in Alice. During its 13 years in Alice, FedSem not only developed a good tradition in theological education, it also helped to stimulate black theological thinking related to the South African scene. An inevitable result was that students at Fort Hare found in FedSem a window on the world concerned about helping the black community fight racism. In 1974, however, the government decided to expropriate the land and buildings of the seminary for use by the university. In doing so, they not only went back on their word, but also aroused the anger and disgust of those who knew the story behind the headlines. An editorial in *South African Outlook* described the action of the state as follows:

> In expropriating the Seminary the Government is breaking its word; it is taking by force, nay violence, land which has belonged to the black community since long before white men came to this country; it is marching with hobnailed boots over the history of a people; it is high-jacking the Church.[31]

There was little the churches could do to prevent this from taking place. Despite government compensation for the land and property in Alice, the churches were penalized for providing the black community with spiritual leaders opposed to the system. But the churches held fast to their convictions. In 1976 the Congregational and Presbyterian colleges at FedSem united to form the Albert Luthuli College, thereby honouring one who believed that the Christian faith is central to the black struggle for political rights. The Seminary moved to a new home in Pietermaritzburg, where it continued to train young ministers for the English-Speaking churches. Sadly, it was closed in the early 1990s.

At the end of the 1970s, we expressed our opinion about black theology in this way:

> It is our conviction that black theology is an authentic attempt to understand the gospel of Jesus Christ in South Africa, and to spell out its implications for witness and mission. No one, not even its opponents, can doubt its significance for the future of the gospel in our land. It is a tragedy, then, that many white Christians have too

---

[31] *South African Outlook* (November 1974).

often overreacted, and seen it as a threat, rather than as a genuine attempt to express the Christian faith. This has meant that its creative possibilities have too often turned to protest, and its prophetic insights been rejected. It is important to realize that we are witnessing a result of the great missionary enterprise which, for all its faults, brought the gospel to South Africa in the first place. Like all theologies, it must not be allowed to turn in on itself or lose the ability of self-critique in the light of the Word of God, but it needs the freedom to express and fulfil itself for the sake of the church and society.[32]

It was clear that for white South African Christians, black theology should have had a significance, though few were able to recognize it. Whites were generally critical of and closed to the possibility that God was speaking to the church through black prophets. Before we deal with this, however, we will need to consider the impact of Soweto upon South Africa, for the word of the black theologian could not be separated from the anguished cry of the black community.

Soweto: Symbol of Black Protest

Until the middle of 1976 the black township of Soweto, on the southwestern border of Johannesburg, was largely unknown outside of South Africa. In June that year, black students took to the streets in protest against government educational policies that required the use of Afrikaans in the teaching of high school subjects. Soon the original reason for the protest was largely forgotten, for by then Soweto was in turmoil and South Africa was confronted with a situation of graver significance than even Sharpeville. Within a very short time, young black students, as well as Coloureds and Indians throughout the country, joined in solidarity with their Soweto counterparts, especially in the sprawling townships of the eastern and western Cape. Soweto became a symbol of protest against apartheid, a new symbol generated by young blacks who were no longer prepared to accept the situation in which they found themselves.

Government action in Soweto and throughout the country was immediate and draconian. Riot police were sent into every troubled

---

[32] See de Gruchy, *The Church Struggle*, 2nd edn, p. 168.

area. Soon there were reports of scores of students killed or badly injured by police action. Hundreds were arrested and detained. The action of the police became the focal point for new waves of protest, and by this stage the reticence of the older generations to join in with the students had changed to support and participation. The ugly escalation of violence and counterviolence grew apace as the tactics of the authorities met with continued resistance and rejection. The concerted attempts by black leaders to bring order into the chaos were hamstrung time and again by insensitivity on the part of government authorities and provocative police action as well as by continued boycotts of schools and burnings of community buildings. Arrests and detentions without trial added fuel to the fires. Though there were periods of relative calm, sporadic outbursts of protest indicated that the tension and conflict had by no means been resolved. This state of uncertainty and violence plagued the black townships of Johannesburg and elsewhere for more than a year. A hiatus came with the death in September 1977 of student leader Steve Biko, the arrests of many black community leaders, and the bannings of 19 October 1977.

In retrospect, Soweto was a moment of truth for white South Africa which they largely failed to grasp, and a powerful symbol of the black struggle for liberation which heralded the beginning of the end for apartheid. This could be understood in several ways. First, Soweto became an international symbol. By the time of Biko's death, Soweto was already a household word throughout much of Europe and North America. The death of Biko gained prominence largely because of the awakening of intense interest in South Africa and in young blacks in the aftermath of Soweto. For the outsider, Soweto stood for the total rejection of apartheid by blacks. It suggested that revolutionary change was only a matter of time. It reinforced all that the anti-apartheid movements in the Western world had been claiming through the years in their attempt to expose South Africa. Indeed, on the admission of government spokesmen, Soweto did far more to damage the reputation of white South Africa than anything else in its history. It also did far more to awaken sympathy and support for black South Africa than any political rhetoric has managed in the councils of the nations.

Second, Soweto was a symbol of a new generation of politicized blacks who were in revolt against the system of apartheid. Over the preceding years, there were other signs of black protest. The large-scale strikes by workers in Natal and confrontations on the mining compounds near Johannesburg from late 1972 onwards, were obviously of great signifi-cance. But they did not have the same impact on South African consciousness as Soweto, nor did they stir the sympathetic imagination of others throughout the world. Soweto began as a children's crusade. Black students were protesting against their educational curriculum and system. But all of a sudden, the demonstration flared up into a situation of total confrontation on a massive scale. Observers in Soweto spoke of the bewildered spontaneity of the eruption. Everyone seemed surprised. But even more remarkable was the persistence and endurance of the protesters against immense police odds. Indeed, it is a remarkable thing that young people still at school virtually took on the might of the police force by themselves, and persisted in spite of heavy casualties. Hundreds were killed.

How are we to explain this? It is a dubious analysis to suggest that Soweto was the result of careful planning by the African National Congress or the Black People's Convention, or some other black politi-cal organization. Such bodies may have played a role during and after-wards, but it seems unlikely that they were the instigators of the protest. Soweto, it appears, was not the result of some organization's planning, but was part of an interconnected web of circumstances and events. And central to this was the rise and impact of black consciousness within and upon the black community. Soweto could not have happened if the mes-sage of black dignity and protest, a message that had its greatest impact upon young black students, had not been preached and heard during the years before it took place. Black school teachers subsequently remarked on the fact that most of their pupils, even in junior school, were highly politicized. And, if some were not politically aware before Soweto, they were soon deeply affected by it. This was a new phenomenon in the South African situation, and it was of tremendous consequence for the future. To use a Latin American term, the younger generation of blacks were 'conscienticized'.

Third, Soweto symbolized the failure of separate development, espe-cially in the urban areas. In an interview early in 1977, Bishop Manas Buthelezi, a resident of Soweto, made it clear that the Soweto protests went far beyond education. He stated:

> Separate Development is not acceptable to the black community. The recent happenings in Soweto were evidence of that. We would like to

have a share in the decision-making process of the country. Even concerning separation; if we came together and then agreed that the solution is that we should separate, then separate development would have a moral basis. But now only one section says we must separate and dictates how we should separate. As a Christian I also find some problems with this.[33]

Fourth, Soweto was a symbol of the violence that lurked so near the surface of apartheid South Africa. Many white South Africans were living with an illusion in this regard. They surveyed the major trouble spots of the world, Northern Ireland, the Middle East, Southeast Asia, and the long hot summers of civil rights protests in the United States and elsewhere, and concluded that there was an absence of violence in our own country. The facts were quite different, as both the government and those working for change clearly recognized. If this were not the case, there would have been no need for the vast array of security legislation and the immense strengthening of the police force and its powers. The average white person had confused law and order with genuine peace, and so was caught by surprise when violence erupted in Soweto in 1976.

This myopic condition of many whites in the early 1980s is not surprising, given the movement towards isolation, the growth of censorship, and an unwillingness to face reality. It is true, of course, that the nationalist government was able to maintain order during its 45-year period in office, but order does not mean the absence of violence. Over the years, people had been banned, detained, imprisoned without trial, and died, all for the sake of maintaining the present order. Unfortunately, too few whites were aware or even willing to become aware of this reality. Soweto was the overflowing of a volcano. What most whites refused to acknowledge was the suppressed frustration and fury that lay beneath the surface in the black community. Soweto burst that illusion, at least for those willing to hear the anguished cry, and it indicated as never before the lateness of the hour.

Finally, Soweto was a powerful symbol of black protest against the church itself in so far as it identified with white power and white domination. Before exploring this challenge to white Christianity, however, let us consider how the churches themselves reacted to Soweto.

---

[33] In an interview published in *To the Point*, 4 February 1977, p. 46.

Shortly after the initial protests began in Soweto, the moderature of the General Synod of the NGK expressed itself as follows:

> To a great number of innocent people, White and Black, who suffered these losses, the Church expresses its sincere sympathy, and trusts that local church councils and other bodies charged with the task, will make the necessary support and emergency aid available. Further, the Church calls its members to a worthy plan of action in which the example of the Lord can be followed, and the Christian demand of love of God in one's neighbour can be practised. The younger churches are assured of our Church's sympathy and prayer in these times of tension.[34]

The leaders of the NGK also indicated that they would make representations to the government on the issues affecting Soweto and other townships. But there was little if any attempt to express an opinion on the underlying causes of Soweto, or on such matters as police action. This was not the case with the reaction of such churches as the Roman Catholic or those belonging to the South African Council of Churches.

Church leaders meeting in the Greater Durban Area on 21 June 1977, expressed their convictions by attempting to provide a 'true interpretation of the riots':

> We urge all our members to listen to the anguished plea of Black people which has so often gone unanswered and has now resulted in violence. Though we deplore violence as a means of effecting change or of preventing change, we have little difficulty in understanding why such an explosion of rage has taken place. We realise, however, that many of our White Christians will not understand, and that they see in the riots an unjustified outburst. While we recognise that in any situation of violence irresponsible elements will be involved, we earnestly urge our members to take note of the deep groundswell of bitterness and resentment that exists among Black people throughout our country, and that can so easily be fanned into violence. If attention is not paid to well-known causes of that discontent, no

---

[34] *Ecunews*, 21/76 (7 July 1976), Appendix A; cf. 'Soweto Disturbances: Attitude of the D. R. Church', *NGK Africa News*, vol. 2, no. 3 (March 1977).

amount of security legislation, repression, deportations, detentions or bannings will give this country genuine and lasting peace.[35]

On the subject of police responsibility, the church leaders said: 'That there is profound hostility to the police in the black community may not be widely known among whites, but in all the legal harassment and suppression it experiences, the black community sees the police as agents of white power.'

It is unnecessary to quote from all the statements and resolutions uttered and adopted by the churches on the subject. Virtually all those who were critical of apartheid over the years expressed sentiments similar to those of the Durban church leaders.[36] We shall refer to just two documents which seem to sum up the feelings of the churches. First, the following statement was issued by the General Secretariat of the South African Catholic Bishops' Conference in September 1976, following the arrest of two black Catholic priests, Father S'mangaliso Mkhatshwa and Father Clement Mokoko. After protesting against their arrest, the statement went on to say:

In expressing sympathy and solidarity with them, we express the same with dozens of others so detained under excessively harsh security laws against which we protested last year and also previously . . . We consider the present wave of unrest sweeping the country to be at most the inevitable result of unjust and oppressive laws against which we with other churches have continually witnessed for almost three decades. We renew our protest against these laws in the strongest possible terms and urge that they be repealed forthwith. At the same time we request that it be recognised that the phenomenon of Black Consciousness correctly understood is an inevitable demand by the Black Community for recognition of their human dignity and legitimate aspirations. We appeal to the Government to relieve the present tension not by repressive acts but by rapid and practical moves towards full citizenship and shared responsibility.[37]

---

[35] *Ecunews*, 20/76 (30 June 1976), p. 8.

[36] Cf. *Ecunews*, 20/76, 25/76, 36/76, and 37/76.

[37] *Ecunews*, 28/76 (3 September 1976), p. 9.

Second, we refer to the pastoral letter of the president of the Methodist Church, the Revd Abel Hendricks, written in October 1976:

> South Africa stands on the threshold of war and peace. The last three months have seen the outpouring of years of Black frustration, suppression and anger that has burst into manifestations of protests, strikes and peaceful marches, but also violence, death and destruction. The White status quo has in turn allowed their fear, confusion and ignorance of Black suffering and aspirations to manifest itself in violence, brutality and the detention of those crying out for liberation ... Time is running out and the Church of God must raise her voice for justice so that there may be peace. If we fail here, we will not only be disobeying the call of the Lord, to cry aloud and lift up our voices like a trumpet in declaring to our people their transgression (Isaiah 58:1), but we will be judged by history to be simply irrelevant ...[38]

Clearly, the churches in opposition to apartheid saw the cause of the Soweto protests as apartheid itself. They regarded the escalation of violence as generated in varying degrees by the tactics of the police and the enforcement of security legislation.

Those churches that responded to Soweto in the way we have just described were also positive about the role of black consciousness itself. This does not necessarily mean that black consciousness was approved without qualification, but neither does it mean that it was rejected by the churches as contrary to Christian faith. On the contrary, in spite of government action against its proponents within and outside the churches, notably on 19 October 1977, an editorial in *Kairos*, the monthly paper of the South African Council of Churches, could state:

> Many Christians see Black Consciousness as being directly in line with the Biblical doctrine of creation – that all men are created in the image of God. This doctrine and concept has received particularly strong emphasis among Black South African Christians – something clearly attributable to their reaction to apartheid, which, even in its most sophisticated 'separate freedom' guise, is still humiliating to Blacks.

---

[38] *Ecunews*, 34/76 (15 October 1976), p. 8.

Polarization, the editorial maintained, is not caused by black conscious-ness, but is the result of apartheid. It went on to say, 'Indeed, it has been said by Afrikaner academics that in many ways Black Consciousness resembles the emergence of Afrikaner nationalism as a reaction to the humiliations imposed by British imperialism', and it concluded:

> Yet, in choosing the path of confrontation and seeking to bind Black Consciousness, the authorities will be shown in time to have been merely trying to wish away reality. Out of Christian convictions we and others will continue to accept Black Consciousness as naturally as we breathe. No State can prevail against a mass spiritual movement in the long run.[39]

Whatever the perceived dangers of black consciousness, and whatever its significance for the black community, let us turn to the challenge it presented to white Christians in South Africa. In particular, the chal-lenge focused on two things. On the one hand, it raised the questions: How Christian have white Christians been in South Africa? Is it not they, perhaps, who need to be liberated? Has their Christianity become cap-tive to their own interests, culture, and ideologies? On the other hand, it raised the question: What kind of society do white Christians want? In other words, it forced whites to face the implications of Christian faith for their own existence, and therefore for the structures of social life, human rights, and economic justice. We turn now to these questions as we explore the connection between black and white liberation.

Connecting Black and White Liberation

Long before the rise of liberation or black theology, or Marxist treat-ments of colonial history, black South Africans had the feeling that, whatever its benefits, the Christianity of the white settlers was concomi-tant with their sense of superiority and linked to their socio-economic dominance. The early opinions of leaders in the African Initiated Churches provide evidence for that. And this feeling has been strength-ened over the years. It was eventually given penetrating expression from

---

[39] *Kairos*, vol. 9, no. 10 (November 1977).

a Christian perspective in Bishop Manas Buthelezi's 'Six Theses on Evangelism', which we quoted earlier. Let us sum up our discussion thus far in this chapter by reflecting on South African history again, but this time attempting to see the development of Christianity and the church from the perspective of many black South Africans today.

The Dutch settlers regarded the indigenous peoples as culturally inferior heathen destined by God to be the 'hewers of wood and the drawers of water' for their superior masters. The settlers prospered; the indigenous peoples and imported slaves suffered. The Christian faith seemed to provide the rationale necessary to justify the situation. As the white settler community pushed into the interior, notably at the time of the Great Trek, Christianity was used to justify and explain what happened.

Whatever the Christian virtues of most of the Trekkers, they were by no means missionary-minded, driven by a desire to evangelize the 'heathen' in the interior. Indeed, Daniel Lindley, the American Board missionary in Natal, whom the Trekkers invited to be their pastor, wrote the following to his board in Boston in July 1839, justifying his accept-ance of the call:

> I do sincerely believe that the cheapest, speediest, easiest way to convert the heathen here is to convert the white ones first. More, the whites must be provided for, or we labour in vain to make Christians of the blacks. These two classes will come so fully and constantly in contact with each other, that the influence of the whites, if evil, will be tremendous – will be irresistible, without a miracle to prevent. To their own vices the aborigines will add those of the white man, and thus make themselves two-fold more the children of hell than they were before.[40]

The Great Trek arose out of a desire for freedom from British domina-tion and out of the effects of the emancipation of the slaves, an emanci-pation regarded as detrimental to Christian faith. The vision of the Trekkers was the establishment of a Calvinist republic in which neither white alien nor black native would be eligible for a meaningful role in the social and political life of the community.

---

[40] Quoted by Arthur F. Christofersen in Richard Sales (ed.), *Adventuring into God: The Story of the American Board Mission in South Africa* (Durban: privately printed, 1967), p. 22.

A great deal has been written about the role of the nineteenth-century European missionaries in South Africa. They have been variously depicted as the defenders of the blacks and the critics of the colonists. More recently it has become fashionable to decry them as handmaidens of colonial power. The truth is far more complex than either of these polar views will allow.[41] Yet, it seems clear that many were at fault in at least two respects. First, they were far too insensitive to African culture, and second, they allowed themselves to be used by the agents of European colonial expansion. The result of cultural insensitivity was that the gospel contributed to the undermining of the foundations of African culture. This produced an identity crisis, hastened by urbanization and industrialization, that was traumatic for the African community. Once again, the rise of African indigenous or initiated churches was a sign of missionary failure. The result of being part of colonial expansion, wittingly or not, aroused suspicions that the church had ulterior motives. This suspicion erupted with a vengeance throughout Africa during the 1960s, and led some to reject Christianity in favour of Islam or Marxism. Thus, in spite of the laudable intentions of the missionaries, and their courageous deeds of compassion and service as well as their many achievements in education and evangelism, many blacks came to regard white Christianity, if not Christianity itself, as a form of European domination.

British rule at the Cape and in Natal, and the imperial push north en route to Cairo, were also bound up with the idea of extending Christian civilization into 'darkest Africa'. But the diamond and gold rush, and the ensuing wars between the British and the Boer republics, were hardly edifying for those whom they labelled 'heathen'. There was nothing Christian or civilized about the concentration camps or the grasping for economic gain and power. Just as two world wars between so-called Christian nations raised serious questions about Christianity in the Third World, so the clash between British and Afrikaner Christians demonstrated how religious faith was easily set aside and sacrificed on the altars of political and economic interest. The cause of God's

---

[41] Cf. Monica Wilson, *Missionaries: Conquerors or Servants of God*, an address published by the South African Missionary Museum (Kingwilliamstown: South African Museum, 1976); and Peter Hinchliff, 'The "English-Speaking Churches" and South Africa in the Nineteenth Century', *Journal of Theology for Southern Africa*, no. 9 (December 1974), pp. 28–38.

kingdom and the integrity of the church are always the casualties in this kind of conflict.

And then, to cap it all, Christianity became identified by many blacks with apartheid. In protest against government policy and action in the name of Christianity, a small group of black ministers staged a march in Johannesburg in 1977. They were arrested and charged in the Magistrates Court with breaking the law. The following is the statement they made in court:

> The Honourable Minister of Police and Prisons, Mr. Jimmy Kruger, has stated that people who do not accept the concept and policy of APARTHEID can say so without fear of being PROSECUTED, harassed and intimidated. It is on the strength of his words and of the truth of the Gospel of Jesus that we stage this PROTEST MARCH as testimony of our non-acceptance of APARTHEID and its attendant evil effects. This march registers our TOTAL AND ABSOLUTE REJECTION of the Bantustan Apartheid Policy. We want to say that this policy is responsible for a great deal of unhappiness in our country: Detentions without trial, Banning orders, the unjust enforcement of Bantu Education, mass removals, job reservation, muzzling of the Black Press, a disproportionate and disastrous military budget, etc . . .

> In the face of these injustices perpetrated by the White Christian Government, we have great difficulty as Ministers of Religion in explaining the Gospel to our Black people.

> The White people came here and told us they were bringing a Gospel of brotherhood. But they will neither live in the same areas as us, nor sit in the same coach in a train.

> They told us that they believed 'you must love your brother as yourself', but they will allow us none of the things they wish for themselves, no equal opportunity in work, no say in Government, no free movement.

> They told us their Gospel was one of sharing, yet they have taken more than three quarters of the whole land for a small minority, and force us to work so that they always gain ten times as much as us.

> They told us that Christian life was based on the family, yet there are a million of our men working with them not allowed to have their families where they work, driving our people to sin.

They told us Christianity brought the light of civilised culture, yet they oblige our children to a form of Education that is narrowed and impedes their access to the education and culture of the world.

They told us the Grace of Christ made the human person priority No. 1, yet in a country full of wealth they leave hundreds of thousands out of work and with no unemployment benefit, their children starving.

They told us it was a Gospel of kindness, yet they push us so far from our work that parents are fourteen to sixteen hours away from home and do not see their children awake between Monday and Saturday.

They told us that Christ had broken down all barriers between peoples, yet their Christian Government is forcing us who have worked together for a hundred years and more to become separate nations.

They told us 'truth would set us free', yet when we try to speak the truth of all this as we see it, our spokesmen are detained or banned, our free associations crushed, quotation of our leaders forbidden.

The result of this is that our voices sound hollow when we preach this Gospel in Church. We implore the White Christian Government to examine its Conscience and heed the voice of the Gospel.[42]

Shortly after the Soweto Uprising, a series of random interviews with black students conducted by a black newspaper reporter confirmed what many had half-suspected: 'Most blacks regard the Church in South Africa as an irrelevant institution if not an extension of the status quo.'[43] This may be an exaggeration, but it was true of many young blacks nonetheless. Religion was scornfully rejected as a drug that induced apathy towards apartheid. When a black Dutch Reformed minister was asked why church buildings were gutted by the rioters, he replied: 'Because the Black people identify the D.R. Church with the political

---

[42] Quoted in *CHURCHSOC* (the Church and Society Report of the United Congregational Church of Southern Africa), no. 18 (April 1978).

[43] Revelation Ntoula, 'Church Must Reach out to Youth', *The Voice*, black newspaper founded by the South African Council of Churches (October/November 1976), p. 16.

[44] Dr F. E. O'Brien Geldenhuys, 'Appraisal: New Issues and Challenges Facing the Church in South Africa', *NGK NEWS*, vol. 1, no. 9 (October 1976), p. 6.

dispensation in our country.'[44] In a way strongly reminiscent of the classic Marxist critique of religion, a young black person was reported as saying: 'The white man's god has been used to tame the black people.'[45] Even if this was only a partly true, emotive response, it was surely a damning indictment of the Christian presence and witness in South Africa after more than 300 years. It dramatically portrayed that the path chosen by many younger blacks was becoming radically different from that of whites, and even from that chosen by their Christian parents. They had chosen a secular terrain for their struggle. Indeed, as the sociologist Archie Mafeje indicated at the time, 'because they have rejected the status quo and have no wish or way of going back to the African past, they are destined to produce the necessary revolutionary paradigms, even for the un-liberated African Christians.'[46]

This black protest against the racial bondage of Christianity was not directed only against the advocates and defenders of government policy. For many blacks, the English-speaking and Catholic churches were also regarded as part of the problem rather than the solution. For them, Christianity itself needed to be liberated before it could become mean-ingful for their situation, liberated, that is, from bondage to white interests in church and society.

Thus, the relationship between younger blacks and Christianity rapidly become problematic for the churches, especially in the urban townships. It is true, of course, that black Christian student organiza-tions and church groups still flourished. Indeed, even the more radical students of Soweto and elsewhere had a love/hate relationship with the church, rather than one of total rejection. This ambivalence was true of Steve Biko himself. Throughout the disturbances in 1976 and 1977, black protesters sought the counsel of their pastors and looked for refuge within the precincts of the churches. They were aware that time and again it was the gospel itself that inspired blacks to break out of bondage and to struggle and endure with courage and hope. However, it was also evident that some blacks had moved away from Christianity and found in Marxism an attractive alternative. Without a doubt this was

---

[45] Margaret McNally, 'Portrait of a Black Youth', *The Argus*, Cape Town, 6 November 1976, p. 17.

[46] A. B. M. Mafeje, 'Religion, Class and Ideology in South Africa', in Michael G. Whisson and Martin West (eds.), *Religion and Social Change in Southern Africa* (Cape Town: David Philip, 1975), p. 176.

stimulated by other events in southern Africa during those years, notably the Frelimo victory in Mozambique. This meant that the church in its struggle against racism had to contend not only with injustice but also with the growing power of a hostile ideology.

This rejection of the church by some younger blacks included a rejection of the African indigenous churches as well. Indeed, the mainline churches were often regarded as more relevant to the black struggle than these African Initiated Churches. In his classic study of the latter, particularly in his treatment of 'Zionist healers', Sundkler had observed that these churches were 'a very definite threat to the progress of the African'.[47] A theme reiterated by Mafeje who wrote: 'They are unable to confront structure with structure but instead take refuge in self-induced hallucinations'.[48] African Initiated Churches in South Africa, so it was assumed at the time, were apolitical compared to those in some other African countries. In a comparative study of such churches among the Kikuyu, who were largely responsible for winning independence from the British in Kenya, and of others among the Zulu in Natal, Robert Janosik came to the conclusion that although the situations regarding white domination were very similar, the Kenyan sects were deeply involved in the political struggle, while the Zulu sects, both 'Zionist' and 'Ethiopian', were politically indifferent and quiescent.[49] This assessment would, however, soon become a matter of considerable debate when it was recognized that the role of these churches was different, but as political as any others, and sometimes more so.

Black theologians were fully aware of the fact that many younger blacks were turning their backs in increasing numbers on Christianity and the church. They were very conscious of the challenge of Marxism within the South African context, but unlike some liberation theologians, they did not want to form an alliance with Marxism. Their concern was to rescue the gospel from ideological captivity to white interests, and thereby show its relevance to both black aspirations and, as it happened, to white fears and expectations as well. Indeed, some black Christians were convinced that the power of the gospel could not only

---

[47] Bengt Sundkler, *Bantu Prophets in South Africa* (London: Lutterworth, 1948), p. 237.

[48] Mafeje, 'Religion', p. 183.

[49] Cf. 'Religion and Political Involvement: A Study of Black African Sects', *Journal for the Scientific Study of Religion*, vol. 13 (1974), p. 169.

help bring about their liberation but also that of their white fellow men and women. But they were also convinced that the church itself had to be liberated from ideological bondage and self-interest if this was to happen. Black theologians did not only speak to blacks, they also had a potent message for whites.[50] Black theology was, in fact, a powerful challenge to white Christianity, and a catalyst for Christian renewal and change in society.

Bishop Alphaeus Zulu, one of the first black bishops in the Anglican church, often expressed the dilemma of the black South African Christians in their relationships with whites. In his T. B. Davie Memorial Lecture at the University of Cape Town in 1972, he put it like this:

> Some black people find strength from appreciation of the humanity of the white man. They refuse consciously and deliberately to retaliate by shutting their eyes and calling a white man a beast because he regards them as such. They consider it a duty and privilege to strive to help open the eyes of their fellow men to values presently closed to them. Such people will endure, at least for a time, criticism and disparagement from their fellows on account of their continuing against odds to expect brotherly relationships to be forged across the colour barrier.

But he warned:

> At the same time it would be a grave mistake to presume to think that such attitudes will survive callous white discrimination indefinitely. And even if the patience of such persons should be strangely endless, it may be necessary for them to act with severity in the way that God himself deals with the humanity he loves . . .[51]

That was four years before Soweto. A year after Soweto, speaking at the South African Renewal Conference in Johannesburg, Bishop Zulu

---

[50] J. Moltmann, 'The Liberation of Oppressors', *Journal of Theology for Southern Africa*, no. 26 (March 1979). Clark H. Pinnock, 'A Call for the Liberation of North American Christians', in Carl E. Armerding (ed.), *Evangelicals and Liberation* (Philadelphia: Presbyterian and Reformed, 1977), p. 128; 'Liberation' was the theme of the January 1977 Congress of the S.A. Missiological Society; see *Missionalia*, vol. 5, no. 2 (August 1977).

[51] Alphaeus Zulu, *The Dilemma of the Black South African* (Cape Town: Cape Town University Press, 1972), p. 4.

returned to this theme. He told the vast audience that many blacks no longer felt it possible to be reconciled with whites, that blacks now spoke openly about whites as their oppressors, and that this made the position of black Christians working for reconciliation extremely difficult.[52]

Yet, in spite of Soweto and other events which have black attitudes, it was almost incredible how much concern there was among black Christians for their white fellow citizens. Reporting on the Annual National Conference of the South African Council of Churches in 1977, Dr Wolfram Kistner wrote:

> Towards the end of the Conference the question was raised whether it could be expected for black people to love their oppressors in the present situation. It was pointed out that this question was often asked by young people in the black community. The way in which a considerable number of black delegates responded to this question was a surprise. In a very pronounced manner they expressed their commitment to unconditional love in a time of crisis. This to them was an integral part of the Christian faith and of the Christian message. In some cases such statements assumed the form of a very personal compassion.[53]

Kistner's account was substantiated by that of black journalist Obed Musi, who reported on the openness of black delegates to whites. He quoted a black leader, Constance Koza, Director of InterChurch Aid for the SACC, who in opposing a motion condemning detentions and bannings of blacks said: 'It's not blacks alone who have been suffering. Whites too were involved. So I'd rather see the wording in the motion changed to read just "people" who have been banished, banned or detained . . .' Musi commented: 'And there was not a single voice of dissent. Rather the movers of the motion looked sheepishly at their rough drafts and later gleefully accepted the change in wording.'[54]

It would be wrong to read this as a sign that black attitudes towards whites were without rancour, bitterness, or hatred. But, largely as a result of black consciousness, blacks had once again become liberated as persons, they no longer felt inferior, and believed that their God-given

---

[52] Cf. *Ecunews*, 34/77 (6 September 1977), p. 2

[53] *Ecunews*, 30/77, p. 18.

[54] *Ecunews*, 30/77, p. 20.

dignity could not be destroyed again. They were therefore free to take the risk of loving whites in a way that was as far removed from sentimentality as is the love of the cross. And rising out of this love was a deep and profound concern for white liberation. As Manas Buthelezi put it in his 'Theses': 'It is now time for the black man to evangelise and humanise the white man. The realisation of this will not depend on the white man's approval, but solely on the black man's love for the white man.' In a similar vein, Bishop Desmond Tutu, General Secretary of the SACC, declared (in the sexist language of the time):

> We are involved in the black liberation struggle because we are also deeply concerned for white liberation. The white man will never be free until the black man is wholly free, because the white man invests enormous resources to try to gain a fragile security and peace, resources that should have been used more creatively elsewhere. The white man must suffer too because he is bedevilled by anxiety and fear and God wants to set him free, to be free from all that dehumanises us together, to set us free for our service of one another in a more just and open society in South Africa.[55]

So, too, Boesak insisted at the time that black theology should include whites. 'Blacks', he wrote, 'know only too well the terrible estrangement of white people; they know only too well how sorely whites need to be liberated – even if whites themselves don't.'[56] In the same vein he later wrote:

> We want to share our dreams and hopes, for a new future with whites, a future where it must not be necessary to make a Christian theology an ideology or a part of a cultural imperialism . . . One is only human because of others, with others, for others. This is what we mean. It is authentic, it is worthwhile, it is in the most profound sense of the word gospel truth.[57]

With such sentiments, there was a sense in which the story of the church in South Africa had come full circle.

---

[55] Desmond Tutu, 'God-given Dignity and the Quest for Liberation in the Light of the South African Dilemma', *Liberation*, the papers of the Eighth National Conference of the SACC (July 1976), p. 59.

[56] Boesak, *Farewell*, p. 16.

[57] 'Coming in out of the Wilderness', in Torres and Fabella (eds.), *Emergent Gospel*, p. 93.

Black consciousness and theology thus radically challenged white Christians; despite a general antipathy they could not avoid being affected by it. But whereas before, whites in the church called the tune and blacks played their expected role, now blacks refused to play a 'non-white' role, with the result that whites were forced to face reality in a new way. What they did with reality was, of course, another matter. There was still a long and hard road ahead before South Africa would fundamentally change and whites would discover that their freedom was contingent upon that of blacks. But at least more whites were getting the message that they themselves were in bondage to racism, privilege, and fear, and therefore in need of liberation.

As the Spro-cas Economics Commission report *Power, Privilege and Poverty* expressed it,

> The economically secure are suspicious of the aspirations of the insecure, and become repressive and resistant to change, especially where poverty is seen to be related to social and economic impotence. On the other hand, the economically insecure (supposing them to be not sunken in total apathy) have nothing to lose by militancy and intransigency in their growing demands.[58]

Few white South Africans were, at that time, without fear for the future. As far back as 1945, Jan H. Hofmeyr, then Deputy Prime Minister of South Africa, pointed to this powerful phenomenon. In his Hoernlé lecture that year, he quoted Hoernlé's own words: 'The price which the white caste pays for its domination is fear – fear for the continuance of its own domination, fear for its future.'[59]

In many ways, whites at that time lived in a world of pseudo-innocence. It is far easier to live with fear and an unjust situation if you refuse to acknowledge them or the factors which cause them. Very many white people, for example, did not want to know what was happening in the black townships, what blacks were really thinking and experiencing, how many people were in detention without trial, what new legislation implied for civil rights, and so forth. Such disturbing facts were pushed down into the unconscious. But, of course, the effect of this constant

---

[58] *Power, Privilege and Poverty*, Report of the Economics Commission of the Study Project on Christianity in Apartheid Society (Johannesburg: Spro-cas, 1972), p. 103.

[59] Jan H. Hofmeyr, quoting Hoernlé in *Christian Principles and Race* (Johannesburg: SA Institute of Race Relations, 1945), p. 16.

sublimation was not less anxiety, but more. Moreover, part of this pseudo-innocence was a lack of a sense of guilt for what was happening to black people as a result of white attitudes, actions, and policies. In the name of maintaining security whites were constantly informed that they had nothing for which they need feel guilty. Such a refusal to acknowledge what history plainly described did not mean an absence of guilt, only an absence of admission and acceptance of it. So what could have been one of the most potent forces for healing society's wounds, became one more burden which prevented change and reconciliation. As Archbishop Bill Burnett said in his open letter to Mr Vorster in September 1976: 'Unless White Christians in particular admit the wrongs they have done to Black people and take action to redress them, there can be no possibility of healing in our land.'[60] Indeed, Christianity for many whites, not least those in power, had become a form of escapism and self-deception which prevented them from recognizing reality.

White people belonged, as Nadine Gordimer put it back then, 'to an imported cult that they have not had the will to transform'. This 'lack of will to transform their imported culture', she continued, 'has been – under so many different names – the carapace of white supremacism.'[61] The question whites faced was thus traumatic: How were they to resolve their identity crisis and respond to the black challenge in such a way that the result would be reconciliation rather than destruction, a growing together rather than a splitting apart into polarized oblivion? It was sobering to recall at that time the words of a Cape Town clergyman written in 1900:

> To neglect the black man, or keep him down as a mere servile dependent of the white man, spells ruin to our South African community. A huge black democracy will some day assert itself, as all democracies are bound to do; and if it has been neglected or unfairly treated it will assert itself in a way terrible to think of, and then the black terror will be to our children what the red terror has been to France.[62]

---

[60] *Ecunews*, 30/76 (September 17 1976), p. 4.

[61] 'From Apartheid to Afrocentrism', *South African Outlook*, vol. 107, no. 1278 (December 1977), p. 181; cf. Nadine Gordimer, 'What Being a South African Means to Me', *South African Outlook*, vol. 107, no. 1273 (June 1977).

[62] Quoted by Hinchliff, 'The "English-Speaking Churches"', p. 34.

The first part of this prophecy came true when, in 1994, a new democratic government was elected with an overwhelming black majority. But thankfully the second part of the prophecy was avoided. How that happened, and the role of the churches in preventing it, is the story of the next chapter.

5

Resistance, Repression and the
Transition to Democracy

The Soweto Uprising in 1976 was a watershed in the struggle for liberation in South Africa. From then on the tempo of resistance increased, infused with fresh energy. Over the next few years the liberation movement in exile gained new heart and a dynamic was set in motion that eventually led to the downfall of apartheid. But the transition to a new democratic South Africa did not come without considerable cost, nor did it come soon even though it came suddenly. Increasing resistance led to more brutal and determined repression. Though light was discernable at the end of the tunnel, the tunnel itself remained dark and threatening. 'The outlook is very dark indeed', wrote Lesslie Newbigin, an ecumenical leader from Britain who visited South Africa in 1980, and 'it is getting worse and not better.' Apartheid, he continued, creates a 'vicious circle of fear, resentment and oppression'.[1]

Government counter-revolutionary measures were twofold. On the one hand, every effort was made to give apartheid a 'human face' and to co-opt into the system all those black leaders who were prepared to work within it. The classic technique of divide-and-rule became the order of the day. On the other hand, there was a strengthening of state security institutions, a side stepping of parliamentary procedures, and the implementation of whatever measures were deemed necessary to combat the 'total onslaught' of 'communist aggression'. State terror was the result.

The cycle of violence that erupted as resistance grew and repression intensified spread throughout the region, threatening to escalate into a civil war that would have brought even greater chaos to southern Africa. But South Africa eventually pulled back from the brink of disaster. Many

---

[1] Mimeographed report on a visit to the Republic of South Africa, August 1980.

factors contributed to this outcome, but a crucial one was the role played by the ecumenical church[2] that, together with the trade unions, had assumed the role of leadership in the internal struggle against apartheid.[3] The church struggle and the struggle for liberation were now inter- *prophet effect* twined, and the more this was the case, the more the ecumenical church became the target of both government action and opposition within its own ranks, often aided and abetted by the state] The struggle for justice and the struggle for the soul of the church were the same —[a struggle for ✳ an authentic Christian witness against apartheid. So the ecumenical church had to fight on two flanks: it had to engage state-sponsored injustice and repression in all its many forms, and it had to engage those who sought to undermine its witness to the gospel. As such, the church was both an agent and a site of the struggle. \

The struggle took various forms and occurred in many places around the country, and its story can be told at various levels. Indeed, it would be impossible within the confines of this chapter to document every event and the people involved in the myriad of micro-histories that made up the church struggle as the struggle for liberation entered its final decisive stage.[4] At the macro-level, which is largely the focus of this book, the story concentrates on major representative figures and institutions. Thus, much of what we examine concerns people like Desmond Tutu or Beyers Naudé, or the SACC and other national church structures. However, that macro-story is only part of the story of the church struggle. [Indeed, it is integrally related to the many micro-stories of courageous pastors and parishes, para-church organizations, and people in all walks of life who, out of Christian conviction, participated in the

---

[2] By 'ecumenical church' I refer to those churches and related institutions that found common cause in the struggle against apartheid through their membership of the South African Council of Churches and the World Council of Churches. This includes what previous chapters called the 'English-speaking' churches, the Lutheran churches, the 'daughter' churches of the NGK, and even some Evangelical and Pentecostal bodies. The Roman Catholic Church was a constant partner.

[3] A detailed account of this period in the church struggle is Tristan Anne Borer, *Challenging the State: Churches as Political Actors in South Africa, 1980–1994* (Notre Dame: University of Notre Dame Press, 1998).

[4] For some in-depth analysis of key moments and individuals see the essays in the third volume of the social history of Christianity in South Africa, *From Dark Days to Liberation: Perspectives on the Social History of Christianity in South Africa, 1936–1994*. This was published as a special issue of the *Journal of Theology for Southern Africa*, vol. 118 (March 2004).

struggle, often suffering greatly in doing so, and without which the church struggle would have had little significance at the grassroots. Not all these stories of faith and courage, suffering and martyrdom, have been recorded. But those that have provide detailed and often harrowing accounts of what transpired in many places where local pastors and priests together with their congregations joined together to oppose apartheid. Two immediately come to mind. One is the story of St Anthony's United Church, a small multiracial congregation in downtown Johannesburg,[5] whose remarkable witness for justice, reconciliation and peace was a beacon of hope for many in the city in the 1970s and '80s. Another is the dramatic story of the churches in the Vaal Triangle, which includes Sharpeville and Boipatong, names associated with infamous massacres, from the early 1980s right through to the birth of the new South Africa. These stories are but two of many that could be told and which document the role of the churches in caring for and empowering people whose daily lives were continually threatened by apartheid and conflict. Of necessity, a book of this scope has to focus on the macro-history, the story of those people and events who gave direction to the struggle, weaving the rest into a common narrative. This leadership itself took different forms, sometimes catapulting church leaders into protest marches and imprisonment. At other times, the battle was ideological in character, not least because the state claimed to be Christian and those churches that supported apartheid claimed biblical sanction for the policy.

Our telling of the story of the final two decades of the church struggle begins by recounting how this ideological battle was waged and finally won. The battle had begun years before, most notably at Cottesloe and then with the publication of the *Message to the People of South Africa*. The *Message* had declared apartheid a 'false gospel'; the next step was to reject any attempt to justify it theologically as heretical, a small, long overdue step, but a significant one nonetheless. Indeed, at first glance this might seem of little relevance to the struggle for liberation, but within the context of South Africa it had far-reaching consequences. The fact that the state and its surrogates reacted so vehemently to such theological attacks on its Christian claims, is indicative of the extent to which they

---

[5] Rob Robertson, *St. Anthony's Activists* (Cape Town: privately printed, 1999).
[6] Patrick Noonan, *They're Burning the Churches* (Bellevue, Gauteng: Jacana, 2003).

undermined its attempt to gain credibility while implementing its policies. This was, in fact, a step in the direction of the ecumenical church declaring the state itself illegitimate, though that step was as yet some distance down the road.

Apartheid is a Heresy

The Lutheran World Federation met in Dar-es-Salaam in 1977 not long after the Soweto Uprising. At the instigation of Manas Buthelezi, now the Lutheran bishop in Soweto, the LWF adopted a motion declaring a *status confessionis* in South Africa.[7] This peculiarly Reformation theological notion meant that it was no longer adequate for the church to regard apartheid as sinful or immoral; it had to be unequivocally and publicly rejected as a heresy that undermined the Christian faith at its core. There could be no compromise with the ideology or co-operation with those who supported it. This decision had particular and immediate significance within the Lutheran family of churches, isolating those white Lutheran congregations that refused to unite with the wider multiracial but largely black Lutheran Church. But the Lutheran decision, as we shall see, had wider ramifications for the ecumenical church.

Meanwhile the South African Council of Churches, relatively unscathed by the banning of the Christian Institute and its leadership, but isolated and vulnerable, was now at the centre of the church struggle.[8] Those churches and organizations associated with the Council, which we broadly describe as the 'ecumenical church', were not always

---

[7] Prasanna Kumari Jens Holger Schjorring and Norman A. Hjelm (eds.), *From Federation to Communion: The History of the Lutheran World Federation* (Minneapolis: Fortress Press, 1997), pp. 71–2. On the meaning and significance of the '*status confessionis*' in South Africa, see D. J. Smit, 'A "Status Confessionis" in South Africa?', *Journal of Theology for Southern Africa*, no. 47 (June 1984), pp. 21–46.

[8] On the work and witness of the SACC during this period see, inter alia, Desmond Tutu, 'God's Strength – in Human Weakness', in Margaret Nash (ed.), *Your Kingdom Come: Papers and Resolutions of the Twelfth National Conference of the SACC, Hammanskraal, May 5–8, 1980* (Johannesburg: SACC, 1980), pp. 11–23; *The Divine Intention*, presentation by Bishop D. Tutu, General Secretary of the SACC to the Eloff Commission of Enquiry, 1 September 1982; Hans Brandt (ed.), *Outside the Camp: A Collection of the Writings by Wolfram Kistner* (Braamfontein: SACC, 1988); Sol Jacob (ed.), *Hope in Crisis*, SACC National Conference Report, 1986.

supportive of its stand on issues or the role it played. In fact, the relationship between the member churches and the SACC was not an easy one, for the stand taken by the SACC often resulted in tension and conflict within them. But there was also mutual benefit in the relationship. The member churches provided a protective shield for the SACC, while the SACC stuck its neck out in prophetic leadership, drawing the churches into a community of common purpose and action. And as the churches came increasingly under the influence of their black constituencies, and as the black NGK mission churches began to flex their growing muscle, so the SACC became both the symbol of church resistance and a spearhead for the internal liberation struggle, and a major link to the resources of the wider ecumenical church beyond South Africa. If nothing else, the SACC was a conduit for much needed financial assistance to many ecumenical projects around the country.

In 1978, following the appointment of Bishop Desmond Tutu as its general secretary, the SACC took on a new dynamic. The already large and now predominantly black staff grew in size, and its programmes diversified and extended to meet the urgent needs that intensifying resistance and repression created. In particular its support for activists in detention, its lead in calling for an intensification of international sanctions against South Africa, and its growing links with the liberation movement leadership in exile, meant that the SACC was under greater and constant state surveillance. It was also the target of covert security police action, much of it illegal and violent. Right-wing church opposition to the ecumenical church also grew more intense and vociferous, aided and funded by the state and anti-ecumenical sources overseas.[9] In particular, organizations such as the Gospel Defence League, along with the South African Broadcasting Corporation, continued to foster dissension within denominations, trying to discredit their leaders as 'communists' and 'liberation theologians'.

Tutu was a special focus of state attention and attack. In his annual Report to the SACC National Conference in 1980 he referred to the various ways in which the regime had sought to undermine his work and influence. Not least among these was the confiscation of his passport and public vilification. But Tutu was not one to take things lying down.

---

[9] On 'right-wing Christianity' in South Africa, see articles in the *Journal of Theology for Southern Africa*, no. 69 (December 1989).

'I want to warn the authorities, as I warned Mr Le Grange (then Minister of Justice), that they are not gods.' He went on to say:

> They are just ordinary mortals who exercise power through draconian laws. But God will not be mocked, and tomorrow they will be just faint scrawls on the pages of history . . . We are engaged in a glorious liberation struggle even for their sakes, to liberate them from their fears so that they too can enjoy their heritage, their glorious freedom as the children of God.[10]

Recognizing the threat that the SACC and Tutu presented both inside the country and abroad in providing Christian theological and moral support for the liberation struggle, the state eventually in 1983 appointed the Eloff Commission of Inquiry to investigate its activities. The state was particularly concerned about the extent to which the SACC provided legal and financial aid to political detainees and trialists, a ministry that had mushroomed after the Soweto Uprising with the establishment of the Asingeni Fund. In 1979 this was renamed the Dependants' Conference, a project which by then had managed to raise large sums of money from donor organizations overseas. There can be no doubt that without the assistance of the Dependants' Conference, which had staff workers and offices around the country, many activists who had been arrested, along with their families, would have had little recourse to legal or financial aid.[11] The state argued that such assistance encouraged people to engage in actions that threatened law and order. But in a submission to the Commission provocatively entitled *Here We Stand*, the SACC President, Peter Storey, a Methodist leader, answered the criticisms of the state on this and other points of contention, challenging its leaders to recognize that what the SACC was doing was of God, and God alone would judge it.[12] Under Tutu's leadership as

---

[10] Tutu, 'God's Strength', p. 16.

[11] For a detailed examination of this work of the SACC, see Jonathan Eugene Klaaren, 'A Contextual History of Christian Institutional Involvement in Legal Aid Assistance to the Victims of Apartheid, 1960–1982' (MA dissertation, University of Cape Town, 1988).

[12] Peter Storey, *Here We Stand: Submission to the Commission of Inquiry into the South African Council of Churches, 9th March 1983* (Johannesburg: SACC, 1983).

General Secretary, the work of the Dependants' Conference expanded even further with Archbishop Robert Selby Taylor of Cape Town as its chair. And following Tutu's reception of the Nobel Peace Prize 1984, his new international status not only enabled him to gather more support for the cause but also gave him a certain immunity in doing so. Despite state opposition and harassment, the work of the Dependants' Conference continued after the Eloff Commission completed its work, becoming increasingly multi-faceted as state repression grew in intensity.[13]

While the Soweto Uprising, like the Sharpeville Massacre before, should have been a wake-up call for other churches beyond the orbit of the SACC, few recognized the seriousness of the situation and the need for fundamental change. The NGK and the other Afrikaans Reformed Churches remained solidly in support of the government, while some other churches, notably the Baptists and Pentecostals, chose to adopt an untenable neutral position. Nonetheless, critical voices gradually began to challenge the NGK from within,[14] and the emergence of the Black Baptist Convention and similar organizations led to a decisive shift in consciousness and focus within the more evangelical sectors of the church. This gradually brought some evangelicals, especially those who were black, into alliance with the ecumenical struggle against apartheid.

In 1979, in continuity with the Congress on Mission and Evangelism held in Durban in 1973, African Enterprise made a further attempt to bring the various church constituencies together at the South African Christian Leadership Assembly (SACLA) held in Pretoria that July.[15] Part of the rationale was to overcome the polarization between 'evangelicals' and 'ecumenicals' that was undermining Christian witness in the country. More than 6,000 participants from a vast array of cultural, language and denominational backgrounds met to consider ways of responding to the crisis in the country. Among its achievements, SACLA helped to generate a more radical evangelical witness among student participants leading to the establishment of SUCA, the Student Union

---

[13] The extent of the work of the Dependants' Conference can be seen from the Report of the DC to the National Conference of the SACC in 1986. See Jacob (ed.), *Hope in Crisis*, pp. 112–17.

[14] See, for example, F. E. O'Brien Geldenhuys, Nico J. Smith and Piet Meiring (eds.), *Stormkompas* (Cape Town: Tafelberg, 1981); Adrio König, David J. Bosch and Willem D. Nicol (eds.), *Perspektief Op die Ope Brief* (Cape Town: Human & Rousseau, 1982).

[15] See articles in the *Journal of Theology for Southern Africa*, no. 29 (December 1979).

for Christian Action, a non-racial body that sought to engage in direct acts of Christian witness against the state. Significant as the event and some of its outcomes were, SACLA was too theologically diverse and politically divided to reach consensus on the issues at stake or on action required. Like the Durban Congress, SACLA demonstrated the extent to which the churches had become even more polarized by politics and especially by the question of appropriate political action.

One of the key issues facing young white Christian students at the time of the SACLA conference was the question of Conscientious Objection. The earlier theological and political debate that had been sparked by the Hammanskraal resolution of the SACC in 1974, had been thrown into ethical relief by the use of white military conscripts in policing the black townships of South Africa following the 1976 Soweto Uprising. This was now reaching a climax as young white Christian students began to reflect on what their faith had to say about serving in a military force that was upholding apartheid, and being used in Namibia and Angola as an army of occupation. In 1979 and 1980 two cousins, Peter Moll and Richard Steele, were the first in a line of young men who went to prison rather than serve in the military. Their courageous witness inspired others to follow suit, called forth the admiration and support of the ecumenical churches, and brought into being a network of support groups located in the major centres of the country, which over time coalesced with a more general white opposition to the South African military into the End Conscription Campaign. The ECC, in which a wide range of Christians participated, was perhaps the most creative and 'popular' of all the white-initiated opposition groups to apartheid in the 1980s, and a range of its leaders were subjected to the repressive actions of the state alongside those of other popular resistance structures. Although the numbers of COs who went to prison never went beyond 20, the ideological destabilization brought about by their Christian witness and the snowballing effect that it was causing, panicked the state into a whole battery of legislation aimed at providing 'alternative service' that was still punitive. By 1985 more and more young Christian men were seeing this alternative service as the key way that they could signal their opposition to the militarized repression of the state, alongside their solidarity with black resistance.

Despite internal dissension, generally along racial lines, the member churches of the SACC continued to oppose apartheid and were drawn

[handwritten margin note: Christians refusing to participate in unjust groups]

ever deeper into the struggle for justice and liberation. Synodical statements were clearer and less ambiguous now than before, though opposition to denominational decisions in white parishes and congregations was sometimes vociferous and bitter. Some white members withdrew from their denominations and joined more conservative churches. The extent of this white backlash was one of the reasons why the SACC convened a Consultation on Racism at Hammanskraal in February 1978. Born out of the frustration and anger felt by black theologians who saw little evidence of change a call was made on 'all white Christians to demonstrate their willingness to purge the church of racism'. This was followed by an ultimatum that: 'if after a period of twelve months there is no evidence of repentance shown in concrete action, the black Christians will have no alternative but to witness to the Gospel of Jesus Christ *by becoming a confessing church*.'[16]

In some ways, the formation of a black confessing church might have been the logical outcome of black theology, but for a variety of reasons it did not happen in precisely the way proposed at Hammanskraal. Even though a 'black church' identity had emerged which united black Christians and theologians across denominations in a common struggle, Catholics and Anglicans in particular had difficulty with the notion of a 'confessing church'. The same was not true for Lutherans and those in the Reformed tradition. Indeed, the time had now come when the black NGK mission churches would take on this identity and play a key role in the church struggle, especially within the NGK church family.

Already indicative of this was the formation in 1981 of the Alliance of Black Reformed Christians in South Africa (ABRECSA) under the leadership of Dr Allan Boesak. ABRECSA, comprised of Dutch Reformed, Presbyterian and Congregationalist theologians and pastors, called on their churches to recognize apartheid as a heresy and to unite in opposing it.[17] The various NG mission churches had already signalled their readiness to do this by cutting ties of dependence on the white NGK, and in their desire for greater unity. Already in 1975 the NG Kerk in Afrika, against the expressed wishes of the NGK, had become an observer member of the SACC – a decision followed by the NG Sendingkerk

---

[16] *Ecunews*, 4/80 (27 February 1980), p. 11.

[17] John W. de Gruchy and Charles Villa-Vicencio (eds.), *Apartheid Is a Heresy* (Cape Town: David Philip), pp. 161–8.

in 1978 and the Reformed Church in Africa (Indian) in 1980. That same year, the Revd S. P. Buti, moderator of the NG Kerk in Afrika, became the president of the SACC. All of this brought the SACC back into direct contact with the NG church family. But now it was through its black rather than its white constituency, making the SACC even more representative of the churches in the country.

Boesak played a major role at the meeting of the General Council of the World Alliance of Reformed Churches held in Ottawa, Canada, in 1982. Not only did this result in his election as its president, but also in the decision of the WARC to recognize, just as the Lutherans had done at Dar-es-Salaam, that a *status confessionis* had developed in South Africa.[18] The statement adopted by the Council on 'Racism in South Africa' included this crucial clause: 'We declare with black Reformed Christians of South Africa that apartheid ("separate development") is a sin, and that the moral and theological justification of it is a travesty of the Gospel and, in its persistent disobedience to the Word of God, a theological heresy.'[19] This decision led, first of all, to the further ecumenical and international isolation of the white NGK, but secondly to the drafting of the Belhar Confession by the NG Sendingkerk in 1982. The Belhar Confession was the first confession of faith adopted by a church within the Dutch Reformed tradition since the seventeenth century.[20] But its significance for the church struggle was that it made ethical commitment to justice central to the faith and therefore to the unity of the church. The NG Sendingkerk thus became a black confessing church founded on the rejection of apartheid as contrary to the gospel of Jesus Christ. This meant that the theological justification of apartheid had now been categorically rejected from within the NGK family of churches, and that the future relations between those churches now depended on rejecting apartheid. No longer could the white NGK leadership complain that it was simply the liberal English-speaking churches that were anti-government; now the churches that had been planted through their own missionary endeavours had turned their backs on apartheid.

---

[18] De Gruchy and Charles Villa-Vicencio (eds.), *Heresy*, pp. 168–73.

[19] De Gruchy and Charles Villa-Vicencio (eds.), *Heresy*, p. 170.

[20] On the Belhar Confession see G. D. Cloete and D. J. Smit (eds.), *A Moment of Truth: The Confession of the Dutch Reformed Mission Church, 1982* (Grand Rapids: Eerdmans, 1984).

With the Belhar Confession we have come a long way from Cottesloe, yet the principles articulated in the Cottesloe Statement, as well as in *The Message to the People of South Africa,* were now finally and logically developed in a confession of faith by a church which, after years on the periphery, had come to the forefront in the struggle against apartheid. At the same time, not least through the influence of the NG Sendingkerk's confessional stand, other churches in South Africa followed suit in declaring apartheid a heresy, something fundamentally at variance with the gospel of Jesus Christ. The use of the term 'heresy' to describe a political ideology and programme evoked critical reaction. Political systems may be immoral, unjust or corrupt, but why heretical? But the term was carefully chosen. What was at issue was not simply the policy of apartheid, but its theological justification, the attempt to give it biblical sanction, and to implement it in the life of the church.

Quite apart from the challenge that the black NG churches and the WARC now presented to the NGK, the NGK also had to reckon with a major rift within Afrikanerdom brought to a head by President P. W. Botha's 'reformist' policies. These policies were indicative of the extent to which the government recognized the need for change in the aftermath of the Soweto Uprising, however much they were half-hearted and flawed. Botha was less committed to the strict ideology of apartheid than predecessors like Verwoerd, who remained the hero of the Afrikaner right-wing whether in church or politics. By way of contrast he was prepared to be pragmatic as long as this did not undermine state security or compromise political control. Indicative of this was his willingness to change such racist laws as the Mixed Marriages Act and the Immorality Act. In 1981, church leaders of the Church Unity Commission churches (Anglican, Congregational, Methodist and Presbyterian) were asked by their denominations to meet Botha and present their demand for the repeal of these two laws. In their meeting, with several members of the cabinet present, Botha stated that he would repeal the laws if the church leaders could persuade the NGK moderature to support such a move. The government was perfectly willing to move on this matter, he declared with a flourish, it was the NGK that stood in the way.

In essence, through his 'reformist policies' Botha sought to retain white domination by co-opting Coloureds and Indians into a tri-cameral parliament of separate racially determined houses. Even though the African majority was excluded and whites would retain control, this move was too much for a significant section of Afrikanerdom. Thus the Conservative Party (CP) was launched in 1983 under the leadership of Dr Andries Treurnicht. Treurnicht had long represented the right wing of the National Party and the NGK. A former editor of *Die Kerkbode*, he had kept the church faithful to the principles of apartheid. Moreover, as Minister of Education he was largely responsible for the immediate events that sparked-off the Soweto Uprising. Now, with considerable support from within the NGK, he led the break-up of the National Party in defence of apartheid.

All of a sudden the unity of the NGK was threatened as its members and ministers were forced to take different political sides, albeit still within the broad arena of apartheid politics. This led to a growing reluctance on the part of the NGK to commit itself on social and political issues in a way contrary to the principled position it had previously adopted in its promotion of apartheid legislation. But at its General Synod in 1986 the NGK finally, if timidly, gave up the attempt to provide biblical and theological justification for apartheid in its report on *Church and Society (Kerk en Samelewing)*.[21] If the NGK had not rejected the *Cottesloe Statement* in 1961, it would have anticipated by 25 years much of what was now being stated. History had unfolded in such a way, however, that the new position of the NGK was totally inadequate, in fact, it was nothing more than a theological rationalizing of the government's own attempt to reform apartheid. But apartheid was beyond reform; it was a heresy that had to be rejected as contrary to the gospel of Jesus Christ. There could be no compromise, no 'cheap reconciliation', only the dismantling of apartheid and everything that sustained it.

A Kairos Moment

In 1983 the United Democratic Front (UDF), a broad coalition of anti-apartheid organizations, NGOs, trade unions and faith communities, was formed to oppose Botha's reform proposals. Significantly the patrons of the UDF were Bishop Tutu, Dr Boesak, and the Catholic Archbishop of Durban, Dennis Hurley. The UDF immediately launched campaigns of mass action around the country that ushered in a

---

[21] *Kerk en Samelewing* (Bloemfontein: Pro Christo Publishers, 1987).

new phase of resistance. The increasingly militant mass action, which coincided with the escalation of the armed struggle, and the tightening of international sanctions, aimed to make the country ungovernable. In response, Botha declared two States of Emergency, the second of which started on 21 July 1985 and lasted until his demise in 1989. The already powerful state security system was given even greater powers to crush all opposition, described in state propaganda as a communist-inspired revolutionary 'total onslaught'. Detention without trial, torture, the murder of political activists, and the fomenting of violence in black townships, became the day-to-day business of state security agencies. Thousands of people, including many Christians and people of other faith communities, were detained, tortured, and killed. Funerals of activists, usually held on a Saturday in the black townships, became ecumenical rallying points, as people of all denominations joined together to bury the dead, express their anger at the causes of oppression, and commit themselves afresh to the struggle.

One Christian response to this crisis was the National Initiative for Reconciliation (NIR) launched in September 1985 by African Enterprise.[22] About 400 church leaders, including some from the SACC and the white NGK, gathered in Pietermaritzburg to address the growing conflict situation. In their 'Statement of Affirmation' the church leaders acknowledged that reconciliation without removing the causes of conflict was a fraud. At the same time, the NIR believed that working for reconciliation at the interpersonal level was essential alongside working for justice. Reconciled communities following the 'third-way' of the gospel provided the key to overcoming the political crisis.[23] This marked a step in the right direction for many more conservative church leaders. But it was too equivocal for others who had to minister within the black townships where angry young people were calling for more radical resistance.

For some time a group of pastors and theologians had been meeting in Soweto under the auspices of the Institute for Contextual Theology (ICT) to consider how best to respond to these more radical demands.

---

[22] See Klaus Nürnberger and John Tooke (eds.), *The Cost of Reconciliation in South Africa* (Cape Town: Methodist Publishing House, 1988).

[23] For critical reflections on this position, see Tony Balcomb, *Third Way Theology* (Pietermaritzburg: Cluster Publications, 1993).

The ICT had been formed in 1982 as a means of fostering the development of progressive or prophetic theological responses to apartheid. Its first director, Frank Chikane, a minister of the Apostolic Faith Mission, had been in the forefront of black student politics since the Soweto Uprising. He would later be elected general secretary of the SACC, following Beyers Naudé, who had filled that office when Tutu was elected Anglican Archbishop of Cape Town in 1984. Chikane's appointment was remarkable. Although his own church had withdrawn his ministerial licence because of his political involvement he was, nonetheless, a member of a pentecostal denomination outside the SACC and a product of the black consciousness movement and the Soweto Uprising.[24] But these credentials were ideal for leading the ICT and for launching his role within the ecumenical church. Together with Fr Albert Nolan, a Catholic theologian, Chikane gathered a group of pastors and theologians together in Soweto to formulate a theological response to the burning issues facing them. The result was the drafting of the *Kairos Document*, a document that soon gathered signatures from around the country, and was made public late in September 1985.

Recognizing that the basic difference between Christians in South Africa was not primarily denominational or confessional, but political and economic, the *Kairos Document* perceived that the church itself was a site of the struggle. Thus it not only rejected the 'state theology' of those who gave their support to apartheid, but also opposed what it named the 'church theology' of the mainline multiracial churches, accusing them of promoting 'cheap reconciliation'.[25] In doing so, the *Kairos Document* called for direct Christian participation in the struggle, including acts of civil disobedience in resistance to government tyranny. Government reaction was immediate. Many of its signatories were detained and suffered for their convictions. In countering its claims, the state once again worked in tandem with right-wing religious organizations which continued to flourish, despite the Information Scandal which some years previously had disclosed how such religious organizations were supported by the tax-payer as part of the national security strategy

---

[24] Frank Chikane, *No Life of my Own: An Autobiography* (Johannesburg: Skotaville, 1988).

[25] *The Kairos Document*, 2nd rev. edn (Johannesburg: Institute for Contextual Theology; Grand Rapids: Eerdmans, 1986), art. 3.1.

of the apartheid government. Some of them even became involved in covert support for the Renamo movement that, with the aid of the South African security forces, was involved in the destabilization of Mozambique.

Comparison of the *Kairos Document* with the earlier Cottesloe Statement and the *Message to the People of South Africa* indicates how the parameters of the church struggle had shifted during the past 25 years. Unlike the earlier documents, the *Kairos Document* was largely a black Christian response to the crisis situation in South Africa. Whereas Cottesloe and the *Message* did not challenge the legality of the State, the *Kairos Document* described the state as tyrannical and therefore one that had to be resisted through acts of civil disobedience. While it did not justify the armed struggle, it could certainly be read in support of it. But the *Kairos Document* not only rejected the state theology that supported the status quo, it also turned its back on the more liberal response to apartheid evident at Cottesloe and in the *Message*, a theology that had long characterized the SACC and its member churches.[26] There could be no reconciliation as long as apartheid remained in place.

The *Kairos Document* made an impact far beyond the borders of South Africa. Indeed, it soon became one of the theological documents of the ecumenical church in the late twentieth century. Of all the documents emanating from South African churches and theologians, it was by far the most radical and controversial, prophetically announcing the dying of the old order and the birth pangs of the new.[27] The metaphor is appropriate, because the changes taking place involved considerable suffering as the struggle intensified, and as Christians recognized the need for repentance and transformation. Moreover, heated controversy around the meaning of reconciliation ensued within the churches as state repression against Christian activists associated with the *Kairos Document* intensified. Even churches and church leaders who had rejected apartheid and who were engaged in the struggle to end

---

[26] For a discussion of the liberal tradition in the SACC, see David Thomas, *Christ Divided: Liberalism, Ecumenism and Race in South Africa* (Pretoria: UNISA, 2002).

[27] For a discussion of the *Kairos Document* in relation to other major confessing documents in South Africa, see John W. de Gruchy, 'From Cottesloe to the "Road to Damascus": Confessing Landmarks in the Struggle Against Apartheid', in G. Loots (ed.), *Listening to South African Voices* (Port Elizabeth: Theological Society of Southern Africa, 1990), pp. 1–18.

it were unhappy about the way in which 'church theology' and reconciliation were, in their terms, caricatured and criticized. There was also sharper criticism of the *Kairos Document* emanating from a circle of black theologians who remained faithful to the more radical concerns of the black consciousness movement. For them, the discourse of reconciliation was controlled by the 'ruling class', and the issues at stake were not primarily alienation between white and black, but black alienation from the land, from the means of production, and thus from power.[28] If reconciliation was to mean anything significant for the poor and oppressed, it had to reverse this alienation.

Some of the criticisms were apposite. Yet nothing can detract from the prophetic courage of the *Kairos Document*. If the rejection of apartheid as a heresy undermined the attempt to give the policy theological justification, the *Kairos Document* challenged the legitimacy of the apartheid state as such. Not only was it necessary to reject apartheid; it was now also necessary to declare that the regime was unlawful and tyrannical and, as such, it had to be replaced with a just democratic order. The only debate remaining concerned how this should be done. Simply working for interpersonal racial reconciliation, important as that was, was inadequate given the entrenched nature of state power.

At this point Christians who agreed with the *Kairos Document* were divided between those who identified with the armed struggle, and those who, while sympathetic, believed that non-violent alternatives had to be pursued. One such alternative was mass protest marches. These were illegal under the State of Emergency and were inevitably and brutally stopped. Perhaps the most significant of these was the mass march in October 1985 on Pollsmoor Prison in Cape Town calling for the release of Nelson Mandela. The main march was violently broken up by the police and many of the clergy of different faiths who were leading it were arrested and imprisoned. A smaller group of church leaders managed to get to Pollsmoor to present a petitition, and some of these were also arrested.

Another non-violent alternative was calling for the implementation of comprehensive sanctions against South Africa, something strongly

---

[28] Itumeleng J. Mosala, 'The Meaning of Reconciliation: A Black Perspective', *Journal of Theology for Southern Africa*, no. 59 (June 1987), pp. 19–25. For a discussion on the debate about reconciliation in South Africa, see John W. de Gruchy, *Reconciliation: Restoring Justice* (London: SCM Press, 2002), pp. 10–43.

advocated by Archbishop Tutu. In a press statement in 1986, Tutu concluded with these words:

> I have no hope of real change from this government unless they are forced. We face a catastrophe in this land and only the action of the international community by applying pressure can save us . . . so I call the international community to apply punitive sanctions against this government to help us establish a new South Africa – non-racial, democratic, participatory and just. This is a non-violent strategy that will help us to do so.[29]

The advocacy of sanctions was obviously condemned by the state, but it was also criticized by many liberal church leaders as unhelpful to the cause of reconciliation and change. Yet just as young white Christians had opted to become conscientious objectors as a sign of solidarity with the liberation struggle, so the support for sanctions – whatever their potential effect – was now the only way left, apart from joining the armed struggle, for Christians to express their support for liberation.

The Final Push

Longstanding personal relationships and a common commitment to the anti-apartheid struggle ensured contact between some church leaders and the liberation movement in exile. Some of the leaders of the movement, notably Oliver Tambo, were Christians with strong connections with the ecumenical church both at home and abroad. After all, much of their support in Britain and Western Europe came from church-related groups, and clerics such as Bishop Trevor Huddleston were leaders in the anti-apartheid movement. Furthermore, many of the students who fled South Africa after the Soweto Uprising were church members, as were many of those engaged in the liberation forces. Indeed, in the later years of the struggle the ANC requested chaplains to minister to them. So it was not surprising that there was contact with church leaders who were supporters of the struggle. And as resistance intensified, contact between them became more regular and necessary. Some of this was informal but there were also meetings between denominational and

---

[29] Desmond Tutu, *The Rainbow People of God* (New York: Doubleday, 1994), p. 111.

ecumenical leaders and representatives of the liberation movements in exile. In 1986, for example, the executive of the United Congregational Church met ANC leaders in Bulawayo, Zimbabwe, and that same year the Catholic bishops sent a delegation to meet with ANC leaders in Lusaka, the Zambian capital.

Larger ecumenical consultations were also held to work out a common understanding and strategy. A meeting in Harare, Zimbabwe, in 1986, between church representatives and the liberation movement led to a common declaration of intent set out in the *Harare Declaration*. This identified the ecumenical church in South Africa with the liberation struggle in a common purpose and goal.[30] Then, in May 1987, ecumenical church leaders gathered in Lusaka together with leaders of trade unions, women's and youth organizations, and anti-apartheid groups from around the world. In continuity with the *Harare Declaration*, the *Lusaka Statement* called upon the churches to support the liberation struggle, both in Namibia (which was not yet independent) and South Africa, and declared that the South African government was illegitimate.[31] The SACC adopted the *Harare Declaration* in 1986 at its National Conference, calling for comprehensive sanctions to be imposed on the country as the only remaining non-violent strategy left.

The debate about sanctions and the use of violence to bring about an end to apartheid now dominated most church synods and conferences. Not all the member churches of the SACC were able or willing to identify fully with its resolutions. Some, including the bishops of the Roman Catholic Church, deferred on 'comprehensive sanctions' preferring to call for more 'economic pressure' to be brought to bear on the government.[32] And, of course, the churches remained committed to non-violent strategies for change, even though the debate about the use of violence had become even more intense within them. At the very least, the churches had to recognize the legitimacy of the 'armed struggle' even if they could not directly participate in it.[33]

By this time, the remembrance of 16 June, the anniversary of the

---

[30] 'The Implications of Harare', *ICT News*, March 1986, pp. 3ff.

[31] See the discussion in Borer, *Challenging the State*, pp. 110–12.

[32] 'Pastoral Letter on Economic Pressure for Justice', 1986.

[33] Malusi Mpumlwana, 'Legitimacy and Struggle', in Charles Villa-Vicencio (ed.), *Theology and Violence: The South African Debate* (Johannesburg: Skotaville, 1987; Grand Rapids: Eerdmans, 1988), pp. 89–99.

Soweto Uprising, had become an annual event celebrated in many churches. These services were a blend of politics and piety, with freedom songs interspersed with hymns, and prayers for those in prison as well as for an end to apartheid. The tenth anniversary of Soweto in 1986 provided a special opportunity to remember, reflect and to take the struggle further. With this in mind the SACC called on its member churches to pray for the end to unjust rule. In its rationale it declared:

> The considered judgement of every synod, assembly and conference of the Roman Catholic and mainline Protestant Churches (with the exception of the Afrikaans Reformed Churches), has been that the present regime, together with its structures of domination, stands in contradiction to the Christian Gospel to which the churches of the land seek to remain faithful. We have continually prayed for the authorities, that they may govern wisely and justly. Now, in solidarity with those who suffer most, in this hour of crisis we pray that God in His grace may remove from His people the tyrannical structures of oppression and the present rulers in our country who persistently refuse to heed the cry for justice, as reflected in the Word of God as proclaimed through His Church within this land and beyond.[34]

Opposition to this call indicated that it had touched a raw nerve. And, indeed, with the call to prayer for the end to unjust rule the SACC had gone beyond any position previously adopted, declaring, in unison with the *Kairos Document*, the state to be a 'tyrannical regime' and praying for its removal. This was a decisively new emphasis in the witness of the ecumenical church against apartheid. Many had previously regarded the state as illegitimate; now the SACC and some church leaders were publicly saying so.

Of course, the State of Emergency was still in effect, and as resistance and the armed struggle intensified, so state repression continued to harden. On 24 February 1988 the government clamped down on 17 extra-parliamentary opposition organizations, imprisoning many of their leaders.[35] This led to an emergency meeting of the SACC on 29

---

[34] Allan A. Boesak and Charles Villa-Vicencio (eds.), *When Prayer Makes News* (Philadelphia: Westminster Press, 1986), p. 29.

[35] For an account of these events see 'The Church-State Confrontation: Correspondence & Statements, February–April 1988', *Journal of Theology for Southern Africa*, no. 63 (June 1988), pp. 68–87.

February at which a petition addressed to State President P. W. Botha and Members of Parliament protesting against state action was drafted. This was signed by 25 church leaders representing all the member churches of the SACC, among them Desmond Tutu and Stephen Naidoo, the Catholic Archbishop of Cape Town. The following day, all 25 leaders marched on Parliament in Cape Town to present the petition. All were arrested en route, though released shortly after. In their petition, the church leaders protested 'in the strongest terms' at the restrictions placed on the opposition organizations and their leaders. They went on to say:

> We believe that the Government, in its actions over recent years but especially by last week's action, has chosen a path for the future which will lead to violence, bloodshed and instability. By imposing such drastic restrictions on organisations which have campaigned peace-fully for the end of apartheid, you have removed nearly all effective means open to our people to work for true change by non-violent means . . . Your actions indicate to us that those of you in government have decided that only violence will keep you in power; that you have chosen the 'military option' for our country. It appears to us that you are encouraging the growth of black surrogate forces to split the black community and to smash effective opposition to apartheid.

The church leaders regarded this as undermining the mission of the church:

> We regard your restrictions not only as an attack on democratic activity in South Africa but as a blow directed at the heart of the Church's mission in South Africa. The activities which have been prohibited are central to the proclamation of the Gospel in our country and we must make it clear that, no matter what the conse-quences, we will explore every possible avenue for continuing the activities which you have prohibited other bodies from undertaking.

With considerable boldness, the church leaders told the State President that the week previously they had addressed 'the oppressed people of our land', urging 'them to intensify the struggle for justice and peace', encouraging 'them not to lose hope, for victory against evil in this world is guaranteed by our Lord'. This message, they then declared, applied also to the State President and Parliament. 'Your position is becoming untenable', they declared, and urged them to end the State of Emergency, release political prisoners, allow exiles to return, and 'enter negotiations for a dispensation in which all of us can live together in peace, freedom and justice'.[36]

The action of the church leaders and their petition not only caused considerable reaction inside and outside the country, but it also led to a flurry of correspondence between the State President and Tutu, the bishops of the Anglican church, and the General Secretary of the SACC, Frank Chikane. Botha's response was blunt, challenging the church leaders to acknowledge that they had become lackeys of the 'communist onslaught':

> You owe all Christians an explanation of your exact standpoint, for we are all adults and the time for bluffing and games is long past. The question must be posed whether you are acting on behalf of the kingdom of God, or the kingdom promised by the ANC and the SACP? If it is the latter, say so, but do not then hide behind the structures and the cloth of the Christian church, because Christianity and Marxism are irreconcilable opposites.[37]

The same theme was developed at greater length in a letter sent to Chikane on 25 March. 'The SACC', Botha wrote, 'in its support of the *Kairos Document*, apparently regards communism as a myth, and in its acceptance of the *Harare Declaration* and *Lusaka Statement*, expressed support for sanctions, disinvestments and boycotts against South Africa, and its support for the Marxist terrorist movements'. Botha, who expressly declared that he was writing as a Christian who loved and served the church, said that the church leaders had insulted God and abused the church, and challenged them to become faithful to Christ and the gospel.[38] The rhetoric suggests the hand of NGK government apologists at work. Tutu fired off the final salvo, quoting Scripture in

---

[36] *Journal of Theology for Southern Africa*, no. 63 (June 1988), pp. 69–70.

[37] Letter from Botha to Tutu, 16 March 1988, in *Journal of Theology for Southern Africa*, no. 63 (June 1988), p. 73.

[38] Letter from Botha to Chikane, 25 March 1988, in *Journal of Theology for Southern Africa*, no. 63 (June 1988), pp. 78–9.

answering Botha's attack on him and the SACC. He categorically rejected Botha's criticism, insisting that his 'theological position' predated 'Marxism and the ANC by several centuries', and was derived from the Bible and the teaching of the church.[39] This exchange of letters reveals the extent to which by this stage the ecumenical church leaders were publicly and unambiguously identifying with the liberation struggle. It also reveals how much the struggle for liberation was related to the church struggle, and the extent to which it was a contest between two very different understandings of Christianity and the teaching of the Bible.

Ironically as it appears in hindsight, at this very time exploratory and highly secretive talks had already begun between Mandela, still in prison, and some National Party leaders to consider the possibility of negotiations. There were also other secretive talks between the ANC in exile and members of the Afrikaner Broederbond, with the Institute for Democracy (IDASA). Botha was aware of the talks with Mandela as were some of the liberation leaders in exile, and both sides were extremely wary about the consequences and implications. But little about them was known beyond this small circle.[40] The fact that Mandela initiated the talks, the way in which he entered into them, and the response he received from those with whom he met, indicates not only his acknowledged stature within the liberation movement, but also his understanding of what needed to be done at that moment. Neither the state nor the liberation movement had the capacity to achieve a decisive victory, and the prolonging of the vicious stalemate could only spell disaster for the country. Just as the turn to the armed struggle had been determined by both strategic and moral considerations, as Mandela at the Rivonia Trial[41] and Z. K. Matthews at a World Council of Churches Conference in 1964, had so powerfully stated,[42] so now seeking its termination was

---

[39] Letter from Tutu to Botha, 8 April 1988, in *Journal of Theology for Southern Africa*, no. 63 (June 1988), pp. 82–7.

[40] The story of these talks is told in Nelson Mandela, *Long Walk to Freedom: The Autobiography of Nelson Mandela* (Johannesburg: Macdonald Purnell, 1994).

[41] Nelson Mandela, 'Second Court Statement, 1964', in *The Struggle is my Life* (London: IDAF Publications, 1990), pp. 161–81.

[42] Z. K. Matthews, 'The Road from Nonviolence to Violence', World Council of Churches Conference, Kitwe, Northern Rhodesia, May 1964, in Thomas G. Karis and Gail M. Gerhart (eds.), *From Protest to Challenge: Nadir and Resurgence, 1964–1979*, A Documentary History of African Politics in South Africa, 1882–1990, vol. 5 (Pretoria: Unisa Press, 1997), p. 356.

based on political realism and a moral commitment to the common good. Thus the pursuit of reconciliation as a means to restore justice became part of the strategy of liberation. It was by no means clear to those engaged in the struggle that such a strategy had any chance of success. For while the State of Emergency enabled the government to prop up its authority and maintain control, it was clear that it could not resist both internal and international pressure for much longer. By the same token, if the liberation struggle continued to make the country ungovernable and civil war erupted, it would destroy so much that was needed to make the transition to democracy feasible.

[margin notes: restoration / civil war]

In May 1988 the leaders of the member churches of the SACC launched the 'Standing for the Truth Campaign'. The campaign sought 'to engage in effective non-violent actions' which would 'force the regime to stop its violence and repression and negotiate with the legitimate leaders of the people'.[43] In initiating the campaign, the SACC was identifying the churches with the Mass Democratic Movement (MDM) that was then sweeping the country in a series of illegal mass protest rallies, marches and strikes. Government reaction was severe, but it was evident that, as in countries in Eastern Europe at that time, something had to give way. Indeed, there was a link between these events, for the collapse of the Soviet Union had far-reaching repercussions in southern Africa. All of this together provided the final push that brought down the edifice of apartheid. But, of course, in retrospect it needed Mandela's initiative, something that had inserted a totally new and unexpected dynamic in the process. As long as pressure was maintained on the State, these 'talks about talks' had the potential to break the deadlock.

Eventually Botha was forced to resign in the closing months of 1989 to be replaced by F. W. de Klerk. Some members of the cabinet, as well as leaders within the Broederbond, recognized that something else was needed than meeting resistance with more force and repression. But few observers anticipated what was about to happen. After all, de Klerk, a member of the Gereformeerde Kerk and son of a former National Party leader, was widely regarded as a conservative. But in a remarkable speech at the opening of Parliament on 2 February 1990, de Klerk announced the unbanning of the ANC, PAC, and South African Communist Party, as well as the imminent release of Mandela and other political prisoners.

---

[43] Frank Chikane, foreword to the SACC Pamphlet 'Standing for the Truth' (1991).

Observers in and beyond the country were taken by surprise. So too were those participants in a mass protest march that had gathered outside Parliament, that auspicious day in February 1990, with a set of demands and an ultimatum. De Klerk's announcement met them all.

Political analysts and historians will long debate precisely what finally brought an end to apartheid. As we have already intimated it cannot be attributed to any single factor; it was a combination of all the elements of the struggle over many long years, and eventually the result of tough negotiations. Some churches, church organizations and church leaders undoubtedly contributed significantly to the process, and it goes without saying that many Christians on the ground were involved in various ways.[44] However, the sudden change in political fortunes brought about an equally rapid change in their political role. After years of the church struggle, during which the identity of the ecumenical church had been shaped, how were they to respond to the emerging new reality?

Midwives of Democratic Transition

During the years of the struggle, ecumenical church leaders had assumed a political role by default due to the banning of the liberation movement. The time had come to give way to political leaders who had now been released from prison or who had returned from exile. But for some observers both within and outside the ecumenical church it appeared that there was an unseemly haste on the part of some church leaders to withdraw from political involvement. It also appeared as if the churches were now redirecting their efforts more into their institutional needs, regrouping as it were after the years of energy-sapping and divisive struggle. This was partly true but also partly a misperception. Many church leaders and pastors who had been actively engaged in the struggle continued to be involved, recognizing that while their precise role had changed, there was still an urgent need for their contribution in the ongoing process of democratic transition and social transformation. At the same time, there were several significant church leaders and theologians who now decided that the time had come for them to enter

Mid wife phase

---

[44] For a detailed examination of the role of the churches, see Dee F. Matreyek, 'The Birth of Democracy in South Africa: The Churches Respond' (PhD dissertation, Claremont Graduate University, Claremont, California, 1998).

the political and public arena more fully. Their shift into politics, public service and government institutions, undoubtedly contributed significantly to the development of the emerging new South Africa. But it also left the churches bereft of their leadership at a critical juncture. As most of those who made this decision were black church leaders and theologians, this exodus also created a serious vacuum in the churches' capacity to respond to the issues.

But there were several other factors that also began to affect the public profile of the ecumenical church. One of the most significant was the extent to which international support for the SACC began to lessen. New financial demands made upon the WCC and its member churches, especially in Germany, as a result of the changes taking place in Eastern Europe redirected much of the funding that might have gone to South Africa. At the same time many of these partner churches, which had so strongly supported the SACC during the years of struggle, were experiencing their own financial constraints. Of course, not all funding dried up. But there was a sense abroad that the need was no longer so great and urgent. This was part of the process of 'normalization' that affected many NGOs in post-apartheid South Africa which had been dependent on overseas funding. In short, the Council was forced to reduce its staff and programmes, and reconsider its role in society.

At the same time media attention switched from the role of church leaders and the SACC to the returning exiles and those released from prison. Whereas over the previous decades church pronouncements on the struggle gained attention, this was now far less the case. There were new spokespeople for the struggle, returned exiles, freed political prisoners, unbanned leaders, whose voices needed to be heard. At the same time other, new 'mega-churches' had emerged, largely charismatic and fundamentalist in character, which had entered the public arena after years of silence and which, with a remarkable ability, gained media attention for their own conservative agendas. This meant that 'the Christian' voice in the media, with the notable exception of struggle stalwarts like Desmond Tutu, increasingly referred to those whose opinions attracted the attention of a media hungry for comment that would reinforce fundamentalist stereotypes. The ecumenical church was not very good at countering this changing image of Christianity, especially at a time when world-wide attention was focusing on religious fundamentalism of all kinds.

A further important factor that began to reshape the political role of the churches was the shift from a state-supported Christian hegemony to a situation in which all religious traditions were regarded equally within a secular state. After all, despite the preponderance of Christians in the country, there were other significant faith communities that had contributed to the ending of apartheid and were committed to democratic transformation. Creating a secular state did not imply the downgrading of religion to a purely personal and private affair, but it did mean not favouring one above another. Nonetheless, the numerical strength of Christianity inevitably meant a greater potential for helping in the transition to democracy and social transformation. Mandela had this in mind when, in December 1992, during an address to the Free Ethiopian Church of Southern Africa, one of the oldest African initiated churches in the country, he called on the churches in South Africa 'to join other agents of change and transformation in the difficult task of acting as a midwife to the birth of our democracy and acting as one of the institutions that will nurture and entrench it in our society'.[45] But what precisely was that role?

Two ecumenical events sought to provide guidance on this role and signalled the beginning of a new phase in the political involvement of the churches in South Africa. The first was the National Conference of Church Leaders held at Rustenburg in November 1991. This brought together leaders from across the whole spectrum of the church, from Roman Catholic to NGK and African Initiated, from the English-speaking to the Pentecostal and independent Charismatic churches. It was estimated, in fact, that the leadership represented more than 90 per cent of South Africa's Christians, and more than 70 per cent of the population.[46] For the first time Christian leaders of such diversity, many of whom had been in bitter political opposition during previous years, sought to reach a common mind on the witness and role of the church in the shaping of a new South Africa.

The presence at the Rustenburg Conference of Beyers Naudé, who we recall was a key participant at the Cottesloe Consultation so many years

---

[45] Speech delivered by Nelson R. Mandela, President of the ANC to the Free Ethiopian Church of Southern Africa, Potchefstroom, 14 December 1992.

[46] Louw Alberts and Frank Chikane (eds.), *The Road to Rustenburg* (Cape Town: Struik, 1991), p. 10.

before, provided a link between these two seminal events. In his address to the Conference, Naudé insisted that the church now had the responsibility of getting its own house in order, and that at the same time it had to participate quite concretely in struggling to overcome the legacies of apartheid.[47] Naudé, as always direct and to the point, made a special appeal to the NGK to acknowledge its guilt and to apologize to the World Council of Churches for the serious wrong done in turning its back on Cottesloe in 1961. Naudé was given a standing ovation after his address, vindicating his courageous stand through the wilderness years. A few years after Rustenburg, it should be noted, Naudé was warmly welcomed back into the NGK and received its apology for the way in which he had been treated. But at this stage the NGK leadership was still struggling to come to terms with the new political reality.

Ever since Botha began to implement his 'reformist policies', the NGK had been increasingly divided between those who wanted the church to remain faithful to the ideology of apartheid and those who wanted change. Many were also caught in between, not really knowing which way to move. These divisions had been clearly evident in March 1989 at the Vereeniging Consultation in which representatives of all the churches of the NGK family were present to discuss the changes taking place in the country, and especially their unity. Gone were the days of defending apartheid on the basis of Scripture, indeed, there seemed to be a major breakthrough in relationships. Yet, despite what was said and confessed, the white delegates were still cautious in unequivocally rejecting apartheid and doing so publicly, and there was some diffidence about satisfying the demands of the black NG constituency.[48] At this stage de Klerk had yet to assume leadership of the National Party and to make his celebrated speech to Parliament. So the NGK leadership, so closely aligned with the National Party government for so long, was in a quandary. It was already evident that many younger members of the NGK were disillusioned and had either left to join other denominations or simply opted out of the church altogether.

There were two alternatives that the NGK could take into the future. It could withdraw into its shell and simply serve the pastoral needs of the

---

[47] Beyers Naudé, 'The Role of the Church in a Changing South Africa', in Alberts and Chikane (eds.), *Road to Rustenburg*, pp. 220–31.

[48] See Douglas Bax, 'The Vereeniging Consultation', *Journal of Theology for Southern Africa*, no. 68 (September 1989), pp. 61–73.

white Afrikaner community, a position that was adopted by many congregations. Or it could continue to fulfil a public role by responding positively to the new situation. This meant helping its members to come to terms with the changing political terrain and enabling them to make a positive contribution to the new South Africa. The emerging leadership of the NGK was generally committed to this approach. But it had to take its constituency with it if it was to make such a contribution; it also had to acknowledge its guilt, as Naudé indicated, for the sins of the past. This was reflected at Rustenburg in the speech given by Professor Willie Jonker of the NGK theological faculty in Stellenbosch.

Jonker, who had always been on the more progressive wing of the NGK, expressed deep sorrow for the way in which the NGK had supported apartheid. 'On the human level', Jonker said, 'the NGK can do little more than to acknowledge its guilt and ask for forgiveness and acceptance.' But he then went on to say:

> I confess before you and before the Lord, not only my own sin and guilt, and my personal responsibility for the political, social, economical and structural wrongs that have been done to many of you, and the results of which you and our whole country are still suffering from, but *vicariously* I dare also to do that in the name of the NGK of which I am a member, and for the Afrikaans people as a whole. I have the liberty to do just that, because the NGK at its latest synod has declared apartheid a sin and confessed its own guilt of negligence in not warning against it and distancing itself from it long ago.[49]

Tutu's warm embrace and words of acceptance following Jonker's speech demonstrated what many others felt. But there were some who were not yet able or willing to forgive all. This was especially true of participants from the NGK mission churches who believed that the white NGK, as evident at the Vereeniging Consultation, was still dragging its feet in rejecting apartheid. At the same time, many members of the ruling National Party and the NGK were furious with Jonker's act of 'betrayal'.

Rustenburg was not only problematic for some black participants but like so many other church conferences during the apartheid years it

---

[49] Alberts and Chikane (eds.), *Road to Rustenburg*, p. 92.

failed to deal with gender issues in the life of the church and society.[50] This was symptomatic of the fact that for so many church leaders and other males engaged in the struggle such issues were regarded as of secondary or peripheral importance. A statement issued by the women delegates at Rustenburg put it clearly. Referring to the fact that the victims of the legacy of apartheid were 'mainly people from the oppressed community, mainly black women' the statement went on to say; 'yet the representation at the Conference reflects the old order of selective justice! . . . While the Conference has grappled with the issues of justice, the humanity of women has been gravely neglected.' All delegates were called on to 'confess and repent of the sin of dehumanising and belittling of women through discriminatory practices'.[51]

Women had long played a key role in the struggle against apartheid. The celebrated Women's March on Pretoria in 1956 in protest against the Pass Laws had set a pattern for subsequent political action, including the protest that led to the massacre at Sharpeville in 1961, and later to the mass action of the 1970s and '80s. Many women members of the churches were involved in these protests and also in the *Black Sash*, a nation-wide organization of white women engaged in the struggle.[52] In many instances women often took the initiative in organizing boycotts against increased rent, electricity, and transport tariffs, and rises in the price of consumer goods. Yet sexism in the church and in the broader society was largely ignored in both the church struggle and the struggle for liberation. Not even the *Kairos Document* referred to the oppression of women or to women's theologies of liberation. Indeed, in previous editions of this book, the role of women in the history of the South African churches and in the struggle against apartheid was not mentioned. That was a serious oversight for which apology, though far too belated, is made. Yet during the period under consideration in this

---

[50] For a critique related to the Rustenburg Conference, see Betty Govinden, 'No Time for Silence: Women, Church and Liberation in Southern Africa', and Sheena Duncan, 'Some Reflections on Rustenburg', in Denise Ackermann, Jonathan A. Draper and Emma Mashinini (eds.), *Women Hold up Half the Sky* (Pietermaritzburg: Cluster, 1991), pp. 274–98, 386–90.

[51] 'Statement by Women Delegates', in Alberts and Chikane (eds.), *Road to Rustenburg*, p. 269.

[52] Denise M. Ackermann, 'Liberating Praxis and the Black Sash: A Feminist Theological Perspective' (PhD dissertation, University of South Africa, 1990).

chapter, women increasingly took the initiative in claiming what was their right within the life of the church and the broader community. Just as black theology had previously reshaped the agenda of the ecumenical church, so now women theologians began to challenge patriarchy in both society and the church. Women's voices began to be heard in new ways, reflecting developments in feminist and womanist theologies in other parts of the world, but always related to the South African context.[53]

Within the church, the focal point became the ordination of women to the priesthood.[54] A few women had been ordained to the ministry in some English-speaking churches as early as the 1930s, but this was unthinkable in the Catholic and Anglican Church as well as the NGK. However, during the 1980s the debate intensified within these churches leading eventually to the decision in 1992 to ordain women in the Anglican Church (CPSA), and shortly after in the NGK. Of course, ordination was only one of a range of issues affecting women in the church that had to be addressed in the struggle for a 'non-sexist' and not only a 'non-racial' church. The problem of the relationship between black and white women in the struggle was particularly acute, as Denise Ackermann so clearly stated:

> In South Africa belonging to the ruling class involves both class and racial distinctions. A white feminist liberation perspective must therefore both seek freedom for *white* women (indeed for all whites) who are trapped in the situation of being oppressors, while at the same time articulating alongside black woman *our* struggle for our liberation from patriarchal oppression.[55]

The connections between the liberation struggle and the struggle for the liberation of women, between the violence that was endemic to apartheid, and the violence that was experienced by women as women, between the struggle for human rights in society and equality in the church, were thus increasingly brought into clear focus by women

---

[53] See the essays in Ackermann, Draper and Mashinini (eds.), *Women.*

[54] See Phoebe Swart-Russell, 'The Ordination of Women to the Priesthood' (PhD dissertation, University of Cape Town, 1988).

[55] Denise Ackermann, 'Feminist Liberation Theology: A Contextual Option', *Journal of Theology for Southern Africa*, no. 62 (March 1988), p. 25.

theologians whose critique of church praxis highlighted the connections between all forms of oppression.[56]

Quite apart from its failure to deal with gender justice, Rustenburg had other shortcomings and compromises which watered down the prophetic demands of some participants.[57] Yet while tensions remained, the Conference moved towards consensus on key issues that had previously polarized the churches, reflected in the declaration that was adopted at its conclusion.[58] These included a confession of guilt for the sins of apartheid, the need to work for justice, especially economic justice, restitution in health, education, housing, employment and especially land ownership, the need for the exclusion of 'racial, gender, class and religious discrimination in the implementation of justice' in the new South Africa; the 'acceptance of the Rule of Law under an independent judiciary'; the 'entrenchment of a Bill of Rights'; and the 'establishment of a democratic elective process based on one-person, one-vote ... in a multi-party democracy in a unitary State'.

The second ecumenical Conference to which we earlier referred was convened by the South African member churches of the WCC, a significant fact if we recall that it was precisely these churches that had convened at Cottesloe 30 years previously under the auspices of the WCC. The Conference met in Cape Town in October 1991, and in its concluding Statement listed five dimensions to the task of the church in the process of democratic transition and transformation.[59] The first was the exposure and eradication of all persisting forms of apartheid, exploitation and discrimination; the second was the liberation of church and society from an obsession with apartheid, to deal with the urgent and life-threatening issues facing the country (poverty, development, education, pollution, AIDS, and technological challenges); the third was to participate in the reconstruction of society on the basis of values

---

[56] See the essays in Ackermann, Draper and Mashinini (eds.), *Women*; Denise Ackermann, Eliza Getman, Hantie Kotzé and Judy Tobler (eds.), *Claiming our Footprints: South African Women Reflect on Context, Identity and Spirituality* (Stellenbosch: EFSA, 2000). See also the increasing number of issues on women's issues and feminist theology in the *Journal of Theology for Southern Africa* from the mid-1980s.

[57] Malusi Mpumlwana, 'The Road to Democracy: The Role of Contextual Theology', opening address to the AGM of the Institute for Contextual Theology, May 1993.

[58] Alberts and Chikane (eds.), *Road to Rustenburg*, pp. 275–86.

[59] 'Cape Town Statement', October 1991, *Journal of Theology for Southern Africa*, no. 77 (December 1991), pp. 84f.

determined by the kingdom of God and in solidarity with others committed to those values; the fourth was to express solidarity with those who suffer in other parts of the world; and the fifth was the need to transform the structures of the churches themselves.

The Statement then went on to challenge the churches to become involved in peace-making and the monitoring of the violence; in working for reconciliation, restitution, reconstruction and justice, including justice for women and the enabling of young people to participate more fully in the democratic process. The Statement also dealt in more detail with specific issues: the need for the churches to be involved in peace-making and the monitoring of violence, and work for reconciliation, restitution, reconstruction and justice, including justice for women; the need to enable young people to participate more fully in the democratic process; a call for a general amnesty for unreleased political prisoners and exiles; the need for sanctions to remain in place until there was agreement on an interim government and a democratic constitution; the need for a more just democratic order; the need for multi-cultural respect and tolerance; and finally, the need for the renewal of the church, its unity and ecumenical solidarity.

The Cape Town Statement was more prophetically focused than the Rustenburg Declaration, reflecting the fact that those involved were more united in their social analysis and their theological convictions. Yet taken together, and also with the many other documents that subsequently emerged on the witness of the church in democratization,[60] they indicate an overwhelming consensus on the need for a genuinely multi-party representative democracy, but one which is economically just, participatory, and fully inclusive. The importance of this role in the process of democratization was widely recognized.

While there has been considerable conflict between Christians in South Africa, there has been very little conflict between believers of different religious communities. Fortunately in the struggle against

---

[60] See, for example, 'Democracy and Voting in South Africa', an information manual, SACC, n.d.; 'Democracy and the Churches', the Pastoral Letter of the South African Catholic Bishops' Conference, April 1993; Dawid Venter (ed.), *Towards a Democratic Future: The Church and the Current Situation* (Johannesburg: Institute for Contextual Theology [ICT], 1993); 'The Road to Democracy' (ICT, May 1993); *Christianity and Democracy*, Lenten Lectures, 1992, published by the Justice and Peace Commissions of the Roman Catholic dioceses of Johannesburg and Cape Town.

apartheid people of different faiths discovered that they shared basic values and concerns even though they differed on matters of faith and doctrine. It was therefore of considerable significance that the South African chapter of the World Conference on Religion and Peace meeting in 1992 in Johannesburg should have produced a Declaration on Religious Rights and Responsibilities, as a result of two years of discussion and consultation among religious groups, and that this should have received such widespread support. For not only did the declaration affirm the freedom of conscience, and the equal rights of religious communities, which are fundamental to any truly democratic society, but it also called on all religious communities to exercise their moral responsibility in society in ways that are essential for the nurturing of a just democracy.[61] Indeed, the freedom of religion was understood not only as the freedom to worship and engage in other religious activities, but also the freedom 'to criticize and challenge all social and political structures and policies in terms of the teachings' of each religion.

The problem of violence as a major stumbling-block en route to a new democratic South Africa was, as we have seen, high on the agenda of all forums in which the role of the church was debated during this period. The fact is, that between February 1990 and the decision by Parliament in September 1993 to establish a transitional executive council in preparation for the first truly democratic election, the country was plunged into a cycle of violence that threatened to tear it apart.[62] The causes of the violence varied from one part of the country to another.[63] But as became evident later during the Truth and Reconciliation Commission, a 'third force' with links to the government and the security forces was directly involved.[64] This harsh reality overshadowed everything else at the time.

---

[61] Declaration on Religious Rights and Responsibilities, adopted by the National Inter-Faith Conference, Pretoria, 22–24 November 1992, under the auspices of the World Conference on Religion and Peace.

[62] For an analysis of the violence, see David Chidester, *Shots in the Streets: Violence and Religion in South Africa* (Cape Town: Oxford University Press, 1992).

[63] See Heribert Adam and Kogila Moodley, *The Negotiated Revolution: Society and Politics in Post-Apartheid South Africa* (Johannesburg: Jonathan Ball, 1993), pp. 121ff.; for a critical response to the response of the government, see the report *South Africa: Half-Hearted Reform* (published by Africa Watch, New York, May 1993).

[64] The Institute for Contextual Study took this position in identifying violence as 'the new kairos'. *Violence: The New Kairos: Challenge to the Churches* (Braamfontein: ICT, n.d).

There was a growing awareness on all sides that unless the escalating violence was stopped, the democratization process itself would prove impossible. Addressing the issue at the beginning of 1992, the Roman Catholic bishops noted that violence was part of the evil heritage of the past. 'Violence', they said, 'was used to impose apartheid and violence was used to resist it. Still today – violence wastes lives, destroys property, separates families and blights our very souls.' They also referred to the alarming extent to which 'people are being attacked and even killed for disagreeing about political parties or ideas'.[65] The situation on the East Rand, near Johannesburg, and in the province of Natal, was particularly disturbing, where clashes between supporters of the ANC and the Inkhata Freedom Party regularly erupted into violence. And the assassination of Chris Hani, leader of the South African Communist Party, by right-wing whites, in March 1993, threatened to plunge the country into chaos which would have made progress towards the planned elections extremely difficult if not impossible.

Many church leaders, congregations and Christian activists played an indispensable role in seeking to deal with the violence, not least through the various National and Regional Peace structures which were established. Methodist Bishops Mmutlanyane Stanley Mogoba and Peter Storey, the General Secretary of the SACC, Frank Chikane and, notably in KwaZulu-Natal, several Anglican bishops led by Michael Nuttal and Catholic Archbishop Hurley, together with Diakonia and PACSA,[66] played key roles in the leadership of these initiatives. The peace-making role of the churches in the Vaal Triangle, to which we have already referred, was also of crucial importance, involving a wide range of denominational lay and clergy participation in dealing with a particularly explosive situation.[67] Without this mediating intervention it is doubtful whether South Africa would have been able to hold its first democratic elections. Indeed, the role of the churches as mediators between conflicting parties became crucial to both the negotiating process and the

---

[65] 'A Call to Build a New South Africa', Pastoral Letter of the South African Catholic Bishops' Conference, January 1992, 2.7.

[66] Diakonia is an ecumenical agency based in Durban, and PACSA one based in Pietermaritzburg. Through this period they spearheaded ecumenical action in dealing with violence and transition to democracy.

[67] See Noonan, *Burning the Churches*.

attempt to deal with the violence.[68] In effect it was this need that plunged the churches once again directly in the political arena.[69] Lines of communication were essential if the conflict was to be managed, and this required mediators who could be trusted. For this reason, the bishops of the Church of the Province (Anglican) decreed in 1990 that no priest should belong to any political party or organization. This controversial decision was not intended as a withdrawal from the political arena, but as a necessary step if the churches were to act in a mediating capacity in situations of conflict, especially in Natal, until normalcy was achieved.

Various churches, ecumenical agencies and other faith community organizations also became involved in extensive voter education programmes in order to prepare the way for free and fair elections with the maximum of informed participation.[70] Along with other churches, the Roman Catholic bishops in South Africa called on their membership 'to be good democrats' by keeping informed 'about political parties and policies' and evaluating them in terms of justice and the teaching of the gospel. They also called on the Catholic community itself to promote democracy by providing 'an example of justice, respect and equality'. The bishops went on to encourage the building of a civil society in a variety of spheres 'without domination by either the market or the state',

---

[68] John Aitchison, 'The Conflict in Natal – Prospects for Democracy', in Klaus Nürnberger (ed.), *A Democratic Vision for South Africa: Political Realism and Christian Responsibility* (Pietermaritzburg: Encounter, 1991), p. 369; Stanley Mogoba, 'The Role of the Church in the Formation of Democratic Assumptions and Behaviour', in Nürnberger (ed.), *Vision*, p. 569.

[69] Ironically, some church leaders who were deeply involved in peace-making efforts were held responsible by some analysts for having sown the seeds of the violence. Rachel Tingle, *Revolution or Reconciliation: The Struggle in the Church in South Africa* (London: Christian Studies Centre, 1992); John Kane-Berman, *Political Violence in South Africa* (Johannesburg: SA Institute of Race Relations, 1993). See the critical response to and rejection of Tingle's argument, 'ICT Replies to Accusations', in *Challenge* (September 1992), pp. 8f.; Brian Brown, 'The Churches and Violence in South Africa', *CCSA Occasional Paper*, no. 1, 1993 (published by Christian Concern for Southern Africa, London).

[70] Sheena Duncan, *The Church's Role in Preparing for Free and Fair Elections* (Durban: Diakonia, 1992); among the many documents being prepared by the churches for use in educating voters, see *Democracy and Voting in South Africa*, an information manual, no. 2, published by the SACC as part of its Education for Democracy Programme. See Frank Chikane, *The Church's Role During a Period of Transition*, an address given on 12 August 1992 (Durban: Diakonia).

and 'to seek to empower the poor and handicapped, the aged and youth, and women from every group'.[71]

There was, it must be acknowledged, a certain malaise in the ecumenical churches during this period of transition. After years of conflict and controversy, there was a sense of relief on the part of many that, at last, it was possible to get back to normalcy, to 'being the church'. While understandable, this attitude reflected a failure to recognize that it was precisely in struggling for justice and reconciliation that the church had in many ways become more truly the church. The challenge now was how to be the ecumenical church in the emerging new South Africa.[72] At a conference in Leeds, England, in 1993, Tutu reflected back on what had happened in the ecumenical church since the heady days of the 'Standing for the Truth' campaign in 1988 and de Klerk's momentous speech in 1989. Whereas previously the ecumenical churches, together with people of other faiths, had been united in standing *against* apartheid, now they were finding it difficult to define what they were *for*.[73] As Charles Villa-Vicencio expressed it: 'The challenge now facing the church is different. The complex options for a new South Africa require more than resistance. The church is obliged to begin the difficult task of saying "Yes" to the unfolding process of what could culminate in a democratic, just and kinder social order.'[74]

Many conservative Christian groups were strongly against South Africa becoming a secular democracy, fearful of losing a previously privileged status and ability to control moral values. But the overall ecumenical consensus was that truly democratic forms of government provide the best means we know for achieving just, equitable and free societies, and therefore societies which best approximate the Christian vision of a just world order. Of course, no political system – including democracy – is perfect and none can be equated with the kingdom of

---

[71] 'A Call to Build a New South Africa', Pastoral Letter of the South African Catholic Bishops' Conference, January 1992, III/13–15; IV/26.

[72] See the discussion in John W. de Gruchy, 'Becoming the Ecumenical Church', in Barney Pityana and Charles Villa-Vicencio (eds.), *Being the Church in South Africa Today* (Johannesburg: SACC, 1995), pp. 12–26.

[73] Desmond Tutu, 'Identity Crisis', in Paul Gifford (ed.), *The Christian Churches and the Democratisation of Africa* (Leiden: E. J. Brill, 1995), pp. 96–7.

[74] Charles Villa-Vicencio, *A Theology of Reconstruction: Nation-Building and Human Rights* (Cambridge: Cambridge University Press, 1992), p. 7.

God.[75] Those in government are fallible human beings, just like those who vote them into power. But insofar as democracy is about human rights, the due process of and equality before the law, the need for truth and accountability in public life, and so forth, then the church can and should be in critical solidarity with the system, ensuring that the system delivers what it promises, and thus keeping those in power accountable.

Throughout sub-Saharan Africa churches had struggled to change gear after de-colonization and liberation, and to continue to exercise a prophetic ministry.[76] This was obviously a particular challenge now for the ecumenical church in South Africa. No one said this more powerfully than the General Secretary of the SACC, Frank Chikane:

> I am calling on the Church that we all stand up and say we will go to prison again, we will die again if any person gets victimised because of colour, or for any other reason that contradicts our commitment to justice. And so our taking sides is vital, and I will go back to cell No. 20 in John Vorster Square if the ANC take over and practise injustices against other people . . . It is important that the Church of Christ say it now – we stood for justice and we will continue to do so in the new era that is coming. Even if we eventually have a legitimate system in South Africa the struggle for the ideals of the reign of God will not stop.[77]

How to exercise critical solidarity would become one of the more problematic issues during the next decade. There was the need, as Barney Pityana put it, for the church to 'keep the flame of justice alight in the new South Africa'. It could not be neutral, but had to become 'the watchdog' directing 'public discourse about policy' and keeping 'South Africans debating their future as it evolves'.[78] Pityana, an Anglican priest,

---

[75] On the relationship between Christianity and democratic transformation, and the role of the Churches in the transition to democracy in South Africa, see John W. de Gruchy, *Christianity and Democracy: A Theology for a Just World Order* (Cambridge: Cambridge University Press, 1995).

[76] Gifford (ed.), *Christian Churches*.

[77] Chikane, 'The Church's Role', p. 6. Chikane later became the Director General in the Office of President Mbeki.

[78] Barney Pityana, 'The Evolution of Democracy in Africa', *Journal of Theology for Southern Africa*, no. 86 (March 1994), p. 13.

became the Director General of the Human Rights Commission that was established soon after the new government came to power.

The Central Committee of the World Council of Churches met in Johannesburg in January 1994. This was the first time that it had met in South Africa, and it provided an opportunity for the ecumenical movement as a whole to reflect on what had been achieved over the long years of engagement in the struggle against apartheid. It also provided the occasion for reflection on what still had to be done to curb the violence and to bring stability to the country. Just as the WCC had been engaged, chiefly through the Programme to Combat Racism, in the struggle to end apartheid, it was now committed to reconstruct a just new South Africa in partnership with its member churches in the country.[79] That same year Ms Brigalia Bam was appointed the first female General Secretary of the SACC in 1994 in succession to Chikane, bringing with her years of ecumenical experience both overseas and in South Africa, quite apart from her own skills, to the task. In an address to a SACC-sponsored conference on 'South Africa in Global and Regional Context' the next year, she reflected on what it meant to be the church at this time of transition in South Africa:

This is a complex time in the history of our land; it is hard to choose priorities. In the days of apartheid we knew *exactly* what we were doing – we were fighting the evil of legalized racism. We now face hidden racism, the need for truth and reconciliation, a demand for housing and jobs, healing and hope . . . We need to ensure that these issues do not paralyse us. Our ancestors who gave so much, sometimes life itself, for the creation of a new South Africa will not let us rest. The faces and voices of the marginalized and hungry people of our land will not allow it.[80]

'We remain prisoners of hope in the service of a loving God', she went on to say, but time 'is catching up with us and there is a new urgency facing the churches of South Africa'.[81]

---

[79] See the WCC Statement on South Africa, adopted by the Central Committee, Johannesburg, 20–28 January 1994, *Journal of Theology for Southern Africa*, no. 86 (March 1994), pp. 88–91.

[80] Brigalia Bam, 'The Church in South Africa', in Pityana and Villa-Vicencio (eds.), *Being the Church*, p. 43.

[81] Bam, 'Church in South Africa', p. 44.

Bam, who had the confidence of Mandela, was a key person in enabling the SACC and its member churches to play a leading role in preparing South Africa for its first free democratic elections in 1994. Indeed, the ecumenical peace monitoring task force established by the SACC, with the help of overseas ecumenical partners, was of considerable importance in this process as part of the wider monitoring task force provided by the United Nations and by the National Peace Committee. As a church-based project it had its own unique and specific contribution to make because of its direct connection to grass-roots communities and their leadership, thus helping to prepare the way for free and fair elections with the maximum of participation.[82] Bam personally played a key role as part of the leadership within the Independent Electoral Commission that oversaw the elections, and would eventually become the Chief Electoral Officer of the Commission.

On 27 April 1994, 20 million South Africans of all races went to the polls for the first truly democratic election in the history of the country. Against all expectations, the election was virtually free of violence. Indeed, the election proved to be a cathartic experience in turning from the past, and a nation-building, consciousness-raising event in turning to the future. With Nelson Mandela as President of the new South Africa the scene was set to build a just, non-racial society based on a Constitution that was widely regarded as one of the most democratic in the world. Instead of a 'rule of law' that oppressed the majority of people, a culture of human rights was being fostered that had far-reaching implications for all sections of the community. But in order to achieve its goals of reconciliation and justice a great deal had to be done to heal the past, to overcome the many dehumanizing legacies of apartheid, and to ensure a sustainable and secure future for all.

---

[82] John Aitchison, 'The Conflict in Natal – Prospects for Democracy', in Nürnberger (ed.), *Vision*, p. 369; Stanley Mogoba, 'The Role of the Church in the Formation of Democratic Assumptions and Behaviour', in Nürnberger (ed.), *Vision*, p. 569.

6

From Church Struggle to Church Struggles

STEVE DE GRUCHY

The tragic irony of the church struggle against apartheid was that an ideology of apartness and exclusion provided the churches in South Africa with a sense of unity and cohesion. As the previous chapters have illustrated, the hegemonic reach and power of the system and its agencies, together with the overwhelmingly black membership of South African churches, meant that they had no option but to be drawn into its ambit and to orientate their life and witness in response to the system. Furthermore, as we have also identified in the earlier chapters, as the anti-Christian character and brutality of the system became increasingly evident the churches were forced, in defence of the very truth of the gospel itself, to devote more and more time to the struggle against apartheid. A high degree of unity of purpose was forged between the churches, coalescing most visibly in the work and witness of the SACC, but also in many other local ecumenical and fraternal networks and organizations.

It is not altogether surprising then that the end of the all-embracing apartheid system would lead on the one hand to the emergence of denominational myopia and internal ecclesial concerns, and on the other hand to a diffusion of focus in regard to the witness of the church in the face of a plethora of concerns in the public arena. On top of this it must also be remembered that the ending of apartheid coincided with the ending of international isolation for the country – both self-imposed and externally enforced – and thus South Africa was thrust into a whole range of global and international concerns with which it previously had little contact and experience. Most noteworthy of such change was the reconnection with the rest of Africa, and the role South Africa could now play regionally and continentally around such concerns as peacekeeping, economic development and the formation of the African Union.

As we consider South Africa's re-insertion into the wider world, we must also consider that this happened at the same time as this wider world experienced a realignment of global geopolitics following the end of the Cold War and the emergence of global tensions between the 'West' and certain Muslim states. Furthermore, the dominance of the neo-liberal economic vision driven by the USA and its partners in the G8, the World Bank, World Trade Organization and the International Monetary Fund, meant that many of the socialist and populist presuppositions of the struggle to end apartheid would be considered 'outdated in the face of reality', and that the global trade regime would have an impact on the socio-economic fabric of a country that through sanctions, divestment and closed markets had developed thorough-going import-substitution practices.

Thus, as the victory over apartheid created a sense of euphoria and closure to a long-range struggle, such an ending created its own new challenges and opportunities for the country and the churches. One of the first and most pressing had to do with national reconciliation.

National Reconciliation: The TRC and the churches

The final clause of the Interim Constitution, approved late in 1993, was entitled 'On National Unity and Reconciliation'. This paved the way for the Truth and Reconciliation Commission, speaking as it did of the need for understanding not revenge, reparation not retaliation, *ubuntu* not victimization. The SACC captured its motivation in these words:

> The Commission for Truth and Reconciliation is not another Nuremberg. It turns its back on any desire for revenge. It represents an extraordinary act of generosity by a people who only insist that the truth, the whole truth and nothing but the truth be told. The space is thereby created where the deeper processes of forgiveness, confession, repentance, reparation and reconciliation can take place.[1]

---

[1] *The Truth Will Set You Free* (SACC Brochure, 1995), p. 24.

The establishment of the TRC was approved during the first session of the new South African Parliament in October 1994. Its mandate was to provide a record of gross human rights violations committed by both the upholders of apartheid and the liberation movements; to identify the victims and their fate; to recommend possible measures of reparation; to process applications for amnesty and indemnity; and to make recommendations with regard to measures necessary to prevent future gross human rights violations.[2]

The SACC had long called on its constituency to acknowledge and confess its own guilt for apartheid and its failure to be more active in combating it. This was the topic at the SACC Soweto Conference on 'Confessing Guilt' in 1989, and it was a major theme at both the Rustenburg Conference and the Cape Town Consultation. There were, moreover, regular calls by the SACC and its member churches for national repentance and reconciliation. So while the ecumenical church cannot take credit for the establishment of the TRC, it helped create and nurture an ecumenical consciousness around the issues.

The work of the TRC began in February 1996 under the chairmanship of Desmond Tutu. His deputy, Alex Boraine, a theologian by training, had at one time been President of the Methodist Church. A large number of the other commissioners were prominent church leaders, a cause of some concern to those who felt that the TRC was too churchly in orientation. Certainly it is true that it would have been a very different institution if Tutu was not in the chair and if its commissioners were not largely Christians. But many regarded the appointment of Tutu by President Mandela as an inspired choice. In any case, as Tinyiko Maluleke has pointed out, the commissioners were appointed not as church representatives, but as people whose credibility was respected and who could represent those who had been engaged in the struggle for liberation.[3] Nonetheless, the language and conceptualization of the TRC was largely Christian, and its mode of operation sometimes resembled a pastoral counselling chamber presided over by a father confessor rather

---

[2] On the formation and work of the TRC see Alex Boraine, *A Country Unmasked: Inside South Africa's Truth and Reconciliation Commission* (New York: Oxford University Press, 2000).

[3] Tinyiko Sam Maluleke, 'Truth, National Unity and Reconciliation in South Africa', in Mongezi Guma and Leslie Milton (eds.), *An African Challenge to the Church in the Twenty-First Century* (Johannesburg: SACC, 1997), p. 115.

than a court of law chaired by a judge.[4] This led cabinet minister Kadar Asmal to refer perceptively to the TRC as a 'civic sacrament'.[5] Certainly all the elements we associate with the sacrament of penance were present in one form or another, from confession of sin and guilt, through absolution and amnesty, to penance or reparation.

Apartheid had not been conceived and implemented only by the National Party Government and its agencies; there were many other groups that had supported the policy and, at the very least, benefited from it. With this in mind the TRC, towards the end of its work, invited various constituencies, including the churches and other faith communities, to attend special hearings, to give an account of their role during the apartheid era, and to indicate how they planned to contribute to the building of a reconciled and just nation. A wide range of Christian denominations and other religious communities responded to the invitation to participate in the three-day 'Faith Community Hearings' that were held in East London in November 1997.

From the outset of the hearings it was clear that a great deal of soul-searching had already begun among some of the churches.[6] Some, notably the NGK, acknowledged that they had given legitimacy to apartheid; others, like many of the evangelical and Pentecostal denominations, confessed that they had tried to be neutral instead of taking a stand, acknowledging the fault of their position. The member churches of the South African Council of Churches, who had generally opposed apartheid, confessed to the TRC that they were nonetheless, in varying ways and to varying degrees, guilty. Whatever their criticisms of the ideology of apartheid and its implementation, they had not done as much as they should have to combat it. Church leaders confessed that

---

[4] For an extensive discussion of the TRC from a theological perspective, see John W. de Gruchy, *Reconciliation: Restoring Justice* (London: SCM Press, 2002).

[5] Kadar Asmal, Louise Asmal and Ronald Suresh Roberts, *Reconciliation through Truth* (Cape Town: David Philip, 1996), p. 49.

[6] See John W. de Gruchy, James C. Cochrane and Stephen Martin (eds.), *Facing the Truth: South African Faith Communities and the Truth and Reconciliation Commission* (Cape Town: David Philip, 1999); for a personal account by one of the TRC Commissioners and a NGK theologian, see Piet Meiring, *Chronicle of the Truth Commission* (Vanderbijlpark, RSA: Carpe Diem, 1999), pp. 265ff. 'Declaration on Religious Rights and Responsibilities', adopted by the National Inter-Faith Conference, Pretoria, 22–24 November 1992, under the auspices of the World Conference on Religion and Peace.

too many of their members had connived with apartheid, and some had been among those who had perpetrated atrocious crimes. Hence a major emphasis in their statements was that of penitence for past failure, and a commitment to work for national reconciliation and justice in the future.

At the same time it was acknowledged that certain churches, church leaders, and many Christians played major roles in the liberation struggle. Moreover, in so far as the majority of Christians in South Africa are black, many of the victims of apartheid were Christian, and many local church communities suffered at the hands of the regime. This connection between the victims and Christianity was often evident during the TRC when those present, encouraged from the chair, sang hymns or offered prayers – a matter of some concern to those of others faiths. But the representations made to the TRC highlight the extent to which, more than any other faith community, the Christian churches represented the broad spectrum of South African society. Victims, benefactors and perpetrators were members together in the churches, an indication of both the failure of the church to be a community of reconciliation, but also of its potential to help bring about national reconciliation and restore justice in reconstructing South Africa.

Several pledges or commitments were made in this regard. The first was a willingness to engage in the public task of reconciliation and not simply regard reconciliation as a private matter between individuals. A second was a willingness to make use of their resources in working to restore justice. For example, some churches who owned large tracts of land that they obtained for mission work during the colonial period indicated their willingness to engage in land redistribution and development programmes. A third was in terms of liturgical practice. During the struggle years, liturgies of resistance as well as confession emerged that were important in raising the consciousness of congregations. Now some churches indicated that they would seek to ensure that the issues facing the church and nation at this time would also inform their worship. A fourth was speaking out prophetically on issues such as poverty. And a fifth was a commitment to becoming more engaged in the moral reconstruction of the nation.

The work of the TRC would only finally came to an end in 2003. Whether South Africa is a more reconciled nation as a result of its work is a contested issue.[7] Obviously it could not and did not fulfil all the hopes of those who long for justice and peace in South Africa. But its mandate was not to achieve reconciliation; its mandate was to promote reconciliation and serve as a catalyst for what must of necessity be a long-term process. So the question is not whether the TRC succeeded, but whether the government and the country as a whole made the most of the opportunity. In this regard, the expectation of many that reparations would be forthcoming in the short term was not met by the state, leading to a disillusionment and impatience with the process. Some victims of apartheid also felt that too many perpetrators of crimes were given amnesty too readily. All of this is true, and it led some church leaders to criticize the tardiness of government in not following through speedily enough on the recommendations of the TRC. Yet national reconciliation is a huge project and a long-term process of restoring justice. The transformation of education, health services, and every other aspect of public life in such a way that justice and equity is achieved, is essential if justice is to be a reality, and the churches at the TRC hearings indicated that they would want to be involved in this process in whatever way is appropriate.

It is to the credit of the SACC that it has sought to provide leadership for the churches around these new challenges. In 1995 a joint consultation with the World Council of Churches was held at Vanderbijlpark, near Johannesburg, and a follow-up conference was held a year later. The papers at these conferences were published in two books, and are an important pointer to the issues that were on the agenda at that stage, and that still confront the church ten years later. These include locating the South African church in the global and regional context, rethinking church and state relations, human values, culture, ethnicity, race and gender and national security and the global arms trade;[8] and African culture, the land, morality, values, reconciliation and koinonia.[9] Sadly, however, planned follow-up strategies have not materialized, and the SACC has itself had to struggle for its own existence in the face of budget cuts, and the changed political and ecclesial landscape. One of these key

---

[7] For responses to this question from religious leaders see Audrey R. Chapman and Bernard Spong (eds.), *Religion and Reconciliation in South Africa: Voices of Religious Leaders* (Philadelphia: Templeton Foundation; Pietermaritzburg: Cluster, 2003).

[8] See Barney Pityana and Charles Villa-Vicencio (eds.), *Being the Church in South Africa Today* (Johannesburg: SACC, 1995).

[9] See Guma and Milton (eds.), *African Challenge.*

changes has been the growing diversity of the churches in South Africa whose voices now demand public attention. The fact is that the face of the church in South Africa has changed dramatically over the past decade. The perspectives of the churches that led the struggle against apartheid, led largely by the SACC, are now challenged by the voices of charismatic, independent, Pentecostal and indigenous churches who have a growing hold on TV, radio, and bookshops, and who are making inroads into the membership of the 'mainline' churches. This has an obvious effect upon the coherent witness of the church, the loss of an 'institutional memory' that the ecumenical witness against apartheid provided, and the depth of theological vision that is needed to respond to the new challenges.

Thus in 2004, as the nation had closed the chapter of the TRC and celebrated the tenth anniversary of the victory over apartheid with a great deal of pride and satisfaction over what had been achieved under the ANC-led government, all citizens were conscious that there yet remained a range of challenges that face the nation, and by implication those churches that had helped the demise of apartheid. It is helpful perhaps to think of this as a shift from the one church struggle to many church struggles. This chapter does not have the benefit of hindsight, and so time will yet tell as to whether our analysis is correct, but we can suggest four significant and interlocking challenges that have emerged for the church in South Africa at the start of the twenty-first century: the livelihoods of the poor; human sexuality and gender justice; the impact of pluralism; and the effects of globalization. We turn now to each of these, not to provide an exhaustive analysis but to sketch some broad contours of these key struggles that are likely to dominate the work of the churches in South Africa in the coming decades, fully aware that we are dealing now with a highly fragmented witness.

Concerns for the Livelihoods of the Poor

Apartheid placed a profound burden upon people's livelihoods by controlling their access to resources such as land and water, determining where and when they could use their labour, manipulating their health and education, and severely undermining the freedoms that are necessary to live a life that one would choose to live. The struggle to end apartheid was thus not only a moral struggle (shaped, as we have seen, by Christian convictions) for good government, but also a human struggle for survival driven by the desire to build homes and communities in which people could flourish. This hope for a 'time-after-apartheid' – articulated by many in the churches as an anticipation of the kingdom of God – provided the energy for perseverance in the dark night of despair. Indeed, it is precisely on such hopes that liberation struggles are fought and won.

However, in retrospect, it was somewhat naïve to believe that the demise of apartheid would of itself generate the range of assets and human capabilities that are required if livelihoods are to be sustainable. The end of apartheid was absolutely necessary but not sufficient in itself to provide the wherewithal for people to live in the kind of society envisioned in the midst of the struggle and articulated in such a document as the *Freedom Charter* of the ANC of 1955.[10] The post-apartheid state thus continues to be faced, in an acute sense, by the challenge of the livelihoods of the poor around such issues as unemployment, poverty, disease, poor housing, poor education, food security, access to land, and access to water. Each one of these is of major concern; but taken together they represent an 'axis of evil' that terrorizes the lives of many South Africans and that therefore constitutes a key element in the ongoing church struggles in this country.

It is not just the gap between reality and desire that contributes to this livelihoods crisis; but it is shaped by two other vital issues – one rooted in the past, and the other a dramatically new factor. In the first instance, as apartheid became isolated and undermined ideologically by the churches, the link between this ideology and the historical-material base upon which it fed was often forgotten. Apartheid, with its ideological and state apparatus was certainly a 'thing in itself', but it was, nevertheless, a particular manifestation of colonialism, a perfected version of those power relations between Europe and Africa that had been shaped in the horrors of slavery, honed in the extraction of natural and mineral wealth, and perfected in the arrogance of empire. In other words the end of apartheid did not mean the end of colonial power relations, or more

---

[10] The text of the *Freedom Charter* can be found at <www.anc.org.za/ancdocs/ history/charter.html>.

precisely, the power relationships that had been established in the colonial era along racially discriminative lines.

This is illustrated in matters to do with the lack of access that black citizens still have to such livelihood factors as education, health care, decent housing, and start-up capital; but it is perhaps nowhere as clearly and emotionally articulated as in terms of access to land. Patterns of land ownership that were laid down long before the advent of apartheid – in terms of the policies and practices of the Boer Trekkers and then the Boer republics, and of the British colonies, and then the two Land Acts of the Union of South Africa (1913 and 1936) – were not undone by the collapse of apartheid. Thus a fundamental element that could aid the livelihoods of the poor, both in terms of a productive asset and an emotional resource, remains unresolved. As the situations in Zimbabwe and Namibia make clear, this issue is a time-bomb that demands resolution and the attention of the churches, not the least because – taken together – the churches own a large amount of land in South Africa.

The land issue is therefore one of the fundamental issues that the post-apartheid government has had to face, but it has had to do so under two constrains. First, the Bill of Rights in the new Constitution – which was agreed to in the negotiations around the political transition with the National Party – protects private property rights. This means that the 'willing seller, willing buyer' principle has had to be the cornerstone of its policy, and this has made whole-scale land restitution and redistribution impossible even where the land was clearly 'stolen' through apartheid laws. And second, the political decision was taken by the ANC itself to use the 1913 Land Act as the time limit for land restitution. This means that land ownership established prior to the Union of South Africa in 1910, during the period of the Boer republics and the British colonies, and which laid the foundations for black land dispossession, was not under scrutiny. Through the Restitution of Land Rights Act of 1994, and a number of other policies to do with land redistribution, home-ownership subsidies and security of tenure, the state has sought to deal with this issue.[11] However, ten years after the ANC has come to power the land issue remains unresolved, possibly because of these two significant constraints, but also because of bureaucratic inefficiencies in

---

[11] See Gcobani G. M. Vika, 'Land Reform and Development in Post-Apartheid South Africa', *Journal of Theology for Southern Africa*, vol. 110 (July 2001).

the administration of the Act. The emergence of the Landless People's Movement (LPM), a social movement to the left of the government, as a network connecting a range of angry, poor, rural communities, is a reminder to the government of the seriousness of the matter.

From the Church's point of view, the SACC and the National Land Committee jointly hosted a national conference on church land in November 1997, drawing together a range of role-players, to develop a policy for the utilization of church-owned land.[12] The work of the Church Land Programme has taken forward this concern, and has sought to help the churches in South Africa respond in an adequate way both to their own land and to the wider land issue.[13] The issue itself has generated some important theological reflection in which black theologians have made significant contributions, particularly pointing to the way in which the political compromises that led to the new South Africa of 1994 legitimized the white colonial dispossession of the land from blacks.[14] Takatso Mofokeng puts it like this:

A brutal dispossession of African land has been legitimized and legalized in Codesa agreements.[15] This means that a white theology that attributes the criminal act of dispossession to God viz. that God gave them land, has been given State sanction. In this regard instead of calling that violent dispossession a *sin*, it has been turned into God's *blessing*. This further means that our dispossession has been turned into God's act of punishment which Africans have to painfully accept . . .

We also have to conclude that socially speaking, a Black Theology of land that is developed on the basis of the fundamental illegitimacy

---

[12] See David Gillan, *Church, Land and Poverty: Community Struggles, Land Reform and the Policy Framework on Church Land* (Johannesburg: SACC and National Land Committee, 1998).

[13] See the issue of the *Bulletin for Contextual Theology* on church and land, vol. 5.3 (September 1998). See especially the essay by Graham Philpott and Phumani Zondi, 'Church Land: A Strategic Resource in the War against Poverty'.

[14] See, for example, Takatso Mofokeng, 'Land is our Mother: A Black Theology of the Land', and Itumeleng Mosala, 'Ownership or Non-Ownership of Land', both in Guma and Milton (eds.), *African Challenge*. See also, Tinyiko Maluleke, 'The Land of the Church of the Land: A Response to the Whole Issue', *Bulletin for Contextual Theology*, vol. 5.3 (September 1998).

[15] The Codesa conferences were those that set in motion the process that led to the democratic elections of 1994.

and sinfulness of dispossession, has to oppose the political compromise that provided the basis for legalization of the sin of land dispossession. That compromise is a sin because it legalized a sinful act of land dispossession. It is also a sin because it legalized the creation of a perpetual state of poverty and loss of culture and identity of the African people. It laid the political basis for the development of a heretical theology of land . . .[16]

While the land issue predates apartheid, and yet now outlives the death of apartheid, the tragic awfulness of the HIV/AIDS pandemic is that it has newly arisen like a demonic spirit from the funeral pyre of apartheid, as if to taunt and terrorize us in our moment of joy. For indeed, while the task of 'reconstruction and development' after 46 years of National Party rule was always going to be massive given the issues we have noted above, the impact of HIV/AIDS on the livelihoods of the poor could make it well-nigh impossible.

Because of the nature of the pandemic, facts and figures are constantly changing, and between the writing of this text and its being published, the data will have changed yet again. Nevertheless, a *Special Report on a Decade of Democracy – HIV/AIDS* (published in April 2004 by the UN Office for the Coordination for Humanitarian Affairs) describes the situation as follows:

By the end of 2002, an estimated 5.3 million South Africans, in a population of more than 42 million, were infected with the virus.

As a result of HIV/AIDS, the South African Bureau for Economic Research predicted in 2001 that growth would decrease by half a percent for each year though to 2015, production costs could rise by up to 2.3 percent annually, and prime interest rates could increase to 2.9 percent per year between 2002 and 2015.

According to the Bureau, by 2015, South Africa's total labour force would decrease by 21 percent, including a 16.8 percent decline in highly skilled workers, a 19.3 percent drop in skilled workers and a 22.2 percent decrease in semi-skilled and unskilled workers.

Not only the work force is being affected: a recent survey revealed that one in every five young South Africans aged between 15 and

---

[16] Mofokeng, 'Land is our Mother', p. 53.

24 are infected, with the epidemic disproportionately affecting women.

The study, conducted by the University of the Witwatersrand's Reproductive Health Research Unity, found that nearly one in four women aged 20 to 24 were testing HIV positive, compared to one in 14 men of the same age. By the age of 22, one in four South African women has HIV.[17]

The challenge of AIDS is more than just a livelihoods challenge to the church, of course. It raises a whole range of theological issues to do with sexual ethics, patriarchy, stigma, suffering, exclusion, care, death and bereavement, issues to which the church brings an array of resources and energies. Yet, as children find themselves uncared for by sick parents and then orphaned, as young people start becoming unwell and drain scarce resources on medical care, and as breadwinners are buried leaving their impoverished families with funeral debts to cover, the impact that AIDS has and will continue to have on the livelihoods of the poor over the next generations is almost too staggering to contemplate. Together with the colonial imbalance of land it conspires to place the livelihoods of the poor near the top of the agenda for the church in post-apartheid South Africa.

It is difficult to get an overall picture of the response of the churches in South Africa to the AIDS crisis. As in the struggle against apartheid, it is clear that while the leadership structures in the churches have issued the necessary statements and pastoral letters, the actual involvement of local congregations in responding to the pandemic varies enormously. There are some inspiring stories about local churches and Christian organizations that have established care centres and clinics, home-based care programmes, and interventions for orphans and vulnerable children. Theologians have begun to think and write about the pandemic, and there have been concerns to integrate the issue into the theological curriculum in seminaries and universities.[18] Yet alongside this it is just as clear that many Christians and local congregations are steering away

---

[17] The report is published on the PlusNews web page, an HIV/AIDS information service for sub-Saharan Africa, run by the Integrated Regional Information Network (IRIN), a news service that forms part of the UN Office for the Coordination of Humanitarian Affairs. See <www.plusnews.org/AIDSreport>.

[18] See, for example, Ronald Nicolson, *God in AIDS?* (London: SCM Press, 1996).

from the crisis. As we shall note below, the link between AIDS and sex, alongside the longstanding Christian link between sex and sin, has bedeviled the response of the church and Christians to the pandemic. Issues of exclusion, stigma, silence and fear have meant that even those who are concerned are not quite sure how to respond. The debates in the Roman Catholic Church in South Africa over the use of condoms have shown just how difficult it is to think about the crisis in terms of the inherited moral categories to do with sexuality.[19]

It is clear, however, that the sheer size of the crisis and the social impact that it is having and will continue to have in the coming decades seems to dwarf the responses of the churches. Like apartheid, the crisis is of national, regional and international proportions, and it requires a wider co-ordinated response that involves the state as a key leader. Yet, for some strange reasons the ANC government has been extremely unwilling to provide leadership in the struggle against AIDS, a fact that has confounded many ordinary South Africans, as well as many in the churches. President Thabo Mbeki and his Health Minister, Dr Manto Tshabalala-Msimang, have played a reactionary and obfuscating role in the whole process by giving undue attention to fringe AIDS dissidents, questioning the link between HIV and AIDS, undermining the seriousness of the pandemic in a range of public statements, vilifying those who opposed their position, and slowing down the government's provision of antiretrovirals.

In a scene rather reminiscent of the struggle against apartheid, a social movement called the Treatment Action Campaign (TAC) was established to mobilize public pressure to persuade the government to change its mind. Once again, and far earlier than anyone could have predicted, the churches found themselves joining together with this movement, alongside trade unions, health organizations, scientific bodies and other political parties, to confront the state on the matter. The Anglican Archbishop of Cape Town and successor to Desmond Tutu, Njongonkulu Ndungane, has played a crucial role in supporting the social movement and in leading the church challenge to the state on this

---

[19] *A Message of Hope from the Catholic Bishops to the People of God in South Africa, Botswana and Swaziland,* the South African Catholic Bishops' Conference, Pretoria, July 2001. See the critique of this document on the issue of condoms by Philippe Denis, a Dominican theologian, and AIDS activist: 'Sexuality and AIDS in South Africa', *Journal of Theology for Southern Africa,* vol. 115 (March 2003).

matter.[20] In a very similar manner to the struggle against apartheid, it is the church's grassroots presence and ministry among those who are suffering, dying and grieving that gives it the courage and conviction to speak prophetically. Even in a democratic South Africa, it is a calling that it cannot evade.

Issues of Human Sexuality and Gender Justice

Given the fact that the HI virus that causes AIDS is transmitted predominantly through unprotected sexual intercourse, it is true to say that the AIDS crisis is part of a crisis to do with human sexuality. The good gift of sexuality, which Christians believe God has given to men and women so that we may participate in the creation of life, is now also a prime instrument of death. One would therefore think that the churches would turn with all haste to consider responsibly the matter of human sexuality. Yet, as we have just noted, the taboos, stigma, and incoherence around precisely this area that have characterized the responses of many churches and individual Christians to the pandemic suggest that, along with anything else one may say about AIDS, it certainly points to a deep inability on the part of the churches to face up to matters to do with human sexuality. In a number of key ways that go beyond just the question of morality – to the issue of the power relations between men and women – this is one of the fundamental church struggles that we now face.

We must start, however, with the issue of sexual morality. In the past 200 years South Africa has witnessed the collapse of two hegemonic sexual ethical systems. In the first instance, colonial conquest, missionary teaching and migratory labour destroyed the sexual ethical system of traditional African culture. At the same time that this former system was collapsing, the colonial powers introduced a conservative sexual ethical mix of dour Dutch Calvinism, British missionary piety and up-right Victorianism. The break-up of this second system seems to have been coterminous with the end of apartheid and our re-entry into the global

---

[20] See 'All African Anglican Conference on HIV/AIDS: Anglican Archbishop Ndungane Opens All-Africa HIV/AIDS Workshop' at <www.anglicancommunion.org/acns/acnsarchive/acns2575/acns2584.html>; and 'Statement Issued by Anglican Archbishop Njongonkulu Ndungane at Bishopscourt, Cape Town on 17 July 2002' at <www.anglicancommunion.org/acns/articles/30/50/acns3064.html>.

world. Whether or not these ethical systems did actually command the allegiance of the majority of the country is perhaps debatable; but what is not debatable is that neither shapes the contours of public discourse any longer. From television through to pop songs, movies through to magazines, escort agencies through to adult gift shops, on matters of public sexuality the new South Africa is a remarkably different place to its predecessor. Yet there has been almost no theological engagement with the implications of such a change from the churches that led the struggle against apartheid.[21]

It is possible that African cultural constraints around the public discussion of sexuality, or the dominance in the public domain around issues of sexuality by conservative evangelical and Pentecostal churches has shaped this silence; just as it is possible that the broader commitment to freedom and a culture of human rights within the framework of a secular state, a commitment in which the language of censorship seems out of place, means that the mainline churches are uncertain of their contribution on this matter. Thus discussions about the legalization of prostitution, or the promotion of condoms in the fight against AIDS, are invariably characterized by knee-jerk reactions in which the church is unable to speak with the criticality and coherence that it did in the struggle against apartheid.

In the light of this, Philippe Denis points to the need for the church to think through sexual ethics in a coherent way if it is going to make any contribution to the AIDS pandemic:

> To change sexual behaviour, one has to talk about it. If those who indulge in high risk activities feel that they are being judged by their families, their teachers, the members of their churches, they will keep silent and will continue to indulge in sex, as before. AIDS touches on the most intimate area of human existence, sexuality. Sexual behaviour – and leading on from that, relationships between men and women – will only change for the better when sexual questions are discussed freely in an atmosphere of respect for each other and with an understanding of the local culture.[22]

---

[21] See Paul Germond, 'Sex in a Globalizing World: The South African Churches and the Crisis of Sexuality', *Journal of Theology for Southern Africa*, vol. 199 (July 2004).

[22] Denis, 'Sexuality and AIDS', p. 75.

However, as Denis himself notes, the AIDS crisis makes it clear that the issue of human sexuality is not just about sexual morality. It points to the deeper social construction of the relationships between men and women in society, to what are known as gender relations.

The links between the struggle against racism, and the struggle against sexism or patriarchy were explicitly made during the struggle against apartheid; and yet while the former has had some measures of success, the latter continues to remain high on the agenda. There is, in the first instance, a deep-seated relationship between the injustice of apartheid and the injustice of patriarchy that is etched in the lives of poor black women who continue to be excluded from the fruits of democracy by the triple prejudice to do with race, sex and class. A report on the extent of poverty in South Africa commissioned by the office of the Reconstruction and Development Programme (RDP) in 1995 made it clear that women-headed households are the poorest in the country. Drawing attention to this feminization of poverty over the past decades, Beverley Haddad notes that 41 per cent of all African households are headed by women:

> yet customary law severely limits land and inheritance rights of women, resulting in land often being handed over to male relatives on the death of a husband in rural areas. The apartheid legacy has further entrenched poverty into the lives of women by denying them formal education with the literacy rate estimated to be a mere 50% in rural areas. Health services for women, which are crucial to their survival, have been totally inadequate in poor communities. In assessing the leading causes of death amongst women, it is asserted that 'the single largest official category of causes of death is simply called "ill-defined causes", probably because so many women have no access to formal health care and their diseases are never diagnosed, let alone treated'.[23]

Haddad goes on to point out that even though the ANC government is committed to a non-sexist society, and has entrenched gender equality in the new Constitution, their macro-economic policy, known as the Growth, Employment and Redistribution Strategy, or GEAR, 'appears

---

[23] Beverley Haddad, 'Theologising Development: A Gendered Analysis of Poverty, Survival and Faith', *Journal of Theology for Southern Africa*, vol. 110 (July 2001), p. 9.

to be making little difference to the material quality of life of poor women who constitute a major proportion of the South African population'.[24] In a later essay, she has pointed to the way that poverty, racism and gender injustice contribute to make poor African women the most vulnerable to the AIDS pandemic, and how this in turn reinforces their poverty and marginalization.[25]

Given the experiences of injustice, exclusion and violence that many women in South Africa face *because they are women*, the search for gender justice is an absolutely crucial task for South Africa today, and for the church in this country. This search is of course rooted in the biblical vision of human rights and the provision of justice for all citizens, matters about which the church usually speaks openly and clearly. But, because gender justice is so entwined with our social construction of what it means to be male and female, and this in turn is rooted in our cultural understandings of sexuality, the incapacity of the church to deal with human sexuality in anything other than a patriarchal mindset has a mystifying effect upon this demand for justice. As Maluleke and Nadar put it:

By and large, experience, religion, culture and gender socialization would have us believe that the place of women in society is established and that violence against them is normal, even though sometimes regrettable. It is the chief function of the covenant of death to maintain and suggest that violence against women is inevitable, necessary, and normal. This is the societal conclusion presented as an established reality in terms of which all – men and women – are supposed to live.[26]

Thus human rights discourse collides with patriarchal cultural convictions buttressed by a wilfully selective reading of the Bible, in such a way that the voice of the church is awfully and awe-fully silent on matters of domestic abuse, rape, and the transmission of AIDS to faithful wives;[27] as

---

[24] Haddad, 'Theologising Development', p. 12.

[25] See Beverley Haddad, 'Gender Violence and HIV/AIDS: A Deadly Silence in the Church', *Journal of Theology for Southern Africa*, vol. 115 (November 2002).

[26] Tinyiko Maluleke and Sarojin Nadar, 'Breaking the Covenant of Violence against Women', *Journal of Theology for Southern Africa*, vol. 114 (November 2002), p. 15.

[27] See the special issue, 'Overcoming Violence against Women and Children', *Journal of Theology for Southern Africa*, vol. 114 (November 2002).

well as women's access to education, health care, land, and financial resources.

One of the significant reasons for this silence obviously lies in the fact that the church in South Africa is itself rooted in patriarchal structures of authority and control, and its leadership is overwhelmingly male. As more and more women have studied theology and gained the necessary recognition for ordination in their churches, however, a clearer and more strident voice is emerging on these matters. Importantly, women in leadership positions in church and theology often work closely with the insights and perspectives of poor women, so that the church's theology will be informed by the faith and convictions of those women who have survived the worst that society could inflict upon them. It is abundantly clear then that the struggle against patriarchy is a vital challenge for the church, and will require of the church a greater maturity in dealing with matters of human sexuality within the framework of human rights.

An even sharper tension between issues of human sexuality and human rights that throws into bold relief the church's struggle to navigate between the two has to do with homophobia, homosexuality and the rights of gay and lesbian people. There are some who feel that this entire 'gay-rights agenda' has been foisted on to Africa by the 'decadent West', and is to be rejected as a sign of just how degenerate and ungodly people have become in such societies. There are others, however, like Archbishop Desmond Tutu for example, who see the continuities between the struggle against apartheid and the struggle against a similar theology that justifies apartness on the basis of sexual orientation. It is difficult to gauge just how significant the debates on these matters will be in the years to come; but what is clear at this point is that they are so passionate and intense because they trigger off crucial issues to do with the interpretation of the Bible; the relationship between nature, grace and sanctification; the role and place of culture; compassion for 'outsiders' and 'aliens'; the insights of science and psychology; the faith and witness of gay and lesbian Christians; the significance of marriage, family and children; and the protection of human rights for all citizens in a secular society.[28] These are not minor matters!

Just as the church has had to learn to listen to, appreciate and be

---

[28] See Paul Germond and Steve de Gruchy (eds.), *Aliens in the Household of God: Homosexuality and Christian Faith in South Africa* (Cape Town: David Philip, 1997).

guided by the insights of black Christians, pastors and theologians on matters of racism and apartheid; and just as it is learning to be guided by women Christians, pastors and theologians on matters of patriarchy and gender justice; so it is faced with the challenge of talking with and being shaped by the insights and faith of homosexual Christians, pastors and theologians – rather than just objectifying them as a problem to be talked about. Yet, because of the confused and confusing way in which human sexuality is theologized about in South Africa, this is an extremely tough task for it seems that where issues of human sexuality are raised, the churches find it difficult to think in terms of human rights. The church is in a difficult position in trying to find its way through these entangled concerns, a difficulty that to some extent is part of the legacy of its struggle against apartheid. That struggle was so all-absorbing and vital to the very witness of the gospel, that it was almost unethical to spend time reflecting on the ethics of human sexuality. Now, however, the reverse would seem to be the case.

The Reality of Pluralism in a Secular State

Our discussion of the interrelationship between human sexuality and human rights in regard to homosexuality points to a key characteristic of the changing context in which the church lives in South Africa today, namely, the reality of pluralism in a secular state; one in which human rights discourse has replaced a particular form of 'Christian' moralism, so that the rights of gays and lesbians are now protected by the South African constitution. Indeed, the most dramatic religious change in post-apartheid South Africa, and the one that has had perhaps the greatest effect upon the public life of the churches, is the recognition by the state and civil-society of the obvious religious plurality of South African life, and therefore the need to base its ethico-legal framework on more than just one privileged religious tradition. The constitution of the Republic of South Africa from 1961 to 1994 had made it clear that South Africa was officially a Christian state, and the Christian faith accordingly enjoyed great favour in national life. The post-apartheid constitution, however, is clear that South Africa is a secular state with no intention to promote any one religion against another.

The first census in the democratic era (1996) identified the relative strengths of various faith communities in South Africa thus:[29]

Christian	74.1%	(30,058,742)
No religion/unstated	18.3%	(7,418,420)
Other	4.8%	(1,947, 406)
Muslim	1.4%	(553,583)
Hindu	1.3%	(537,428)
Jewish	0.2%	(68,060)
Total	100%	(40,583,639)

While the dominance of Christianity is clear, from a legal and political perspective, religious pluralism is acknowledged and affirmed so that Parliament, for example, no longer opens with Christian prayers, but with prayers from a range of religious traditions. This ritual was powerfully introduced in the public ceremony that accompanied the inauguration of Nelson Mandela as the first President of democratic South Africa.

One of the most contested areas in which this shift towards acknowledging religious pluralism in a secular state has taken place has been in the education system, where public schools are no longer allowed to 'teach' or promote the Christian faith to the detriment of others, but are rather to teach 'religion education' as a way of inculcating an attitude of respect and appreciation for the various religions that make up the fabric of South Africa. A second important contested area has been with regards to the multi-faith approach of religious public broadcasting on radio and TV which is in stark contrast to what occurred under the apartheid system.

The polarized response from churches and other Christian bodies to these policies of the state around religion is one of the ways that the growing diversity of the public voice of the church in South Africa is being expressed. Churches from the conservative evangelical and Pentecostal traditions (and to some extent conservative elements in the mainline denominations) tend to see *pluralism itself* as the problem, and

---

[29] The statistical data for this section of the chapter comes from Jurgens Hendriks and Johannes Erasmus, 'Interpreting the New Religious Landscape in Post-Apartheid South Africa', *Journal of Theology for Southern Africa*, vol. 109 (March 2001) pp. 41–65. See also the appendix of this book.

so see the new struggle in the post-apartheid state as focused on keeping South African society 'Christian'. They oppose the policies of the state on the grounds either that as the South African population is overwhelmingly Christian it should not receive equal footing with what are really minority-supported religions, or simply that the self-evident 'truth' of Christianity means that it should be treated as the one and only religion worthy of respect from the state. They argue that the loss of Christian hegemony and the public authority of the Bible is simply the precursor to ungodly policies on abortion, capital punishment, prostitution, and homosexuality; and the nation will therefore stand under God's judgment. Such sentiments have found a political voice in the African Christian Democratic Party (ACDP), which has sought to impose conservative – almost fundamentalist – Christian morality on to the political landscape of South Africa.[30] While this party was superconfident prior to the 2004 general election, only 1.6 per cent of the electorate responded to its vision.

On the other hand, those churches that took a leading role in the struggle against apartheid tend to take a more positive approach to living in a pluralist society. Some Christians are conscious of the fact that Christianity has been burdened by its close association with the discredited apartheid regime, and that this is a time for humility rather than for demanding favoured status; some believe in principle that it is a bad thing for the Christian faith to be closely allied to any government or nation, and that a secular state provides more genuine opportunities for witness; and some recognize with respect and appreciation that many who fought side by side with Christians to get rid of apartheid – and are involved in contemporary struggles in support of the livelihoods of the poor, in the struggle of land or against AIDS, for example – are faithful adherents of other faiths (and of none).

For a range of reasons, then, it would seem that the wish to 'Christianize' the post-apartheid state is misguided. To make such a change now would mean to change the constitution, and the indications are clear that this would require such a political and ideological about-face from the dominant majority, that it simply will not happen. The voting statistics in the 2004 election suggest, in any case, that a high percentage of South African Christians must have voted for the ANC,

---

[30] For information on the ACDP see <www.acdp.org.za>.

and therefore are comfortable with its pluralist approach to religion in the country (or at least do not see it as a big enough issue to register their opposition). The ongoing pestering for such a 'Christianizing', thus seems to be to the detriment of a respectful and adult Christian contribution to the building of a democratic state with a constitution that upholds human rights, and respects diversity. For this must mean that Islam, Hinduism, Judaism and African Traditional Religion (along with other numerically smaller faiths) are respected and provided with the public space to practise and promote their religious beliefs and practices.

Alongside the growing public prominence of other religions, the public affirmation of religious pluralism and the loss of the hegemony enjoyed by settler- and missionary-initiated churches has also created the space for the public emergence of the African Initiated Churches (AICs) in South Africa since 1994. As we noted above, membership of this group is rising. The 1996 census, which is the last one available to us, enables us to divide the Churches into five main categories with their membership as follows:

• African independent	10.66 mil (35.4% of Christians)
• Mainline ('English-speaking', Lutheran and Roman Catholic)	10.65 mil (34.8%)
• Dutch Reformed (predominantly Afrikaans-speaking)	3.91 mil (13%)
• Pentecostal	2.69 mil (8.9%)
• Other	2.14 mil (7.1%)

On this categorization, by 1996 the AICs had the largest membership, fractionally more than the mainline (English-speaking) churches, although quite a bit less if the Afrikaans Reformed Churches are included with the mainline churches. However, when the figures for black South Africans are examined, it is found that slightly more black people are members of the AICs (10 million; 32.2 per cent) than of mainline churches including the DRCs (9.9 million; 32 per cent). Thus the AICs are now the largest black-member group of churches in South Africa, with 33 per cent of all Christians in South Africa being black members of AICs. In terms of the wider picture of South African society, the AICs are also a force to be reckoned with. With 10.6 million members out of a total population of 40.5 million (in 1996), the AICs make up 24.7 per cent or a quarter of the population. This percentage rises within the black population of South Africa to 32.2 per cent.

It should be noted that the AICs are not a homogenous group. The Stats SA *Religion: Summary Code List* contains at least 4,500 names that were found in the census forms. These include names such as New Green Grass Apostolic Church in Zion, Holy Cross Healers Church of Messiah, and Bantu Peace Holiness Apostolic Church in Zion SA. The Zion Christian Church with a membership of 3.8 million is the largest of the AICs, followed by other Apostolic churches with 3 million, and other Zionist churches with 2.1 million. The Ethiopian churches with 474,000 and the *iBandla amaNazaretha* (the Shembe Church) with 454,000 also have large followings. Indicating the importance of the AIC churches in the ecclesial landscape after 1994, it is instructive to note that the ZCC is the largest single denomination in South Africa with its 3.8 million members. It is larger than the mainline churches such as the Dutch Reformed (3.5 million), Roman Catholics (3.3 million), Methodists (2.7 million) and Anglicans (1.4 million). When the African membership is examined, then the relative importance of the ZCC obviously rises. In simple terms, (with the likelihood that their membership has increased in the past nine years) this means that even by 1996:

- 1 in every 4 South Africans was a member of an AIC, and
  1 in every 11 South Africans was a member of the ZCC

- 1 in every 3 South African Christians was a member of an AIC, and
  1 in every 8 South African Christians was a member of the ZCC

- 1 in every 3 black South Africans was a member of an AIC, and
  1 in every 8 black South Africans was a member of the ZCC

- 1 in every 2 black South African Christians was a member of an AIC, and
  1 in every 6 black South African Christians was a member of the ZCC

Thus the mainline churches are being challenged on the one side with relating to a religiously pluralist world outside of the Christian fold, while at the same time dealing with the way in which this has expanded the range of Christian options inside the church. It is a profound challenge for the church – especially for those who are willing to embrace the change – because so much of the theology that has been inherited and imbibed in the South African churches, including the theology that drove the struggle against apartheid in the *Kairos Document*, for example, has been of a monistic kind that assumes that South Africa is a Christian country, that Christian discourse has a privileged status in the public sphere, and that there is one correct way of being Christian. A key theological challenge for the church at the start of the twenty-first century, therefore, involves learning to bear witness in a pluralist world.

This is, of course, not a problem in South Africa alone, as Christians in Asia have always lived out their faith in such a context, and Christians in the West are learning to be Christian believers in a post-Christian society. Thus South African Christians could learn much from other contexts about learning to think and talk in ways that do not privilege the Bible and Christian tradition in the public arena, and that give respect to the insights and commitments of atheists and people of other faiths. Yet this needs to be done in our context with the recognition that the overwhelming majority of South Africans are Christian believers in one or other form, and therefore to both respect the sensitivities of this majority and at the same time remind it of a tendency towards Christian imperialism in public discourse. South Africa, with its range of religious traditions and faith communities, its growing human rights culture, and its livelihoods challenges that require faithful compassion rather than religious dogma, could – if it gets it right – be in a unique situation to provide a model for a pluralist world in which religion too often is a cause of division rather than fraternity.

The Promise and Peril of Globalization

We have just noted that the reality of religious pluralism in South Africa is a pointer to the wider world that we live in, a world that has a greater and greater impact upon our lives with the advent of rapid globalization. So while Islam and Hinduism are minority faiths in South Africa our lives are shaped by this wider world in which such faiths play a much greater role. Now while this has been true for the people of many countries for quite a while, we noted earlier that the end of apartheid meant the end to isolation and a sudden insertion into this global family, and especially the African family. So at precisely the time that all South African citizens were finally taking their destiny into their own hands, we have been thrust into a reality in which the dominant agendas for politics, for culture, for the economy and for religion are no longer set at local and national levels, but are driven by events throughout this wider globe.

Two paradoxical tendencies can be observed in this process, the one promoting uniformity and coherence around the languages, cultures and political perspectives of the North Atlantic states, and particularly the United States of America. The other process, rooted in post-colonial reality, promotes the break-up of the 'grand narrative' of European colonization in favour of the assertion of local cultures, religions, languages and identity. It is driven by the impact of communications and transport technologies, in which previously isolated parts of the globe are able to speak to and have contact with the wider world. In the first case we can speak of globalization as a project designed by those in power to extend their control over more and more of the globe, silencing the diverse voices of opposition. In the second case, we can speak of globalization as a process in which more and more voices are being brought into world conversations, each demanding a respectful hearing. As Konrad Raiser, then General Secretary of the WCC puts it:

> The situation today with regard to the global perspectives created through the electronic technological revolution is not basically different from the challenges presented by previous industrial revolutions. The shrinkage in space and time that the world has experienced as a consequence of the technological revolutions in transport, communication and information processing is a historical fact from which there is indeed no escape. We are still far from having understood the long-term implications of this new configuration for social, political, cultural and religious institutions and forms of life. But this historical fact of the technology-driven process of globalization has to be distinguished from the deliberate use of the new possibilities to promote a specific policy project in the sense of global capitalism.[31]

South Africa is not immune to these dual processes, with the nation and

---

[31] Konrad Raiser, *For a Culture of Life: Transforming Globalisation and Violence* (Geneva: WCC, 2002), pp. 6, 7.

therefore the church facing both the promise and the peril of globalization at the start of the twenty-first century.

The promise of globalization lies in the possibilities for networking and connections that were previously the domain of the colonizers. In the colonial era (and even after independence) communication flowed between the colonial power and the colony in such a way that the colony found its identity (and often its public language) in that relationship. This is so clearly illustrated in the way that Christian mission has worked. In many ways Anglican, Lutheran or Roman Catholic churches in countries in the South have much closer relationships with England, Germany and Scandinavia, or Rome than they do with the same denomination in the neighbouring country, let alone other denominations in their own country. Now globalization has loosened up the power of this umbilical chord so that ex-colonies (and the churches in those colonies) can begin to relate to one another without having that communication mediated by the 'mother nation'. The new horizons opened by travel and communication technologies mean that globalization brings with it the promise that South–South dialogue can begin to become a reality as people can move and communicate outside of the power networks of the ex-colonial nations. This enables information to be accessed and shared, new insights to emerge and ultimately for solidarities to be forged in the light of common experiences of colonization and struggles for liberation and national identity. This carries many new possibilities for the church in South Africa, as the successful struggle against apartheid alongside world-class academic institutions and 'first-world' infrastructure gives South Africa a powerful voice in the international arena.

While the forging of international links and the building of new networks to challenge the power and hegemony of the West represents the promise of the process of globalization, we need to acknowledge that globalization is at the same time a profoundly perilous project driven by the beneficiaries of capitalism. The end of the bipolar world with the collapse of the communist states at the end of the 1980s ushered in the possibility that the entire world could be linked in one great global market driven by the logic of monetarist capitalism. Through the Reagan and Thatcher administrations in the USA and United Kingdom respectively, this anti social-welfare ideology, usually known as neo-liberalism or 'the Washington Consensus', now controls the economic, political and social thinking of the victorious West. It dictates the strategies of the World Bank and International Monetary Fund in controlling the debt-ridden countries of the South through Structural Adjustment Programmes, as it does the promotion of 'free trade' by the World Trade Organization to the detriment of many poor countries. Space does not permit a full discussion of the disasters that this ideology has had upon the poor people of the world; but a simple consideration of such matters as the access that poor people in the South have to adequate health care, education or food would suggest that globalization is experienced in much the same way as slavery, colonialism, and 'development'. It is just the next chapter in the ongoing rape of the South for the benefit of the North.

It is the Reformed community of faith in South Africa, the heirs of the *Belhar Confession*, who have taken forward the most sustained theological critique of global capitalism by their participation in the work of the World Alliance of Reformed Churches known as the *'processus confessionis*: Confessing/Covenanting for Justice in the Economy and the Earth'.[32] A gathering of the Southern African Alliance of Reformed Churches (SAARC) at Mindolo Ecumenical Foundation, Kitwe, Zambia, in October 1995, produced a key four-page document using the See-Judge-Act methodology which is a searing indictment of global capitalism from a Christian perspective. The document includes the following assessment in its section titled 'Seeing':

7. Our general and pervasive experience is that, instead of rivers of economic prosperity and justice flowing season after season in all Africa, poverty and misery, hunger and chronic unemployment have become endemic. Again, we notice that it is because money flows from the poor South to the rich North to enrich the North still further.

8. The systematic impoverishment of Africa has led many people to lose their capacity for self-help and self-employment. This may have disastrous repercussions on future generations.

9. The irony is that Africa is dying at a time when the accumulated global wealth, to which we and our parents have handsomely contributed, is larger than ever before in the history of humankind,

---

[32] See the various reports and documents of the 23rd General Council of the WARC held in Debrecen, Hungary, in August 1997, <www.warc.ch/pc/debrecen/index.html>.

due to the unprecedented high development of technology and know-how. It is tragic that the mass hunger we see every day coexists in the global context side by side with immeasurable opulence, without tearing apart he consciences of those who are beneficiaries.[33]

The statement goes on to say, under the heading 'Judging':

10. It is our painful conclusion that the African reality of poverty caused by an unjust economic world order has gone beyond an ethical problem and become a theological one. It now constitutes a *status confessionis*. The gospel to the poor is at stake in the very mechanism of the global economy today.

And then in the 'Acting' section, specific reference is made to the Confession of Belhar:

6. We affirm life against death. We have to share the dream of a just society, and refuse to let it die. We proclaim the Trine God as the God of life, of creation, of care, of hope. 'We believe that God has revealed himself as the one who wishes to bring about justice and true peace among people; that in a world full of injustice and enmity he is in a special way the God of the destitute, the poor and wronged and that he calls his church to *follow* him in this' (Confession of Belhar).

The WARC process has continued, with the dialogue widening to involve the WCC and the Lutheran World Federation (LWF). Discussion is ongoing, and the input of South African theologians has been important, though the actual engagement of the South African churches in this issue has been minimal.

This is unfortunate, because it has meant that the churches in South Africa have not been able to provide a coherent and theologically astute critique of the attempts by the nations of Africa to reverse the impact of the negative effects of globalization upon Africa, through the

---

[33] *Reformed Faith and Economic Justice.* Statement of the WARC-SAARC Consultation, 12–17 October 1995 (Mindolo Ecumenical Foundation, Kitwe, Zambia).

African Union and the New Partnership for Africa's Development, NEPAD.[34] This ambitious vision and programme illustrates at once both the promise and peril of globalization. The promise involves a greater post-colonial consciousness, a desire for an African-initiated programme to make a difference in the continent, and a willingness to participate in the global economy as an equal partner. Yet, as critics have pointed out, the only way in which it conceives of this possibility is by accepting the rules of the neo-liberal game – a game in which the playing fields are specifically designed to not be level.[35] Because of this prior commitment, the NEPAD documents are forced to concentrate on economic growth and are silent about the role of religion in Africa, gender justice, the history of previous African attempts at 'development' which were undermined by the West, the role of international financial institutions in causing the debt of African countries, the participation of ordinary Africans in shaping their own future, and the suffering of the African environment.

In responding to the NEPAD initiative, the church in South Africa has been drawn into discussions around globalization, yet without being able to articulate a theological alternative to global capitalism, which is the starting-point of NEPAD. Here again, the same theological uncertainty that characterizes its response to the issues of human sexuality or religious pluralism is to be found. The moral indignation and the theological clarity that characterized the struggle against apartheid – and which emerges in the WARC *processus confessionis* – is conspicuous by its absence, and it would seem that the church is keen to be co-opted into what the political leaders have pre-ordained.[36] The constant refrain to be 'critical of some of the details, but to affirm the basic vision' of NEPAD

---

[34] The October 2001 document which lays out the foundational NEPAD vision was available until recently at <www.dfa.gov.za/events/nepad.pdf>; for further information on NEPAD see <www.nepad.org>.

[35] See *Unblurring the Vision: An Assessment of the New Partnership for Africa's Development by South African Churches* (Johannesburg and Pretoria: SACC and SACBC, 2002), and Steve de Gruchy, 'Some Preliminary Theological Reflections on the New Partnership for Africa's Development', *Bulletin for Contextual Theology*, vol. 8.2 & 3 (August 2002).

[36] See, for example, the report of the SACC, WCC, and All African Conference of Churches (AACC), *Behold I Create a New Africa: An Ecumenical Consultation on NEPAD, March 2003* (Johannesburg: SACC, 2003).

seems to have lost sight of what the global churches recommended at the Harare Assembly of the WCC in 1998:

> Globalization is not simply an economic issue. It is a cultural, political, ethical and ecological issue . . . The vision behind globalization includes a competing vision to the Christian commitment to the *oikumene*, the unity of humankind and the whole inhabited earth . . . Although globalization is an inescapable fact of life, we should not subject ourselves to the vision behind it, but strengthen our alternative ways towards visible unity in diversity, towards an oikumene of faith and solidarity. The logic of globalization needs to be challenged by an alternative way of life of community in diversity. Christians and churches should reflect on the challenge of globalization from a faith perspective and therefore resist the unilateral domination of economic and cultural globalization. The search for alternative options to the present economic system and the realization of effective political limitation and corrections to the process of globalization and its implications are urgently needed.[37]

One of the most significant criticisms of the NEPAD documents relates to its weakness in dealing with the environment, or earth crisis. This has been a crucial contribution that the World Council of Churches has made to the global discussion about the future of life on earth, through its focus on Justice, Peace and the Integrity of Creation. For ironically the greatest opponent of globalization is the globe itself! The earth, together with the poor of the earth, experiences the devastating impact of neo-liberal capitalism and material acquisition gone mad. Since the Brundland Commission published *Our Common Future* in 1987,[38] which led to the Rio Earth Summit in 1992, global leaders have been made aware of the environmental consequences of the economic and political choices that they make, and yet there seems to be no stopping the globalized policies and programmes that are having such a profound impact upon such things as deforestation, desertification, loss of biodiversity, water pollution, and climate change.

---

[37] Quoted in Raiser, *Culture of Life*, p. 58.
[38] World Commission on Environment and Development, *Our Common Future* (Oxford: Oxford University Press, 1987).

This is a major issue for the globe, but again the single-mindedness with which the South African church focused on apartheid means that it has had little time to reflect upon and respond to the earth crisis. The links between people's livelihoods and the life of the planet are not easily made, with many thinking of environmental concerns as the domain of rich white people interested in saving the whales. Yet the opportunity for South Africa to host the World Summit on Sustainable Development in Johannesburg in 2002 provided an opportunity for the South African Council of Churches to bring together a range of theologians to reflect on the links between poverty, livelihoods and the earth. A declaration, *This is God's Earth*, was adopted by the SACC and church representatives in June 2002 in preparation for the summit. It drew attention to the way in which the dominant development paradigm has destroyed both the lives of the poor and the earth, and called for an alternative paradigm built on a theological vision that includes recognizing that the earth belongs to God, and that God's wish for the earth is *Shalom*. The declaration ends with a call for a sustainable earth:

> Our commitment to poor and marginalised people and communities is at the same time a commitment to the earth itself, for the future of the poor is dependent upon the future of the earth, and likewise, the future of the earth is dependent upon the future of the poor. We are aware that many communities are wracked with internal power conflicts between ruling elites and the vulnerable poor, between men and women, between old and young people, and amongst communities themselves, often over the increasingly scarce resources of the earth. We speak therefore of sustaining life in communities that embody right relations, equity and justice, and this in the context of sustaining the earth and being sustained by the earth in turn.[39]

An exciting contribution to the witness of the church in South Africa has been the establishment of the Network of Earthkeeping Christian Communities in South Africa, NECCSA. This is a network for local Christian congregations, communities, groups and organizations as well as interested individuals to engage with one another on issues of environmental justice.[40] Furthermore, growing concern about food

---

[39] 'This is God's Earth', *Bulletin for Contextual Theology*, vol. 8.2 & 3 (August 2002), p. 102.

[40] For information on the NECCSA network, contact <wcpcc@iafrica.com>.

security in a time of drought, and food sovereignty in the face of the control of the food chain by giant multi-national biotechnology companies with their genetically engineered seeds;[41] together with the concerns about the land that we noted earlier, are enabling ordinary people to see the links between the earth, the environment, poverty and justice. As the impact of the earth crisis – driven by global capitalism's desire for greater and greater profit – becomes more and more manifest in the lives of ordinary South Africans, the church will find itself drawn deeper into needing to develop an earth spirituality and an earth ethic. Here it will be immeasurably enriched by the insights of African spirituality.[42]

In many ways the church in South Africa has been unprepared to engage with globalization. Yet, it should be clear that as both promise and peril, it has a profound impact upon the life of the church whether the church chooses to recognize the fact or not. Old ways of doing theology are challenged. Prophets do not know who to speak to any longer, because even national leaders feel they are no longer in charge of what happens to their own countries' economy and political fortunes. New abilities need to be nurtured in understanding the workings of such things as global capitalism, international debt mechanisms, the rules governing world trade, genetic engineering, climate change, emissions trading, and food sovereignty. All of this has to take place while also being contextual and incarnational in a South African reality in which the land struggle, AIDS, and poverty are so crucial.

As we think, therefore, about the four important church struggles we have identified, and that now face the churches of South Africa ten years after the demise of apartheid, we are aware of just how overwhelming the task is. Yet, while each challenge is an issue in itself, it is crucial to see the interlocking nature of these issues. Globalization and the earth crisis, for example, have a profound impact upon the livelihoods of the poor.

---

[41] See Steve de Gruchy, 'Biotechnology as Cultural Invasion: Theological Reflections on Food Sovereignty and Community Building in Africa', *Scriptura: International Journal of Bible, Religion and Theology in Southern Africa*, vol. 82 (2003).

[42] See, for example, Harvey Sindima, 'Community of Life: Ecological Theology in African Perspective', in B. C. Birch, W. Eakin and J. B. McDaniel, *Liberating Life: Contemporary Approaches to Ecological Theology* (Maryknoll, NY: Orbis, 1990), pp. 137–47; Emmanuel Asante, 'Ecology: Untapped Resource of Pan-Vitalism in Africa', *African Ecclesial Review* 27 (1985), pp. 289–93; Gabriel Setiloane, 'Towards a Biocentric Theology and Ethic – via Africa', *Journal of Black Theology in South Africa* 9:1 (May 1995), pp. 53–66.

Religious pluralism and matters of human sexuality are given new expression in a global world, while at the same time having an impact upon AIDS – which is further affected by the implications of cost-sharing in health care due to neo-liberal economic reforms. The church in South Africa is called upon to face these challenges with the same passion and compassion with which it faced apartheid, and so as we complete this chapter we can pause for a moment to ask just what it is that we can learn from this successful struggle.

Lessons for the Struggles from the Struggle

We have identified four key struggles that face the church in South Africa ten years after the advent of democracy. As we have noted, many of these struggles have arisen precisely because of the end of apartheid; and in many ways the church's concentrated focus on apartheid alone has not prepared it for the diversity of issues that it is now called upon to address. Nevertheless, as we seek for the continuities between the past and the present we can identify seven key factors that have emerged in the telling of the story of the church struggle against apartheid that contain important lessons for our contemporary struggles, and consti-tute the enduring legacy of the 'great cloud of witnesses' in that struggle.

The first of these lessons is the most obvious, and it is simply the affirmation of the public role of theology and the church. There have been many voices – both inside and outside the church – that have tried to keep the church focused on internal ecclesial matters, or the private matters of the soul. Yet the story of the church struggle against apartheid – both its failures and successes – should teach us how important it is that the church not be afraid to bear witness in the public arena, to speak on matters of state and society, and to translate its faith convictions into political praxis. From the early missionaries through to Desmond Tutu and Frank Chikane; from the tentative resolutions at Cottesloe to the charge of heresy at Belhar, we can see Christians seeking to relate the truth of the gospel to the realities of power and injustice.

A reading of the story reminds us of the sustained work that was undertaken by the Spro-cas I and II processes that emerged out of the *Message to the People of South Africa*. This was an amazingly broad-based and intense initiative to engage with public issues from the perspective of the Christian faith. Perhaps more than any other aspect of the story of the struggle they provide clues from the past as to how the church might engage around such issues as the livelihoods of the poor or globalization. The changed context of the reality of religious pluralism and the secular state may perhaps alter *how* the church can witness, but it does not the fact *that* it must bear witness.

Thankfully we are helped to think about the 'how?' question by the second lesson that emerges from the story of the past, namely *human rights* as a legitimate locus for Christian witness. There were times when the church's witness against apartheid was limited to its own status, as with the Church Clause of 1957, or the loss of denominational influence because of the Bantu Education Act; but to a large extent opposition to apartheid was driven by a concern for what it did to the humanity of black South Africans, whether or not they were Christian. This is surely a central aspect of the gospel, and is an important theme that must connect the struggle of the past and the struggles of the present. A focus on human rights thus provides a three-way connection for the church's witness in South Africa today: it is congruent with the gospel; it draws on the legacy of the past; and it is a language that speaks directly to the public square. We have seen in our earlier discussion about gender justice that the church is not always able to find the clarity it needs to affirm human rights when they collide with some of its prejudices, but the ability to have an public influence in future discussions will depend, by and large, on this ability to draw on the legacy of the Christian struggle against apartheid as a Christian struggle for human rights.

The third important lesson from the past is that this witness for human rights was very often given focus in the witness of individuals who played a leadership role in the life of the church. As much as one likes to believe that the entire fellowship of believing Christians stood up *en masse* against the apartheid regime, that is not what happened! Rather the story of the church struggle points us to the witness of a remarkable pantheon of individuals who exercised a prophetic ministry in this country: A non-comprehensive list would include at least people such as Johannes van der Kemp, John Philip, William Shaw, John Colenso, Albert Luthuli, Z. K. Matthews, B. B. Keet, Beyers Naudé, Trevor Huddleston, Denis Hurley, Theo Kotze, Douglas Bax, Albertina Sisulu, Desmond Tutu, Manas Buthelezi, Allan Boesak, Sheena Duncan, S'mangaliso Mkhatshwa, Margaret Nash, Peter Moll, Richard Steele,

Molly Blackburn, Albert Nolan, and Frank Chikane. Three things need to be noted here. The first is that while being justifiably proud of such prophets we also need to confess that the mere fact that we can name them is a reminder of just how few there were, given the size of the church in this country!

Yet, second, we must thank God that, given the silence of the vast majority of Christians, these people did in fact stand up, often at great personal cost to themselves. In the face of the new challenges that confront the church, we need to find ways to identify and nurture such prophets for today. This immediately raises concerns about the kind of theological education and reflection that is being offered by the churches to do with their ability to develop a critical consciousness and an empowering spirituality (a point to which we return below). But our third point is that there has to be a fundamental change in the over-whelming masculine identity of such leaders. It surely does not escape our attention that the great majority of those mentioned were males, and that this is both a symptom and a cause of our struggle to confront the issue of gender justice. We would do well not to forget that many, many women were engaged in the struggle against apartheid because of their faith; yet their names are too easily forgotten, and their witness was not allowed to shape the public contours of that struggle. For the sake of the gospel this must change as we identify and nurture the prophets that will provide leadership in the coming years.

A fourth lesson from the past has to do with the ecumenical nature of the public witness of the church. There are times when the story had to do with particular denominational matters such as Beyers Naudé's struggle with the NGK after Cottesloe, but to a very large extent the church struggle against apartheid was an ecumenical affair that saw historic confessional differences shelved in favour of united witness. The student of church history in South Africa may be able to identify the denominational home of the key actors, and in some cases this does have a bearing on their actions; yet what marks those people we have just identified above is not that they were Anglican or Reformed or Catholic or Pentecostal, but that they took a stand against apartheid and that they did so in the company of Christians from diverse traditions.

Furthermore, the story of the past reminds us that ecumenical agencies such as the Christian Institute, the South African Council of Churches and the Institute for Contextual Theology played crucial roles in nurturing and shaping the public witness of the churches. These agencies in turn played a crucial role in the production of such key documents as the *Message to the People of South Africa*, and the *Kairos Document*, documents that were signed by people from diverse denominational backgrounds. And beyond these formal relationships, there was also the ecumenism of the streets which saw Christians of all denominations pray together, march together, go to jail together, attend funerals together, and participate together in trade unions, community formations, student movements and political organizations. Given the nature of the contemporary struggles facing the church, this ecumenical witness constitutes an important legacy from the past that has surely to be sustained in the future.

We have just mentioned two crucial documents of the church struggle, and this points us to the fifth lesson of that struggle that emerges in the telling of the story. We can think of those two along with the resolutions of the Cottesloe Conference, the Hammanskraal resolution on Conscientious Objection, the *Belhar Confession*, the Harare Declaration, and the Rustenburg Declaration. There is no doubt that at times the church gave in to the temptation to write documents and adopt resolutions rather than to engage in the hard realities of social and political action. Yet in the final evaluation of the church's witness, if that were all that were said it would be an unfair judgment. In a similar manner to the great confessional documents of the Early Church, written documents bearing witness to the struggle against apartheid played an important role in clarifying the focus of that struggle, educating a new generation of students, clergy and laity, and coalescing support for the wider political and social struggle. Some documents have begun to emerge around the other struggles, and while it is perhaps too early to expect such documents to have the same kind of effect as those against apartheid, this is a valuable part of the church's witness that needs to be encouraged.

What is crucial to note, however, is that these documents did not just emerge out of thin air. They drew upon ongoing contextual theological reflection, and it is this that constitutes our sixth lesson that we can learn from the past. *The Message to the People of South Africa* seems to have been the catalyst for the emergence of a specifically South African theology, one that drew on the historic roots of the Christian faith, but brought them into dialogue with the contextual realities of apartheid South Africa. Three clear theological streams emerged in the past, to do with the idea of a Confessing Church, drawing from the tradition of the church's opposition to Nazism and inspiring the work that led to the *Belhar Confession*; contextual theology, drawing from the insights of the Latin American liberation theologians and inspiring the work that led to the *Kairos Document*; and black theology, drawing from the insights of black theology in the USA and infusing the wider struggle in both church and community with an awareness of the evil of religiously supported racism and the need for black leadership and an integration with the life experience of African people. This was theological reflection of a significant nature. It was explored in seminaries and universities, inspired the leadership and documents that we have noted above, and led to a wide range of research, conference papers, articles and books. It undergirded the prophetic witness of the church against apartheid. This legacy of disciplined theological reflection, even in the midst of suffering and repression, must not be lost in the years that lie ahead and, in the light of the contemporary church struggles, it must be informed by the theological insights of feminist and African women theologians.

Finally, the reference to wider theological influences above, points us to the seventh important legacy that we have from the church struggle against apartheid, namely, the value of international links. From the earliest days, the South African churches have always been linked to wider church networks that were based in the 'home countries' of the mission bodies. With the shift from mission to church, these international links were maintained, so that even the NGK – which has been independent longer than any other church in South Africa – values its relationship to the Reformed Ecumenical Synod and the World Alliance of Reformed Churches. These links were not just limited to denominational relations, however, as the ecumenical links to the World Council of Churches were so valued that the churches refused to bow to government pressure to leave during the crisis over the Programme to Combat Racism. Apart from partner funding for various denomination-based programmes, funding from international agencies was also crucial in sustaining the work of such bodies as the SACC, the Christian Institute, the Institute for Contextual Theology, many other faith-based Organizations and a host of other exchange and scholarship programmes that enabled the church to bear witness in the way that it did.

As we have noted above, these wider international ecumenical links also provided an important source of theological influence so that the insights of theologians such as Dietrich Bonhoeffer from Germany, Gustavo Gutiérrez from Peru and James Cone from the USA, played an important role in stimulating theological engagement. It was not all one-way traffic, however, as the creative theological work being undertaken in the cauldron of South Africa had an important influence upon the global theological agenda, most notably the influence of the early work towards the *Belhar Confession* upon the World Alliance of Reformed Churches' decision to declare apartheid a sin and its theological justification a heresy; and then the *Kairos Document* upon the wider world first through the Road to Damascus Document and then through such bodies as Kairos Europa and Kairos USA. It is clear that the global focus on apartheid facilitated much of this international networking, and that the ending of apartheid alongside crises in other parts of the world has meant that global attention has moved away from South Africa. Nevertheless, given the value of this international networking in the past, the South African churches must not now withdraw into them-selves but need to remain true to this legacy of global dialogue in the face of the fourfold challenge we have identified in this chapter.

Appendix

Religious Affiliation in South Africa in 1996

	Blacks	Whites	Coloureds	Asians	Others	Total
Dutch Reformed churches (Afrikaans)	1,567,654	1,655,294	661,982	2,568	26,025	3,913,523
Mainline churches (English)	8,388,535	1,034,810	1,112,364	37,259	81,078	10,654,046
Pentecostal/-Charismatic	1,732,798	391,982	476,777	59,375	22,386	2,683,314
African initiated churches	10,025,828	174,195	400,441	10,778	57,273	10,668,515
Other Christian	1,643,555	178,515	216,613	84,447	16,214	2,139,344
Total Christian	**23,358,366**	**3,434,796**	**2,868,177**	**194,427**	**202,976**	**30,058,742**
Jewish	10,447	55,733	1,058	360	462	68,060
Hindu	12,871	1,697	2,285	516,228	4,347	537,428
Muslim	43,253	3,741	246,431	236,315	23,843	553,583
Other religion	1,602,479	141,826	154,847	24,080	14,105	1,937,337
No religion unstated/refused	6,094,980	794,498	326,440	1,045,626	129,358	7,418,420
TOTAL	**31,127,621**	**4,434,702**	**3,600,465**	**1,045,626**	**375,225**	**40,583,639**

This table indicates self-identified religious affiliation in South Africa in 1996, just two years after the end of apartheid. The information is drawn from the first census undertaken in the democratic era, and indicates that at that stage black Christians made up 57% of the South African population, with the largest membership being of African Initiated Churches.[1]

---

[1] Further detail can be found in Jurgens Hendricks and Johannes Erasmus, 'Interpreting the New Religious Landscape in Post-Apartheid South Africa', *Journal of Theology for Southern Africa*, vol. 109 (March 2001), pp. 41–65.

Select Bibliography

The select bibliography, which did not appear in the original US edition, was revised for the second edition, and has been revised again for this third edition of *The Church Struggle in South Africa*. It therefore contains many titles that were published after the first part of this edition was written. Although some titles pertaining to the nineteenth and early twentieth centuries are included, the list is by no means exhaustive but rather is a sample that should provide a way into the material. There is a vast literature on the social history of South Africa both past and present that needs to be consulted in order to locate the church in its proper context. This will help fill many of the gaps in *The Church Struggle in South Africa* to which we have referred above.

RICSA Social History and Documentary Archives

The results of this extensive research project are available on CD-ROM from RICSA at the University of Cape Town. This CD includes a three-volume collection of documents and essays concerning the social history of Christianity in South Africa, as well as a database indexing the documentary archives (some 5000+) lodged at the University of Cape Town's Chancellor Oppenheimer Library. The three volumes are:

Villa-Vicencio, Charles (ed.), *Christianity and the Colonization of South Africa, 1652 to 1870* (print-to-order from RICSA).
de Gruchy, John (ed.), *Christianity and the Modernization of South Africa, 1867 to 1936* (print-to-order from RICSA).
Cochrane, James, and Bastienne Klein (eds.), *Perspectives on the Social History of Christianity in South Africa, 1936 – 1994* (published as a special issue of the *Journal of Theology for Southern Africa*, vol. 118, March 2004).

Historical: General Overview

Davies, Horton, *Great South African Christians*, Cape Town: Oxford University Press, 1951.

du Plessis, J., *A History of Christian Missions in South Africa*, London: Longmans, Green & Co., 1911; repr. Cape Town: C. Struik, 1965.

Elphick, Richard, and Rodney Davenport (eds.), *Christianity in South Africa: A Political, Social and Cultural History*, Cape Town: David Philip, 1997.

Gerdener, G. B. A., *Recent Developments in the South African Mission Field*, London: Marshall, Morgan & Scott, 1958.

Hinchliff, Peter, *The Church in South Africa*, London: SPCK, 1968.

Hofmeyr, J. W., and Gerald J. Pillay (eds.), *A History of Christianity in South Africa*, vol. 1, Pretoria: HAUM Tertiary, 1994.

Hofmeyr, J. W., J. A. Millard and C. J. J. Froneman, *History of the Church in South Africa: A Document Source Book*, Pretoria: UNISA, 1991.

Hope, Marjorie, and James Young, *The South African Churches in a Revolutionary Situation*, Maryknoll, NY: Orbis, 1981.

Norman, Edward, *Christianity in the Southern Hemisphere: The Churches in Latin America and South Africa*, Oxford: Clarendon Press, 1981.

Prozesky, Martin (ed.), *Christianity in South Africa*, Cape Town: Southern Book Publishers, 1990.

Regehr, E., *Perceptions of Apartheid: The Churches and Political Change in South Africa*, Scottdale, PA: Herald Press, 1979.

Sales, Jane M., *The Planting of the Churches in South Africa*, Grand Rapids: Eerdmans, 1971.

Strassberger, E., *Ecumenism in South Africa: 1936–1960*, Johannesburg: SACC, 1974.

Historical: Specific Studies

Adonis, J. C., *Die Afgebreekte Skeidsmuur Weer Opgebou*, Amsterdam: Rodopi, 1982.

Alberts, Louw, and Frank Chikane (eds.), *The Road to Rustenburg: The Church Looking Forward to the New South Africa*, Cape Town: Struik, 1991.

Bate, Stuart (ed.), *Serving Humanity: A Sabbath Reflection. The Pastoral Plan of the Catholic Church in Southern Africa after Seven Years*, Pietermaritzburg: Cluster, 1996.

Boesak, Allan A., and Charles Villa-Vicencio (eds.), *When Prayer Makes News: Churches and Apartheid, a Call to Prayer*, Philadelphia: Westminster Press, 1986.

Borer, Tristan Anne, *Challenging the State: Churches as Political Actors in South Africa, 1980–1994*, Notre Dame: University of Notre Dame Press, 1998.

Brain, J., and P. Denis (eds.), *The Catholic Church in Contemporary Southern Africa*, Pietermaritzburg: Cluster, 1999.

Brown, W. E., *The Catholic Church in South Africa, from its Origin to the Present Day*, London: Burns & Oates, 1960.

Bryan, G. McLeod, *Naudé: Prophet to South Africa*, Atlanta: John Knox, 1978.

Chikane, Frank, *No Life of my Own: An Autobiography*, Johannesburg: Skotaville, 1988.

Chidester, David, *Savage Systems: Colonialism and Comparative Religion in Southern Africa*, London: University Press of Virginia, 1996.

Chidester, David, *Shots in the Streets: Violence and Religion in South Africa*, Cape Town: Oxford University Press, 1992.

Clayton, Geoffrey, *Where We Stand: Archbishop Clayton's Charges, 1948–1957*, ed. C. T. Wood, Cape Town: Oxford University Press, 1960.

de Gruchy, John W., James C. Cochrane and Stephen Martin, *Facing the Truth: South African Faith Communities and the Truth and Reconciliation Commission*, Cape Town: David Philip, 1999.

de Gruchy, John W. (ed.), *The London Mission Society in Southern Africa, 1799–1999*, Cape Town: David Philip, 1999.

de Gruchy, Steve (ed.), *Changing Frontiers: The Mission Story of the UCCSA*, Gaborone: Pula Press, 1999.

de Klerk, W. A., *The Puritans in Africa: A History of Afrikanerdom*, Harmondsworth: Penguin Books, 1976.

Denis, P., T. Mlotshwa and D. Mukuka (eds.), *The Casspir and the Cross: Voice of Black Clergy in the Natal Midlands*, Pietermaritzburg: Cluster, 1999.

Denis, Philippe (ed.), *The Making of an Indigenous Clergy in Southern Africa*, Pietermaritzburg: Cluster, 1995.

Denis, Philippe (ed.), *Orality, Memory and the Past: Listening to the Voices of Black Clergy under Colonialism and Apartheid*, Pietermaritzburg: Cluster, 2000.

Denis, Philippe (ed.), *Dominicans in Africa: A History of the Dominican Friars in Sub-Sahara Africa*, Pietermaritzburg: Cluster, 2003.

Dreyer, A., *Boustowwe vir die Geskiedenis van die Nederduitse Gereformeerde Kerke in Suid-Afrika, 1804–1836*, Kaapstad: Nasionale Pers, 1936.

Duncan, Graham, *Lovedale: Coercive Agency. Power and Resistance in Mission Education*, Pietermaritzburg: Cluster, 2003.

du Plessis, J., *Life of Andrew Murray*, London: Marshall Bros., 1919.

du Toit, Andre, and Hermann Giliomee, *Afrikaner Political Thought: Analysis and Documents. 1780–1850*, vol. 1, Cape Town: David Philip, 1983.

Engelbrecht, S. P., *Geskiedenis van die Nederduitsch Hervormde Kerk van Afrika*, Cape Town, 1953.

ffrench-Beytagh, G. A., *Encountering Darkness*, London: Collins, 1973.

ffrench-Beytagh, G. A., *Encountering Light*, London: Collins, 1975.

Florin, Hans W., *Lutherans in South Africa*, Durban: Lutheran Publishing House, 1967.

Gerhart, Gail, *Black Power in South Africa: The Evolution of an Ideology*, Berkeley: University of California Press, 1978.

Guy, Jeff, *The Heretic: A Study of the Life of John William Colenso, 1814–1883*, Johannesburg: Ravan, 1983.

Hewson, Leslie A., *An Introduction to South African Methodists*, Cape Town: Methodist Publishing House, 1951.

Hexham, Irving, *The Irony of Apartheid: The Struggle for National Independence of Afrikaner Calvinism against British Imperialism*, New York: Edwin Mellen Press, 1981.

Hinchliff, Peter, *The Anglican Church in South Africa*, London: Darton, Longman & Todd, 1963.

Huddleston, Trevor, *Naught for Your Comfort*, London: Fontana, 1956.

Hudson-Reed, Sydney (ed.), *By Taking Heed: The History of the Baptists in Southern Africa, 1820–1977*, Roodeport, Transvaal: Baptist Publishing House, 1983.

Hudson-Reed, Sydney, John Jonsson and Christopher Parnell, *Together for a Century: The History of the Baptist Union of South Africa, 1877–1977*, Pietermaritzburg: Baptist Historical Society, 1977.

Jooste, J. P., *Die Geskiedenis van die Gereformeerde Kerk in Suid-Africa, 1859–1959*, Potchefstroom, 1959.

Kinghorn, Johann (ed.), *Die NG Kerk en Apartheid*, Johannesburg: Macmillan, 1986.

Knighton-Fitt, Jean, *Beyond Fear: The Story of Theo and Helen Kotze*, Cape Town: Pretext, 2003.

Kruger, Bernhard, *The Pear Tree Blossoms: The History of the Moravian Church in South Africa, 1737–1869*, Genadendal: Moravian Church Board, 1967.

Lewis, Cecil, and G. E. Edwards (eds.), *The Historical Records of the Church of the Province of South Africa*, London: SPCK, 1934.

Lodge, Tom, *Black Politics in South Africa since 1945*, Johannesburg: Ravan; London: Longman, 1983.

Lombard, R. T. L., *Die Nederduitse Gereformeerde Kerke en Rasse-politiek met verwysing na die jare 1884–1961*, Silverton, Transvaal: Promedia, 1981.

Luckhoff, A. H., *Cottesloe*, Cape Town: Tafelberg, 1978.

Luthuli, Albert, *Let my People Go*, London: Collins, 1962.

Matthew, Z. K., *Freedom for my People*, Cape Town: David Philip, 1981.

Meiring, Piet, *Chronicle of the Truth Commission*, Vandebijlpark, RSA: Carpe Diem, 1999.

Moorrees, A., *Die Nederduitse Gereformeerde Kerk in Suid-Africa, 1652–1873*, Cape Town: Bible Society, 1937.

Nash, Margaret, *Black Uprooting from 'White' South Africa*, Johannesburg: SACC, 1980.

Noonan, Patrick, *They're Burning the Churches*, Bellevue, Gauteng: Jacana, 2003.

Nuttall, Michael, *Number Two to Tutu: A Memoir*, Pietermaritzburg: Cluster, 2003.

Odendaal, Andre, *Vukani Bantu! The Beginnings of Black Protest Politics in South Africa to 1912*, Cape Town: David Philip, 1983.

Paton, Alan, *Apartheid and the Archbishop: The Life and Times of Geoffrey Clayton*, Cape Town: David Philip, 1973.

Phiri, I., D. B. Govinden and S. Nadar, *Her-stories: Hidden Histories of Women of Faith in Africa*, Pietermaritzburg: Cluster, 2002.

Randall, Peter (ed.), *Not Without Honour: Tribute to Beyers Naudé*, Johannesburg: Ravan, 1981.

Reeves, A., *South Africa – Yesterday and Tomorrow: A Challenge to Christians*, London: Gollancz, 1962.

Reeves, A., *Shooting at Sharpeville: The Agony of South Africa*, London: Gollancz, 1961.

Robertson, Rob, *St. Anthony's Activists*, Cape Town: privately printed, 1999.

Saayman, Willem A., *A Man with a Shadow: The Life and Times of Z. K. Matthew*, Pretoria: UNISA, 1996.

Serfontein, J. H. P., *Apartheid, Change and the NG Kerk*, Johannesburg: Taurus, 1982.

Spoelstra, C., *Bouwstoffen voor de Geschiedenis der Nederduitsch-Gereformeerde Kerken in Zuid-Africa, 1652–1804. Parts 1 and 2*, Amsterdam and Cape Town: Jacques Dusseau, 1907.

Stoker, H. G., and F. J. M. Potgieter (eds.), *Koers in die Krisis*, vol. 1, Stellenbosch: Pro Ecclesia, 1935.

Stoker, H. G., and J. D. Vorster (eds.), *Koers in die Krisis*, vol. 2, Stellenbosch: Pro Ecclesia, n.d.

Stoker, H. G., and J. D. Vorster (eds.), *Koers in die Krisis*, vol. 3, Stellenbosch: Pro Ecclesia, 1941.

Strassberger, E., *The Rhenish Mission Society in South Africa, 1830–1950*, Cape Town: C. Struik, 1969.

Thomas, David, *Christ Divided: Liberalism, Ecumenism and Race in South Africa*, Pretoria: UNISA, 2002.

Thomas, David, *Councils in the Ecumenical Movement*, Johannesburg: SACC, 1979.

Verryn, Trevor, *A History of the Order of Ethiopia*, Johannesburg: Central Mission Press, 1972.

Villa-Vicencio, Charles, *Trapped in Apartheid: A Socio-Theological History of the English-Speaking Churches*, Maryknoll, NY: Orbis, 1988.

Walshe, Peter, *Church Versus State in South Africa: The Case of the Christian Institute*, Maryknoll, NY: Orbis; London: Hurst, 1983.

Walshe, Peter, *Prophetic Christianity in Contemporary Southern Africa*, Pietermaritzburg: Cluster, 1995.

Weisse, Wolfram, *Sudafrika and das Antirassismusprogramm*, Frankfurt am Main: Peter Lang, 1975.

Worsnip, Michael E., *Between the Two Fires: The Anglican Church and Apartheid, 1948–1957*, Pietermaritzburg: University of Natal Press, 1991.

Theological

Ackermann, Denise, Jonathan A. Draper and Emma Mashinini (eds.), *Women Hold up Half the Sky*, Pietermaritzburg: Cluster, 1991.

Battle, Michael, *Reconciliation: The Ubuntu Theology of Desmond Tutu*, Cleveland, OH: Pilgrim Press, 1997.

Bax, Douglas S., *A Different Gospel: A Critique of the Theology behind Apartheid*, Johannesburg: Presbyterian Church of Southern Africa, 1979.

Becken, Hans-Jürgen (ed.), *Relevant Theology for Africa*, Durban: Lutheran Publishing House, 1973.

Boesak, Allan A., *Farewell to Innocence: A Social-Ethical Study of Black Theology and Black Power*, Maryknoll, NY: Orbis; Johannesburg: Ravan, 1977.

Bosch, David, Adrio Konig and Willem Nicol (eds.), *Perspektief Op Die Ope Brief*, Cape Town: Human & Rouseau, 1982.

Botha, A. J., *Die Evolusie van 'n Volksteologie'*, Ph.D. thesis, University of the Western Cape, 1984.

Chapman, Audrey R. and Bernard Spong (eds.), *Religion and Reconciliation in South Africa: Voices of Religious Leaders*, Philadelphia: Templeton Foundation; Pietermaritzburg: Cluster, 2003.

Cloete, G. D., and D. J. Smit (eds.), *A Moment of Truth: The Confession of the Dutch Reformed Mission Church, 1982*, Grand Rapids: Eerdmans, 1984.

Cochrane, J. R., *Servants of Power: The Role of English-speaking Churches in South Africa 1903–1930*, Johannesburg: Ravan, 1986.

Cochrane, J. R., J. W. de Gruchy and R. Petersen, *In Word and Deed: Toward a Practical Theology of Social Transformation*, Pietermaritzburg: Cluster, 1991.

de Gruchy, John W., *Cry Justice! Prayers, Meditations and Readings from South Africa*, London: Collins; Maryknoll, NY: Orbis, 1986.

de Gruchy, John W., *Theology and Ministry in Context and Crisis*, London: Collins, 1987.

de Gruchy, John W., *Bonhoeffer and South Africa: Theology in Dialogue*, Grand Rapids: Eerdmans; Exeter: Paternoster, 1984.

de Gruchy, John W., and Charles Villa-Vicencio (eds.), *Apartheid Is a Heresy*, Cape Town: David Philip; Grand Rapids: Eerdmans; London: SPCK, 1983.

de Gruchy, John W., and W. B. de Villiers (eds.), *The Message in Perspective*, Johannesburg: SACC, 1969.

de Gruchy, John W., *Christianity and Democracy: A Theology for a Just World Order*, Cambridge: Cambridge University Press, 1995.

de Gruchy, John W., *Liberating Reformed Theology: A South African Contribution to an Ecumenical Debate*, Grand Rapids: Eerdmans, 1991.

de Gruchy, John W., *Reconciliation: Restoring Justice*, London: SCM Press, 2002.

Desmond, Cosmas, *Christians or Capitalists? Christianity and Politics in South Africa*, London: Bowerdean, 1978.

Draper, Jonathan (ed.), *Commentary on Romans by Bishop William Colenso*, Pietermaritzburg: Cluster, 2003.

Eybers, I. H., A. Konig and C. F. A. Borchardt, *Teologie en Vernuwing*, Pretoria: UNISA, 1975.

Geyser, A. S., *et al.*, *Delayed Action*, Pretoria: NG Kerk Boekhandel, 1961.

Govender, Shun (ed.), *Unity and Justice: The Witness of the Belydende Kring*, Braamfontein: The Belydende Kring, 1984.

Guma, Mongezi, and Leslie Milton (eds.), *An African Challenge to the Church in the Twenty-First Century*, Johannesburg: SACC, 1997.

Hofmeyr, J. W., and W. S. Vorster (eds.), *New Faces of Africa: Essays in Honour of Ben Marais*, Pretoria: UNISA, 1984.

Hurley, D. E., *State and Church: An Approach to Political Action by Christians*, London: Geoffrey Chapman, 1966.

Jabavu, D. D. T., *An African Indigenous Church: A Plea for its Establishment in South Africa*, Lovedale: Lovedale Press, 1942.

Johanson, Brian (ed.), *The Church in South Africa: Today and Tomorrow*, Johannesburg: SACC, 1975.

Keet, B. B., *Whither South Africa?*, Stellenbosch: Stellenbosch University Publishers, 1956.

Kotze, C. S., *Die NG Kerk en die Ekumene*, Pretoria: NG Kerk Boekhandel, 1984.

Kotze, J. C. G., *Principle and Practice in Race Relations*, Stellenbosch: CSA Publishers, 1962.

Leatt, James, Theo Kneifel and Klaus Nurnberger (eds.), *Contending Ideologies in South Africa*, Cape Town: David Philip; Grand Rapids: Eerdmans, 1986.

Loubser, J. A., *The Apartheid Bible: A Critical Review of Racial Theology in South Africa*, Cape Town: Maskew Miller Longman, 1987.

Moodie, T. Dunbar, *The Rise of Afrikanerdom: Power, Apartheid and Afrikaner Civil Religion*, Berkeley, CA: University of California Press, 1975.

Moore, Basil (ed.), *The Challenge of Black Theology in South Africa*, Atlanta: John Knox Press, 1973.

Mosala, I., and B. Tlhagale (eds.), *The Unquestionable Right to be Free: Essays on Black Theology*, Johannesburg: Skotaville, 1986.

Motlhabi, Mokgethi, *The Theory and Practice of Black Resistance to Apartheid: A Social-Ethical Analysis*, Johannesburg: Skotaville, 1984.

Nash, M., *Christians Make Peace*, Durban: Diakonia/PACSA, 1982.

Nash, M., *Ecumenical Movements in the 1960s*, Braamfontein: SACC, 1975.

Nolan, Albert, *Jesus before Christianity. The Gospel of Liberation*, London: Darton, Longman & Todd; Maryknoll, NY: Orbis, 1977.

Nürnberger, Klaus (ed.), *A Democratic Vision for South Africa: Political Realism and Christian Responsibility*, Pietermaritzburg: Encounter, 1991.

Nürnberger, Klaus (ed.), *Affluence, Poverty and the Word of God*, Durban: Lutheran Publishing House, 1978.

Nürnberger, Klaus, *Ideologies of Change in South Africa and the Power of the Gospel*, Durban: Lutheran Publishing House, 1979.

Oosthuizen, G. C., *Pentecostal Penetration into the Indian Community in South Africa*, Pretoria: HSRC, 1975.

Oosthuizen, G. C., J. K. Coetzee, J. W. de Gruchy, J. H. Hofmeyr and B. C. Lategan, *Religion, Intergroup Relations and Social Change in South Africa*, Pretoria: HSRC, 1985.

Paton, David, *Church and Race in South Africa*, London: SCM Press, 1958.

Pauw, B. A., *Christianity and Xhosa Tradition*, Cape Town: Oxford University Press, 1975.

Pityana, Barney, and Charles Villa-Vicencio (eds.), *Being the Church in South Africa Today*, Johannesburg: SACC, 1995.

Prior, Andrew (ed.), *Catholics in Apartheid Society*, Cape Town: David Philip, 1982.

Setiloane, G., *The Image of God among the Sotho-Tswana*, Rotterdam: Balkema, 1976.

Smit, D. J. (ed.), *Theology – Confession – Politics: The Papers and Responses of the Conference of the South African Theological Society, 1984*, Bellville: University of the Western Cape, 1985.

Smith, J. J., F. E. O'B. Geldenhuys and P. Meiring, *Stormkompas*, Kaapstad: Tafelberg, 1973.

Smith, N. J., *Die Planting van Afsonderlike Kerke vir Nie-Blanke Berolkingsgroepe deur die Nederduitse Gereformeerde Kerk in Suid-Afrika*, Stellenbosch: University of Stellenbosch, 1973.

Speckman, McGlory T., and Larry T. Kaufmann (eds.), *Towards an Agenda for Contextual Theology: Essays in Honour of Albert Nolan*, Pietermaritzburg: Cluster, 1991.

Stevens, R. J., *Community Beyond Division*, New York: Vantage Press, 1984.

Storey, Peter, *Here We Stand: Submission to the Commission of Inquiry into the South African Council of Churches, 9th March 1983*, Johannesburg: SACC, 1983.

Sundermeier, T. (ed.), *Church and Nationalism in South Africa*, Johannesburg: Ravan, 1973.

Sundkler, Bengt, *Bantu Prophets in South Africa*, London: Lutterworth, 1948.

Sundkler, Bengt, *Zulu Zion and Some Swazi Zionists*, Oxford: Oxford University Press, 1976.

Templin, J. Alton, *Ideology on a Frontier: The Theological Foundation of Afrikaner Nationalism, 1652–1910*, Westport, CN: Greenwood Press, 1984.

Treurnicht, A. P., *Credo van 'n Afrikaner*, Kaapstad: Tafelberg, 1975.

Turner, R., *The Eye of the Needle: Toward Participatory Democracy in South Africa*, Johannesburg: Spro-cas, 1972; Johannesburg: Ravan, 1980.

Tutu, Desmond, *The Rainbow People of God*, New York: Doubleday, 1994.

Tutu, Desmond, *No Future without Forgiveness*, London: Rider, 1999.

Tutu, Desmond, *Crying in the Wilderness*, London: Mowbray; Grand Rapids: Eerdmans, 1982.

Tutu, Desmond, *Hope and Suffering*, Johannesburg: Skotaville, 1983; London: Collins; Grand Rapids: Eerdmans, 1984.

Tutu, Desmond, *The Divine Intention: Presentation to the Eloff Commission of Enquiry*, Johannesburg: SACC, 1982.

Viljoen, A. C., *Ekumene onder die Suiderkruis*, Pretoria: UNISA, 1979.

Villa-Vicencio, Charles (ed.), *Theology and Violence: The South African Debate*, Johannesburg: Skotaville, 1987; Grand Rapids: Eerdmans, 1988.

Villa-Vicencio, Charles, *A Theology of Reconstruction: Nation-Building and Human Rights*, Cambridge: Cambridge University Press, 1992.

Villa-Vicencio, Charles, and J. W. de Gruchy (eds.), *Resistance and Hope: South African Essays in Honour of Beyers Naudé*, Cape Town: David Philip; Grand Rapids: Eerdmans, 1985.

Villa-Vicencio, Charles, *Race and Class in the English Speaking Churches*, Bellville: University of the Western Cape, 1985.

Villa-Vicencio, Charles, *Saints and Citizens*, Grand Rapids: Eerdmans; Cape Town: David Philip, 1986.

Villa-Vicencio, Charles, *The Theology of Apartheid*, Cape Town: Methodist Publishing House, n.d.

Villa-Vicencio, Charles (ed.), *On Reading Karl Barth in South Africa*, Grand Rapids: Eerdmans, 1998.

von Allmen, Daniel, *Theology-Advocate or Critic of Apartheid? A Critical Study of the 'Landman Report' (1974) of the Dutch Reformed Church (South Africa)*, Bern: Swiss Federation of Protestant Churches, 1977.

Vorster, W. S. (ed.), *Church and Society*, Pretoria: UNISA, 1978.

Vorster, W. S. (ed.), *Church Unity and Diversity in the Southern African Context*, Pretoria: UNISA, 1979.

West, Charles, *Perspective on South Africa*, Princeton: Princeton Theological Seminary, 1985.

West, Gerald, *The Academy of the Poor: Towards a Dialogical Reading of the Bible*, Pietermaritzburg: Cluster, 2003.

West, Martin, *Bishops and Prophets in a Black City: African Independent Churches in Soweto, Johannesburg*, Cape Town: David Philip, 1975.

Wilmore, G. S., and J. H. Cone (eds.), *Black Theology: A Documentary History*, Maryknoll, NY: Orbis, 1979.

Documentation

Being Church in a New Land: A Selection of Papers Presented at the 1995 National Conference of the SACC, Johannesburg: SACC, 1995.

From Cottesloe to Cape Town: Challenges for the Church in a Post-Apartheid South Africa, PCR Information, no. 30, Geneva: WCC, 1991.

Standing for the Truth, Booklet documenting the Campaign, 1991.

Apartheid and the Church, Report of the Spro-cas Church Commission, Johannesburg: Spro-cas, 1972.

Cassidy, Michael (ed.), *I Will Heal their Land. The Content of the South African Congress on Mission and Evangelism, Durban, 1973*, Pietermaritzburg: Africa Enterprise, 1974.

Cawood, Lesley, *The Churches and Race Relations in South Africa*, Johannesburg: Institute of Race Relations, 1964.

Christian Principles in Multi-Racial South Africa, A Report on the Dutch Reformed Conference of Church Leaders, Pretoria, 17–19 November 1953.

Christian Reconstruction in South Africa, A Report of the Fort Hare Conference, July 1942, Lovedale: Lovedale Press, 1942.

God's Kingdom in Multi-Racial South Africa, A Report on the Inter-Racial Conference of Church Leaders, Johannesburg, 7–10 December 1954.

Hewson, Leslie A. (ed.), *Cottesloe Consultation: The Report of the Consultation*, Johannesburg, 1961.

Human Relations in South Africa, A Report adopted by the General Synod of the Dutch Reformed Church, 1966.

Human Relations and the South African Scene in the Light of Scripture, A Report adopted by the General Synod of the Dutch Reformed Church, October 1974, Cape Town: NG Kerk Boekhandel, 1976.

International Commission of Jurists, Geneva (eds.), *The Trial of Beyers Naudé*, London: Search Press; Johannesburg: Ravan, 1975.

Landman, W. A., *A Plea for Understanding: A Reply to the Reformed Church in America*, Cape Town: NG Kerk-Uitgewers, 1968.

Nash, Margaret (ed.), *Your Kingdom Come: Papers and Resolutions of the Twelfth National Conference of the SACC, Hammanskraal, May 5–8 1980*, Johannesburg: SACC, 1980.

Paton, D. M., *Church and Race in South Africa: Papers from South Africa, 1952–57*, London: SCM Press, 1958.

Randall, Peter, *A Taste of Power: The Final SPRO-CAS Report*, Johannesburg: Spro-cas, 1973.

The Christian Citizen in a Multi-Racial Society, A Report of the Rosettenville Conference, July 1949.

The Future of South Africa, A Study by British Christians, London: SCM Press, 1964.

The Kairos Document: Challenge to the Church: A Theological Comment on the

Political Crisis in South Africa, Johannesburg: The Kairos Theologians, 1985. repr. in *Journal of Theology for Southern Africa*, no. 51 (June 1985), pp. 16ff.; 2nd rev. edn, Johannesburg: Institute for Contextual Theology; Grand Rapids: Eerdmans, 1986.

Thomas, David (ed.), *Liberation: The Papers and Resolutions of the Eighth National Conference of the SACC, 1976*, Johannesburg: SACC, 1976.

World Council of Churches, *Report on the WCC Mission in South Africa, April–December 1960*, Geneva: WCC, 1961.

Journals and Periodicals

The following selection of South African journals and periodicals should be consulted for articles and essays on the church and theology in South Africa. Those that are no longer being published are identified.

ABRECSA Newsletter, published by the Alliance of Black Reformed Christians in Southern Africa (discontinued).

Challenge Magazine, published by Contextual Publications, Johannesburg.

Inselelo (previously *Diakonia News*), published by Diakonia, Durban, Natal.

Die Kerkbode, newspaper of the Dutch Reformed Church.

Dimension, newspaper of the Methodist Church of Southern Africa.

Ecunews, the monthly news bulletin of the South African Council of Churches (discontinued).

Grace and Truth, a Catholic theological journal published by the staff of St Joseph's Theological Institute, Pietermaritzburg, South Africa.

ICT News, newsletter of the Institute for Contextual Theology (discontinued).

Missionalia, journal of the Southern Africa Missiological Society.

Ned. Geref. Teologiese Tydsrif, Theological journal of the Dutch Reformed Church in South Africa.

New South African Outlook, published by Outlook Publications and RICSA.

Religion in Southern Africa, published by the Association for the Study of Religion (Southern Africa).

Seek, the newspaper of the Church of the Province of South Africa (Anglican).

South African Outlook, An Independent Ecumenical Monthly journal concerned with political, racial, and economic issues (discontinued: see New South African Outlook).

Southern Cross, the newspaper of the Roman Catholic Church in South Africa.

Journal of Theology for Southern Africa, an ecumenical theological journal.

Theologia Evangelica, journal of the Faculty of Theology, University of South Africa.

Witness, published by Africa Enterprise, Pietermaritzburg (discontinued).

Woord en Daad, an independent journal dealing with socio-political issues from a Reformed perspective.

Bibliographies

For further detailed references of articles and essays see:

Borchardt, C. F. A. and W. S. Vorster (eds.), *South African Theological Bibliography*, vols. 1 and 2, Pretoria: University of South Africa, 1980, 1983.

Chidester, D., J. Tobler and D. Wratten, *Christianity in South Africa: An Annotated Bibliography*, London: Greenwood, 1997.

Hofmeyer, J. W. and K. E. Cross, *History of the Church in South Africa: A Select Bibliography of Published Material to 1980*, Pretoria: UNISA, 1986.

Hofmeyer, J. W., and K. E. Cross, *History of the Church in South Africa: A Select Bibliography of Published Material from 1981 to 1985*, Pretoria, UNISA, 1988.

Research Theses and Dissertations

There have been a large number of significant masters and doctoral theses on themes related to the history of the Church in South Africa, and the titles of these can be accessed from numerous university libraries in South Africa and elsewhere.

Index of Names and Subjects

CPSIA information can be obtained
at www.ICGtesting.com
Printed in the USA
BVHW040938010620
580614BV00014B/341

9 780800 637552